OLYMPIC DREAMS

OLYMPIC DREAMS

THE IMPACT OF MEGA-EVENTS ON LOCAL POLITICS

Matthew J. Burbank
Gregory D. Andranovich
Charles H. Heying

LYNNE
RIENNER
PUBLISHERS

BOULDER
LONDON

Published in the United States of America by
Lynne Rienner Publishers, Inc.
1800 30th Street, Boulder, Colorado 80301
www.rienner.com

and in the United Kingdom by
Lynne Rienner Publishers, Inc.
3 Henrietta Street, Covent Garden, London WC2E 8LU

Library of Congress Cataloging-in-Publication Data
Burbank, Matthew.
   Olympic dreams : the impact of mega-events on local politics /
Matthew J. Burbank, Gregory D. Andranovich, Charles H. Heying.
       p.   cm. — (Explorations in public policy)
   Includes bibliographical references and index.
   ISBN 978-1-55587-903-7 (hc : alk. paper)
   ISBN 978-1-55587-991-4 (pb : alk. paper)
   1. Olympics—Political aspects. 2. Olympics—Economic aspects.
3. International Olympic Committee. I. Andranovich, Gregory.
II. Heying, Charles H. III. Title. IV. Series.
GV721.5.B88   2001
796.48—dc21   00-053325

British Cataloguing in Publication Data
A Cataloguing in Publication record for this book
is available from the British Library.

Printed and bound in the United States of America

          The paper used in this publication meets the requirements
   ∞   of the American National Standard for Permanence of
          Paper for Printed Library Materials Z39.48-1992.

For Mary, Doris, Margaret, and Guido — M.J.B.

*For my parents and all the USDESEA teachers
in Ankara, Turkey, 1969–1974* — G.D.A.

For Lois — C.H.H.

▓▓ CONTENTS ▓▓

■■ ILLUSTRATIONS ■■

■ **Figures**

■ **Tables**

◼◼ ACKNOWLEDGMENTS ◼◼

This project began as a series of questions about the relationship between cities and the Olympic games. Over a period of four years it
evolved into a book about U.S. cities and their Olympic dreams.
Along the way we were lucky enough to receive the assistance of
many people who shared our interest in telling this story.

We would like to thank the many individuals who helped with
different aspects of our research and writing. Mike Gorrell, Robert
Huefner, and Ted Wilson each read the chapter on Salt Lake City
and provided helpful comments. Dan Jones generously provided access to his unparalleled archive of public opinion data on Utah. Bert
Granberg, director of the DIGIT Lab at the University of Utah, provided the necessary assistance and Phoebe McNeally supplied the
expertise and patience to make the maps for each city. Doug McGee
helped with expert research assistance in the early stage of this project. The staff at the Marriott Library, and especially Special Collections, provided help on many occasions. Thanks also are due to
Frank Bell, Chris Bellavita, John Francis, Jim Gosling, Ted Hebert,
Susan Olson, Steve Ott, Lisa Riley Roche, Linda Sillitoe, and Maria
Titze for help with various aspects of the project. In Los Angeles,
the staff at the Amateur Athletic Foundation of Los Angeles, especially Wayne Wilson and Shirley Ito, provided invaluable assistance
while sharing the Paul Ziffren Sports Resource Center's Olympic
Collection archives. The staff of the UCLA Research Library's Special Collections Department provided assistance with documents
early in the project. The thirty-nine students in Political Science 404
at California State University, Los Angeles, during winter quarter

2000 helped bridge teaching and research by enthusiastically examining local tourism politics. Thanks are also due to those who provided assistance with the Atlanta portion of the project: Barbara McTyre for her professional archival work and John Westerman for his help with online research. And we would like to thank Leanne Anderson, Dan Eades, and Lynne Rienner for their professional expertise and encouragement as we completed the project.

We owe a special thanks to four colleagues who read a complete draft of the manuscript: Harvey Newman, Georgia State University; David Olson, University of Washington; Gerry Riposa, California State University at Long Beach; and Wayne Wilson, Amateur Athletic Foundation of Los Angeles. Their comments helped clarify and improve our work, and we are grateful for their assistance. In addition, Michael Barndt, Richard DeLeon, David Olson, and Peter Skerry provided valuable comments and encouragement on various portions of this research that we presented at professional meetings. Thanks also to the faculty of the Department of Political Science at Washington State University for their comments and suggestions on the research design and some of the preliminary findings.

Finally, our respective institutions assisted in numerous ways. A faculty fellowship awarded to Matthew Burbank by the University of Utah research committee provided release time for writing. Greg Andranovich received a sabbatical leave during the summer and fall 2000 academic quarters from California State University, Los Angeles, allowing him to concentrate on this project. Charles Heying received a faculty development grant from the Office of Research and Sponsored Projects at Portland State University to fund archival work in Atlanta.

—*M. J. B.*
G. D. A.
C. H. H.

OLYMPIC DREAMS

The dream of hosting the Olympics evokes stirring images of athletes competing in idyllic settings. Such imagery can be powerfully appealing for cities seeking the world's attention. Yet staging the games takes place on the contested terrain of urban politics. Olympic hosts may aspire to hold the best games ever, but the realities inherent in governing urban America bend and alter the materialization of Olympic dreams. Los Angeles, Atlanta, and Salt Lake City have all sought to fulfill their Olympic dream. By examining their experiences, we can gain a better understanding of the impact of these events on urban politics.

The appeal of hosting the Olympic games for a city ought to be obvious. The games last only a short time but promise many benefits, both tangible and intangible. Among the tangible benefits are thousands of tourists, from suburban families traveling downtown for the award ceremonies to foreign dignitaries and business people staying at the best hotels. The intangible benefits include days of worldwide saturation television coverage and hundreds of glowing media stories about the city. Indeed, Olympic boosters nearly always claim that the real value of the games comes from being associated with the Olympic image.

Of course, image creation can be a fickle endeavor. Consider the case of Salt Lake City. Members of various Olympic bid committees spent years and millions of dollars trying to attract the winter games to the city. In 1995, Juan Antonio Samaranch, president of the International Olympic Committee (IOC), announced that Salt Lake City would host the 2002 winter games. For local leaders, the Olympics represented a symbolic step onto the world stage for their city. Just as quickly, however, the Olympic-sized dream turned into an Olympic nightmare.

The story of Salt Lake City's Olympic scandal broke in late November 1998, when a local television reporter turned up evidence that Salt Lake's Olympic committees had paid the tuition and living expenses for the daughter of an IOC member. In the days that followed, the story took on a life of its own as new accounts of excesses and favors for IOC members were revealed. Officials on the Salt Lake Olympic Organizing Committee (SLOC) tried to downplay the reports by characterizing the payments as "humanitarian assistance" intended to support Olympic activities in less developed countries.

The story exploded in the media, however, when longtime Olympic insider and IOC member Marc Hodler of Switzerland spoke bluntly about the problems in the bidding process. Hodler called the Salt Lake City payments "bribes." Soon the story was big news nationally and internationally as well: "Olympic Scandal Soils a Clean City" (*Philadelphia Inquirer,* 4 January 1999); "Olympic Glory Is Fading in Utah" (*Washington Post,* 16 December 1998); "Olympic Votes Hinge on Bribes" (*Toronto Star,* 13 December 1998); "Salt Lake City Officials Staggered by Bid Scandal" (*USA Today,* 14 December 1998); and "Salt Lake Mayor Quits as Olympic Scandal Grows" (*New York Times,* 12 January 1999). This definitely was not the kind of media attention that Salt Lake's leaders had envisioned.

The story continued to snowball in the months that followed as reports surfaced about lavish shopping trips and expensive vacations, free medical treatments, jobs or consulting contracts, and even direct cash payments to IOC members or their families. The scandal spread beyond Salt Lake as allegations of improper gifts or payments were raised about bids in Atlanta, Sydney, and Nagano. The media storm eventually became so severe that four separate investigations were launched respectively by the Salt Lake Organizing Committee, the United States Olympic Committee (USOC), the International Olympic Committee, and the U.S. Justice Department concerning possible criminal violations.

Many of the charges reported in the media were supported by these investigations. A report issued by the board of ethics of the Salt Lake Organizing Committee documented numerous instances of payments to IOC members or their families, which were intended to influence the selection process (Hall et al. 1999). In the most egregious case, that of IOC member Jean-Claude Ganga, the bid committee paid for trips and medical treatments for Mr. Ganga, his wife, and his mother-in-law. More than $17,000 in medical expenses were paid for directly by the Salt Lake bid committee, and the total expenses for the Ganga family amounted to more than $250,000 (Hall et al. 1999, 37–38).

The aid to Mr. Ganga was hardly unique. The daughter of IOC member René Essomba received $108,000 in rent, tuition, and expenses from the Salt Lake bid and organizing committees while she attended American University in Washington, D.C. (Hall et al. 1999, 31). Some IOC members received direct cash payments for undocumented purposes or lavish vacations, including trips to Las Vegas, Disneyland, and a trip to Florida for the 1995 Super Bowl (Hall et al. 1999, 37). All told, the Salt Lake bid committee reportedly spent more than one million dollars to woo IOC members with inappropriate gifts and assistance.

Why would individuals merely seeking to bring a sporting event to their city resort to such actions? There are certainly many possible motivations. Perhaps officials of the Salt Lake bid were simply unethical and willing to win at any cost. Or bid officials could have been so immersed in the competitive nature of the IOC selection process that they crossed the line between honest and dishonest competition. Or were members of the IOC the real culprits? Perhaps some IOC members were willing to promise votes to a bid city in exchange for material benefits.

In the case of Salt Lake City, any or all of these explanations may be true. But despite the protests of some IOC officials, it is evident that the activities associated with the Salt Lake bid campaign were not obviously out of place in the bid process (Mitchell et al. 1999). Similar charges of excessive favors or even outright bribery have been raised about bid campaigns conducted by other cities, and the USOC's report refers to a "culture of improper gift giving" within the IOC (Mitchell et al. 1999, 36). Clearly, there are broader questions here than simply the motivations of a few people in Salt Lake City.

The key to answering the broader questions raised by the unseemly nature of the bid process, we believe, is to recognize that for the bid cities much more was involved than merely the opportunity to host a sporting event. Indeed, the excesses of bid committees may not be so much an ethical aberration as the logical consequence of efforts to ensure the success of a high-risk strategy. After all, what advantages would there be to a city, tangible or intangible, if there were no high-profile event?

■ Mega-events and Local Politics

The focus of this book is not on the scandalous behavior of Olympic boosters or problems with the IOC selection process. Rather, our concern is with the impact that mega-events have on the politics of American cities. We address the broad issue of how these events affect the governance of host cities by focusing on four questions: (1) How and why do cities seek to host mega-events? (2) How are policy decisions concerning mega-events made? (3) What are the outcomes of hosting a mega-event? and (4) What can the conduct of mega-events tell us about urban politics generally?

The theme we will develop is that efforts by U.S. cities to attract events such as the Olympics are the product of a deliberate strategy for promoting local economic growth—the mega-event strategy. Hosting a premier event such as the Olympics or a world's fair is central to this strategy because city leaders are seeking not just short-term tourist revenues but to change their city's image and perhaps even the city's physical structure (Essex and Chalkley 1998). Despite the enormous amount of attention and even controversy that accompany such events, little attention has been paid to the potential consequences of this strategy. Debate over the pursuit of a mega-event tends to focus on its economic impact—the cost of the stadium, the value of a new hotel, or the tax revenues generated—but rarely on the broader political and social ramifications (M. Roche 1992). We believe that the study of urban mega-events can illuminate questions of enduring importance in urban politics such as what strategies do cities use to pursue economic growth, what role does local government play, and who benefits?

The mega-event strategy is not a new phenomenon. Various American cities have sought to host showcase events in the hope of making their city a tourist destination. In recent years, however, the mega-event strategy has taken on renewed prominence in cities as the result of the confluence of several factors: the success of the entrepreneurial Los Angeles Olympics, the demise of federal urban aid, and the rise of the global economy.

The event that triggered the contemporary focus on using the Olympic games as an urban mega-event was the 1984 Los Angeles Olympics. Despite the inauspicious circumstances of a Soviet boycott of the games, the Los Angeles Olympics were widely regarded as a success. From the perspective of other cities, this success was not because of the level of athletic competition, goodwill among nations, or even a triumph of logistics. The success of the Los Angeles games from the vantage point of other cities stemmed from two factors. First, with their Hollywood-crafted opening and closing ceremonies, the games generated large television audiences and positive publicity for the city and its tourist industry, with little apparent public controversy. Second, the city was able to attract this positive attention with minimal use of local tax dollars because the Los Angeles organizers raised an enormous amount of private money through corporate sponsorships and ended with a sizable surplus. For city leaders looking to refurbish their city's image and get the attention of businesses around the world, hosting the Olympics now appeared to offer a perfect way to do both with little cost to local taxpayers.

Absent other conditions, the success of the entrepreneurial Los Angeles Olympics might have attracted nothing more than the envious attention of mayors from other cities. Another high-profile event the same year, however, sent an important message to the leaders of U.S. cities. In November 1984, Ronald Reagan was overwhelmingly reelected. The election results confirmed a profound shift in federal policy toward American cities. The Reagan administration argued that state and local governments should look to the free market, not the federal government, to improve their material existence (Wolman 1986), and during Reagan's tenure, funding for programs to assist urban areas was eliminated or greatly reduced (Caraley 1992). The reduction of federal funds had a tremendous impact on development policies of state and local governments. While some local governments responded by reducing development activities, others adopted more entrepreneurial policies (Eisinger 1988; Clarke and Gaile 1992, 1998). Clarke and Gaile (1992, 1998) identify the period after 1984 as the "postfederal" era of local economic development. This period is characterized by greater willingness of local governments to take risks, increased cooperation among governments on a metropolitan or regional level, and greater reliance on public-private partnerships or quasi-public agencies to implement development projects. Thus, just as American voters elected a president committed to ending the flow of federal money to U.S. cities, Los Angeles was showing how to attract money and attention to a city through a high-profile sporting event.

Even under ordinary circumstances, the changing nature of federal urban policy coming together with a successful model of an urban mega-event would have sparked the interest of city leaders across the United States. The circumstances facing cities in the late 1980s and 1990s, however, were not ordinary. The global economy, much discussed but little in evidence throughout the 1970s, was rapidly becoming a reality. Creation of the European Union and movement toward a single currency, implementation of the North American Free Trade Agreement, and the creation of the World Trade Organization provided unmistakable signs that world trade in goods and services was becoming more internationally competitive. For business and government alike, it was increasingly evident that competition for jobs and investments would no longer be primarily with the state or city next door but might well be with a nation or city across the globe. In short, the global economy became an important feature of the broader environment within which cities compete for economic growth (Barnes and Ledebur 1998; Fry 1995; Knight 1989).

The combination of declining federal aid and increasing worldwide competition for business meant that American cities not only had to employ more entrepreneurial techniques to promote development but had to do so on the world stage. Thus the global economy intensified interest in international mega-events. After the success of the summer games in Los Angeles, the Olympics became *the* preferred mega-event for U.S. cities because of its appeal to corporate sponsors, the power of its image, and its potential as a catalyst for urban change.

Of course, one factor that makes the Olympics so valuable is its infrequent occurrence. Each set of games is held only every four years, and the IOC has a habit of rotating the location of the games. Further, the escalating amounts paid for broadcasting rights have elevated the Olympics as business, enticing more cities into the competition to host the games. Certainly, local officials contemplating a mega-event strategy have to recognize that getting the games is not easy. The lure of the potential benefits is there, however, for cities willing to accept the odds.

Not all cities are inclined to pursue such a risky path toward economic development, yet some do. What factors lead cities to embark on a mega-event strategy? We argue that two factors are central to its adoption: The first is the existence of an established growth regime in the city; the second is a desire to create or change the city's image. A growth regime is essentially a network of public and private leaders that functions as an informal government within a city (Stoker 1995; Stone 1993). Its goal is to encourage growth within the city, and its existence is vital to an Olympic bid. Without an established government-business network in place to provide authority and resources, an Olympic bid would simply not occur.

The existence of a growth regime by itself, however, is not sufficient to start a city down the mega-event path. Another necessary ingredient, at least among individuals within the regime if not among city residents generally, is a desire to establish or modify the city's image. As many U.S. cities have begun to rely on tourism and other consumption-oriented activities as a component of their local development policy, the issue of how to enhance a city's image has been pushed to the forefront. City image has thus become an important concern for development policy generally (Pagano and Bowman 1995), but image is especially salient in the mega-event strategy (Hall 1996; M. Roche 1992).

■ The Olympic Endeavor in Three Cities

In this book, we investigate the impact of high-profile development events by examining one type of mega-event, the Olympic games, in three American cities: Los Angeles (1984), Atlanta (1996), and Salt Lake City (2002). We could have chosen to focus on several different mega-events or to examine Olympic cities in other nations, but we chose to study the Olympics in these three cities because we believe there are two important stories to tell. The first is about the rise of the Olympics as *the* urban mega-event since the advent of the 1984 Los Angeles games. Although hosting the Olympics has always been an important happening for any city holding the games, it was only after the financial success of the Los Angeles games that U.S. cities began to look at the Olympics as a vehicle for promoting local development without requiring large sums from local tax dollars.

The second story is about urban politics in the United States. As a result of changes in federal policy and in the international economy, American local governments have been driven to entrepreneurial approaches to achieve local economic growth. Although there are similarities with cities in other nations, notably Canada and increasingly the United Kingdom, the combination of weak local governments, strong business interests, and the need for place-specific growth makes U.S. urban politics unique. No other major industrialized democracy puts its cities in the circumstance that American cities face in the postfederal era of needing to attract investment through local entrepreneurial activity. To tell these two stories, we have chosen to examine each U.S. city with Olympic experience in the postfederal period.

The examination of individual cities as case studies is well established in the study of urban politics (e.g., Andranovich and Riposa 1993; Feagin, Orum, and Sjoberg 1991). Our approach here can best be described as a focused comparison of case studies (George and McKeown 1985). Clearly, Los Angeles, Atlanta, and Salt Lake City are very different cities; they differ in size, social composition, economic base, and political history, among other factors. Moreover, the time period of interest in each city differs as well. Despite these differences, we can draw meaningful comparisons by focusing on a common set of theoretically grounded questions on the role of local government and the impact of mega-events, in order to guide the conduct of our case studies. Each study draws upon multiple sources of evidence, including official documents from Olympic bid and organizing committees, local media reports, personal interviews, opinion poll data, and government documents. By focusing on the process of bidding for and conducting the Olympic games, we are able to provide a grounded comparison of the impact of the Olympic experience in each of these cities.

We begin our investigation with the centrality of growth in American urban politics. Chapter 2 outlines the contemporary context in which U.S. cities seek economic growth, with a focus on the demise of federal urban policy and the rise of the global economy. Chapter 2 also introduces the theoretical approach—regime theory—that guides our investigation of local politics. Chapter 3 examines the rise of the mega-event strategy within the context of a shift toward consumption-oriented development in American cities and also discusses the significance of city image and why the Olympics have become the event of choice for U.S. cities seeking to enhance their image. Chapters 4, 5, and 6 provide a detailed look at Olympic politics in Los Angeles, Atlanta, and Salt Lake City, respectively. Each chapter opens with a brief overview of the city, and then describes the politics of the Olympic bid, organization, and legacies. Chapter 7 concludes with our assessment of the impact of mega-events on urban politics and policymaking, linking the evidence from Los Angeles, Atlanta, and Salt Lake City to the theoretical framework of regime theory and consumption-oriented economic development.

■■ 2 ■■
ECONOMIC GROWTH
AND LOCAL POLITICS

Leaders of nearly every city in the United States want to project the image of their city as a thriving metropolis. Whether a city prospers or withers on the vine, however, depends on many factors. Beginning around 1830 and continuing into the early twentieth century, for instance, many cities grew rapidly because of a combination of immigration and internal migration from the farms to the cities (Mohl 1985, 18–26; Monkkonen 1988, 5–6). Industrial expansion provided jobs in cities that could be filled by Americans fresh from the farm or by newly arrived immigrants seeking to get ahead economically. As a result, cities with a strong industrial base, such as New York, Detroit, Chicago, and Pittsburgh, grew substantially in population and wealth.

Patterns of urban growth changed in the twentieth century, however, as manufacturing industries matured and migration into the large cities slowed. The widespread affordability of automobiles coupled with new and better roads allowed Americans to live farther from their places of work. This increased mobility, along with government programs designed to promote home ownership, helped fuel the growth of suburbs in the years following World War II. Internal migration changed as well, as people moved away from the Northeast to the Sunbelt cities of the South and West. A significant consequence of these new patterns, particularly the growth of the suburbs, was that central cities lost a disproportionate number of middle-class residents. Many older cities were left with an aging infrastructure of streets, bridges, and public buildings, and increasingly, their populations were bifurcated between well-off residents in exclusive neighborhoods and poorer residents in older homes of the central cities.

One lesson from this overview seems clear: the economic vitality of cities depends, at least in part, upon the broader economic and political circumstances of their regions and the nation (Barnes and Ledebur 1998; Ladd and Yinger 1989). Yet city leaders have never been content to leave local economic growth to external forces. As long as there have been cities, there have been city boosters willing to extol the business advantages and lifestyle virtues of their city (Boorstin 1965, 115–134; Mohl 1985, 68–73; Molotch 1976). In this chapter, we examine the contemporary dynamic of local economic growth, often pushed along by a city's business and political elite, and the economic conditions and government policies that create the context within which cities seek growth.

■ The Growth Imperative in Urban America

Why is growth so important to American cities? There are essentially two answers. One is that cities need economic growth for fiscal reasons. Economic growth allows cities to meet their obligations to provide city services without having to raise tax rates unduly. The second answer is more overtly political. In most cities at most times, being supportive of economic growth is an easy position for elected officials to adopt. Economic growth is an attractive goal for politicians because of the fiscal considerations and because economic growth offers opportunities for tangible benefits. Ambitious politicians know that holding a press conference to announce the arrival of a new business in the city, staging a groundbreaking ceremony for a new ballpark, or holding a ribbon cutting to open a new downtown skyscraper all help voters associate local prosperity with their elected officials.

We shall return to the political considerations later, but the issue of a city's fiscal condition deserves elaboration. A city's fiscal condition is important because city governments provide essential services to businesses, residents, visitors, and commuters. Among the services that local governments routinely provide are the delivery of water and other utilities, trash collection, police and fire protection, recreation, education, and health care. Of course, cities across the nation differ in the extent to which they provide certain services, but all have the burden of supplying basic services such as street maintenance and police protection.

Local governments have not always provided such an extensive array of services. In the period following World War II, however, city governments began to provide new services and more of their traditional services to meet the demands of urban residents in an expanding economy. Increased demand for government services arose from many factors, but chief among them was the growing prosperity of Americans generally (Herson and Bolland 1990, 353–371). While the expansion of services improved the quality of life for many city residents, it was costly as well. General city expenditures, which pay mostly for public services, grew by 307 percent in constant dollars between 1950 and 1975, compared to an increase of 240 percent in the federal budget during the same period (Herson and Bolland 1990, 318–319).

City expenditures did not continue to increase at such a rapid rate after 1975. But the point remains that city governments faced an increased demand for essential services, and providing these services required more resources. The money to pay for services comes from taxes. In general, city governments rely on three sources of revenue: local tax money, fees, and transfers from state or federal governments. The vast bulk of locally provided tax money comes from three types of taxes: property, sales, and income. Cities traditionally have relied most heavily on property taxes for revenue because the ability of local governments to raise money through sales or income taxes is closely controlled by state governments.

The essential point is that cities need tax revenues to provide services. If the cost of providing services increases, cities must either cut services, which is unpopular, or raise more tax money. Additional tax money can be obtained either by raising tax rates, which again is not politically popular, or by maintaining the same tax rate with an expanding local economy. If the economy is growing, property becomes more valuable, people make more money, and they buy more goods; all of this produces more tax revenue without increasing tax rates.

So city governments can meet the demand for public services either by doing what is politically unpopular—raising tax rates—or by encouraging growth in the economy. The rapid expansion of city services in the postwar period was paid for largely by a growing national economy. Economic growth allowed local governments to collect more in taxes, and since state and federal governments were also collecting more tax money, it also allowed more aid from state and federal governments to cities.

Expansion of the national economy could not and did not last forever. The national economy cooled considerably by the mid-1970s, but the impact of the economic slowdown on U.S. cities was masked for a time by the policies of the federal government. During the 1960s many new federal programs were initiated to assist cities. Even though local tax revenues were falling or not increasing as rapidly as they had been, urban areas could continue to pay for services by using federal money in place of local funds. As with economic conditions, however, federal policies can change.

The Rise and Demise of Federal Urban Policy

The earliest federal programs directed toward cities grew out of the New Deal and reflected the importance of urban voters to Franklin Roosevelt's Democratic coalition. The creation of a national policy for urban areas and the targeting of significant amounts of federal money, however, began in earnest with the Great Society programs of the 1960s. Two programs that promised assistance to urban areas—the War on Poverty and the Model Cities program—were central to President Lyndon Johnson's Great Society initiative. In addition, during the 1960s, Congress created and funded a number of new federal programs to assist local governments. The result of this spate of new programs was that federal assistance to cities increased substantially. In 1957, the amount of federal money going to big cities was about $3.8 billion (in constant 1990 dollars), by 1977, federal aid to big cities had more than quadrupled to $16.8 billion (Peterson 1993, 195).

The money coming from Washington was not a gift but a mechanism for implementing federal policies. Most of the federal programs for cities were created as categorical grants. These grants typically stipulated that the federal government would provide the bulk, usually 80 or 90 percent, of the money needed for a specific project, with the local government paying the remaining costs. Federal money thus became indispensable to cities that sought to undertake a whole range of development activities from constructing sewers to expanding airports. Along with federal money, however, came federal regulations. The federal government was able to stipulate that when cities accepted funding, they would also have to comply with federal laws concerning civil rights, labor conditions, the environment, community involvement, and the like.

During the 1960s, the federal government used the lure of federal money, with substantial strings attached, as a mechanism for shaping how localities dealt with their residents. The intentions of federal officials were not always achieved, however. Federal urban renewal efforts, for example, were captured by local development interests in many cities, and federal funds were used to undertake projects that served the interests of local developers more than goals of federal policy (Anderson 1964; Mollenkopf 1983). Nonetheless, the 1960s were a period during which national politicians had an intense interest in America's cities and attempted to use federal resources to influence local conditions.

Intense federal concern with the problems of urban areas did not last long. The 1970s became a transition period during which federal programs were consolidated, though the level of spending on urban assistance did not decline (Palmer 1984; Peterson 1993, 200–202). This transition was marked by a shift from categorical grants to block grants. Block grants were favored by some members of Congress, particularly Republicans, because they allowed local officials greater discretion in the use of federal funds. Perhaps the most important example of this shift was the Housing and Community Development Act passed in 1974. This legislation, passed by a Congress controlled by Democrats and signed by a Republican president, consolidated seven existing categorical grant programs, most notably the urban renewal and model cities programs, into the Community Development Block Grant (CDBG) program (Palmer 1984, 27). The CDBG program was popular with local as well as federal officials because it reduced the stipulations for using federal money (Dommel 1979).

Another program that encouraged greater local discretion in the use of federal funds was revenue sharing, an idea championed by President Richard Nixon. Revenue sharing was passed in 1972 and thereafter provided federal money directly to state and local governments, with local officials having nearly complete discretion as to how the money was used. Even though giving local officials greater control over federal money was popular politically, in practice local officials often neglected federal policy goals as they sought to use federal money to their political advantage (Wong and Peterson 1986).

Federal funding continued to be an important source of revenue for cities into the early 1980s. The election of Ronald Reagan in 1980, however, challenged the ideological basis of support for federal aid to cities (Barnekov, Rich, and Warren 1981). In a sharp break with the goals of the Johnson administration, President Reagan and his advisors emphasized that the free market, not the federal government, should provide resources to aid state and local governments. During President Reagan's tenure, programs designed to assist urban areas were eliminated or their funding was greatly reduced. Revenue sharing, the program instituted by President Nixon, was completely eliminated during the Reagan budget cuts, and funding for the CDBG program was reduced by more than half (Caraley 1992, 9). Reductions in funding for some social service programs as well as changes to the federal tax code also affected cities negatively. Further, many programs that had previously involved transfers of federal funds to local governments were modified, so that whatever federal funds were available went to the states rather than directly to local governments (Judd and Swanstrom 1998, 238).

From the late 1960s to the early 1980s, federal funds were an important part of state and local development activities, and the reduction of federal funds had a tremendous impact on state and local governments at those levels. Indeed, some scholars have identified the period after 1984 as the "postfederal" era (Clarke and Gaile 1992, 1998). While some local governments responded to reduced federal funds by cutting development activities, other state and local governments responded by adopting more entrepreneurial approaches to economic development (Eisinger 1988; Clarke and Gaile 1992, 1998).

Susan Clarke and Gary Gaile have identified three separate "waves" of local economic development policies (1998, 55–62). In the first wave, cities used traditional policy tools, such as acquiring land for new buildings and issuing bonds to finance infrastructure, to attract businesses to the city. These traditional "smokestack chasing" policies were gradually supplemented by a second wave of policies prompted by the infusion of federal funds in the 1970s. The second wave was a transitional period during which cities used federal money to try more risky, entrepreneurial development strategies, which included creating small business incubators, streamlining permit processes, issuing below-market loans to businesses providing new jobs, and putting revenues from existing programs into new development schemes (Clarke and Gaile 1992, 190–193; Clarke and Gaile 1998, 81–82).

The demise of federal funding for urban programs in the mid-1980s led to a third wave of development programs. Although similar to second-wave policies, third-wave policies evince an even greater concern with stimulating new businesses and expanding markets. According to Clarke and Gaile (1998, 61–63), third-wave development policies are characterized by greater willingness of local governments to take risks, increased cooperation among local governments on a metro or regional level, pooling of public and private financing rather than relying on one or the other, and greater reliance on public-private partnerships or quasi-public agencies to implement development projects.

By the late 1980s, it was quite clear the federal government was no longer going to supply significant resources to help cities provide services to the poor or to assist with traditional economic development. Rather, federal policies encouraged states and cities to seek local growth using entrepreneurial techniques. The election of a Democrat to the presidency in 1992 did little to change the thrust of federal policy toward cities (Mollenkopf 1998). Indeed, President Clinton's primary urban policy initiative, the empowerment zone and enterprise community program, was only a slightly modified version of policy proposals under consideration during the Reagan and Bush years (Mollenkopf 1998, 479–480). Though Clinton's empowerment zone initiative provided some funding for social service programs, the tenor of the program was very much in keeping with the desire to push local governments toward entrepreneurial activity.

In sum, President Johnson's Great Society initiative aimed federal money at cities to ameliorate social and economic problems. By the 1990s, however, federal policy toward cities sought only to encourage local leaders to use the entrepreneurial spirit to find new ways to promote local economic growth. In part, these changes at the federal level reflected an ideological shift among policymakers away from the belief that federal resources could solve social problems and toward the belief that limited federal resources could, at most, encourage local governments to pursue new growth strategies.

The change in federal policy was also partly a response to a larger set of changes gathering steam during the 1980s and 1990s—the globalization of the economy. As Clarke and Gaile (1998, 63) note, "In the context of globalization, local economic development move[d] away from traditional place wars of the industrial era and toward a more facilitating, entrepreneurial approach to encouraging growth processes, structuring markets, and linking local and global economies."

Cities and the Global Economy

In the postwar world, U.S. cities were accustomed to competing against other cities in their state or region. They competed to be the location of a new business or government agency, to host the largest conventions, and to have the tallest building. During the 1980s, however, American cities were increasingly competing with cities at the international level. This new era of global competition is most apparent at the top of the urban hierarchy where cities such as New York, London, and Tokyo have become "global" or "world" cities (Sassen 1991; Friedmann 1995). According to proponents of the world cities thesis, the rise of a global economy is leading to the creation of a handful of cities throughout the world that fill an economic niche. "World cities articulate regional, national, and international economies into a global economy. They serve as the organizing nodes of a global economic system" (Friedmann 1995, 25). Although based primarily on economic criteria, the concept of a world city incorporates culture as well. In order to appeal to the tastes of an international corporate elite, "world cities are richly endowed with the largest variety of cultural and entertainment facilities of the highest quality, such as museums, galleries, opera houses, theaters, and concert halls" (Shachar 1995, 157).

Not all cities, of course, aim to be at the top of the world cities hierarchy. What the world cities thesis suggests, however, is that U.S. cities can no longer simply compete with one another for economic benefits. Whereas city leaders in Los Angeles might once have viewed San Francisco as a regional rival or New York City as a national competitor, now they must contend with Tokyo, Hong Kong, and Singapore for dominance of the Pacific Rim.

The global economy has thus become an important feature of the broader environment within which cities compete for growth (e.g., Barnes and Ledebur 1998; Fry 1995; Knight 1989; Knox 1995). The global economy is characterized by several features that differ from previous patterns of economic activity. Driven by advances in transportation and communications, the business activities of many large and mid-sized corporations are less tied to one nation and instead may be spread across several nations. These changes are evident in traditional manufacturing industries such as automobiles. In the 1960s, automobiles were usually made in one country, such as the United States, Germany, or Japan, and exported to others. By the 1980s, however, automobiles made by a major American or Japanese car company were assembled in one country from parts manufactured in a host of different nations.

Globalization has been especially evident in the service sector. Traditionally, financial services like banking and insurance were provided almost exclusively by local or national companies. By the 1990s, financial services were becoming internationally competitive as a result of the "financial services revolution" (Moran 1991, 10; see also Sassen 1988). Changes in technology, government regulation, and the organization of companies that provide financial services have greatly increased the mobility of investment capital. Along with the easier movement of money has come the greater movement of people. An extraordinary increase in international tourism is yet another dimension of the global economy. According to data collected by the World Tourism Organization, there were approximately twenty-five million international tourists in 1950 and receipts from international tourism totaled $2.1 billion. By 1995, the number of international tourist arrivals had increased to 567 million and receipts had increased to more than $407 billion (World Tourism Organization 2000, 22–24).

Virtually all U.S. cities have been affected by economic restructuring resulting from the global economy. In some cities, a case can be made that the trend toward economic globalization will result in a net benefit. For example, increased trade between the United States and many Latin American nations provides an edge to cities like Miami that function as intermediaries (Grosfoguel 1995). Other cities, however, have not fared so well. Cities such as Buffalo, Cleveland, and Detroit have suffered from the decline of traditional industries, a rash of closed businesses, and fewer high-paying jobs.

While it is possible to look at these circumstances and conclude that American cities are being buffeted by international economic forces far beyond the control of local businesses or city officials, we must be alert to ways in which city leaders respond to economic change (Fainstein 1990; Judd and Parkinson 1990; Logan and Swanstrom 1990). For instance, although Baltimore, Buffalo, and Pittsburgh faced similar circumstances of economic decline in the postwar period, business and political leaders in these three cities responded in very different ways, and as a result, these cities face the next century with different prospects (see Hula 1990; Perry 1990; and Sbragia 1990).[1]

The fortunes of U.S. cities are, to a certain extent, dependent upon national and international economic conditions beyond the control of local leaders. Cities are also affected by the policies of national and state governments, which city leaders try to influence through lobbying but ultimately cannot control. Despite the constraints of economic change and federal policy, the actions of city leaders still matter. Their actions matter not because they single-handedly determine the economic prospects for the city. Rather, these actions matter because they help determine how changes in the economy or federal policy affect the lives of citizens in America's cities.

■ Regime Theory

How can city leaders pursue local economic development given the difficulties they face within the broader political and economic environment? Why do some cities use entrepreneurial, even speculative, growth strategies while other cities seek growth with more modest techniques? The answers to these questions, we argue, can best be expressed through an approach to urban politics known as regime theory.

Regime theory arises from a diverse series of empirical and conceptual studies, but it has been articulated cogently in the scholarship of Clarence Stone (1989a, 1989b, 1993, 1998). Drawing on the work of Charles Lindblom (1977) and Stephen Elkin (1987), regime theory begins with the premise that the American political economy has two basic principles: (1) government institutions are controlled by public officials formally accountable through the process of open elections, and (2) the economy is predominantly directed by private, nongovernmental actors (Stone 1993, 2). Given this division of market and state, it follows that members of these two groups, business and government, will each have a basis of power and an interest in the content of local public policies. An urban regime, then, may be defined as *"the informal arrangements by which public bodies and private interests function together in order to be able to make and carry out governing decisions"* (Stone 1989b, 6; original emphasis).

▓ Actors in an Urban Regime

At the heart of regime theory is a set of "informal arrangements" between political leaders and members of the city's business establishment. These informal arrangements are essentially a network of relatively enduring connections that are built upon shared concerns and trust between individuals in business and those in public office. A regime is not a single, concrete entity that can be touched or measured. Rather, the concept of a regime is intended to capture the structure of well-established connections between business and political leaders that are essential to getting things done in the city. Although the notion of a regime may seem rather fluid, its operation is quite real. When city officials and local property developers meet over lunch to talk about the developers' plans to tear down a dilapidated downtown hotel and replace it with a gleaming new office tower—that is the city's regime in action. In regime theory, these informal, horizontal connections between elites are viewed as more central to understanding which policy objectives receive attention and what actions will be taken than the formal, hierarchical structures of government.

Who are the elite that make up a city's regime? There is no definitive list of individuals who will or will not be part of a governing regime. The way a regime is composed, or even whether one exists, will vary from city to city depending upon conditions such as the structure of local government, the nature of local business, existing social and political cleavages, economic conditions, and the city's history. Still, from existing research on growth politics in U.S. cities, we can identify the likely candidates for inclusion in a city's growth regime.

The most general discussion of who is likely to be part of a growth regime comes from John Logan and Harvey Molotch (1987, 57–85).[2] Logan and Molotch identify two groups of key participants in growth coalitions: politicians and business people. Elected officials such as mayors and members of the city council are the political figures who are most central to the growth regime. Elected officials are particularly inclined to advocate local growth because they rely on business to finance their campaigns and because they have a vested interest in appearing to provide strong leadership (see also Stone 1989a). Although not discussed by Logan and Molotch in any detail, bureaucrats in city agencies that deal with local development are also likely political figures in a city's regime.

Among businesses, the most ardent advocates for local growth are not the leaders of large national or international corporations, but local business people involved in property development, real estate, or property financing (Logan and Molotch 1987, 62; Heying 1995). While corporate leaders are often involved in local growth politics because of a shared commitment to the ideology of economic growth, their interests are not served as directly by local growth because of the mobility of corporate investment capital.

Logan and Molotch single out two types of businesses as likely to have a key organizational role in growth politics: media (particularly newspapers) and utilities. These businesses are crucial because they benefit from growth generally but do not have a strong interest in the particular form of growth. Thus individuals in these businesses are able to take a "statesmanlike position" in their advocacy of growth that allows them to serve as the "arbiter of internal growth machine bickering" (Logan and Molotch 1987, 71). Logan and Molotch also identify a variety of "auxiliary players" who may play a part in the growth coalition. "Key among these auxiliary players are the cultural institutions in an area: museums, theaters, universities, symphonies, and professional sports teams" (Logan and Molotch 1987, 75). People associated with auxiliary organizations may participate in the regime because they regard growth as being in their organization's interest or because of long-standing ties to local business people or politicians (see also Molotch 1976).

▨ Regime Power and Local Development

A regime's purpose is to "make and carry out governing decisions" (Stone 1989b, 6). The informal network of connections between business and political elites is substantively important because it is the mechanism for bringing resources together to accomplish common goals. The emphasis on getting things done is a fundamental feature of how power is understood in regime theory (Stoker 1995). In contrast to other approaches to urban politics, regime theory emphasizes that a regime is a mechanism for overcoming the fragmented power and limited resources that characterize local governments in the United States. A regime thus enables a city to pursue a coherent policy agenda. This type of power is what Stone (1989b, 227) calls the power of social production: "the capacity to assemble and use needed resources for a policy initiative." Social production is the "power to" accomplish goals rather than "power over" the action of others (the power of social control).

Gerry Stoker (1995, 64–66) argues that regime theory recognizes four types of power: systemic power, the power of social control, coalitional power, and social production power. Systemic power is rooted in the arrangement of existing social and political institutions. The concept of systemic power is a recognition that, whatever the institutional arrangements, some individuals or groups will have greater access to power than others. In the context of American urban politics, the institutions that matter most are private economic resources and the electoral system. So in nearly all U.S. cities, business has systemic power because of its control over economic resources. In some cities, certain social groups may also have systemic power because, by virtue of their numbers and ability to mobilize, they can control election outcomes.

The power of social control, in contrast, comes not from position within the system but from using resources to achieve dominance and overcome resistance. In the classical pluralist view, power is the ability to exercise control, and the exercise of control is a matter of expending resources. Whereas this view of power is central to pluralist accounts of urban politics, regime theory sees local governments as too fragmented and too weak to exercise social control except in limited policy areas. "The operating assumption of the regime paradigm is that the authority of a community's official government is too weak to govern autonomously" (Stone 1989a, 148).

The weakness of local governments within the United States leads to the exercise of a third type of power—coalitional power (Stoker 1995, 65). Coalitional power is exercised when political actors come together and use their resources to seek a common goal. The application of coalitional power tends to be ad hoc; that is, individuals or groups come together to pursue short-term and relatively tangible goals. For example, neighborhood residents and small business owners might coalesce to get better street lighting. Having achieved the objective, however, the coalition dissolves because it entails costs to maintain it and it no longer has a tangible goal. Further, the objectives of coalitions are often intended not to obtain a certain good but to thwart action by others. In most U.S. cities, coalitions to improve a neighborhood are much less common than coalitions to block a tax increase. Because the formal power of local governments is fragmented and weak, exercises of coalitional power are often effective. Along with social control, coalitional power is associated with the pluralist understanding of urban politics.

Both regime theory and pluralism recognize systemic, social control, and coalitional power. The distinctiveness of regime theory, however, is that it emphasizes the importance of social production power. Fundamentally, an urban regime is a mechanism for overcoming the obstacles to exercising power at the local level. A regime is thus a way to create policy stability and ensure urban governance. As Stone (1989a, 148) puts it:

> For a community to be governed, group conflict must be managed and personal ambition harnessed. Although governance does not entail comprehensive control, it does require that cooperation and exchange occur and that critical decisions be made. That is what urban regimes are about, and it is through civic organizations and informal networks that much of the essential cooperation, exchange, and consequent mobilization of resources occurs.

In the abstract, the power to get things done in a city could be dedicated to any number of goals—improving the quality of neighborhood life, better housing for the poor, or encouraging citizens to take an active part in political life, to name just a few. In practice, though, the task the regime sets for itself is local economic development. Economic development is a policy that politicians and business leaders regard as a priority (Logan and Molotch 1987, 62–85; Stone 1987, 6–8). Local economic growth benefits local businesses because it increases the customer base and the price of fixed assets such as land. Political leaders prefer to seek growth because it provides tax revenues to keep the city solvent without the need to raise taxes or cut services. The desire for growth impels cooperation because businesses need the formal authority of government to carry out large development projects and because elected leaders gain the opportunity to distribute tangible rewards to supporters and to solidify their public support by demonstrating leadership. Cooperation is necessary because each partner brings part of the means necessary to get things done: government supplies authority and business provides resources.

Although a commitment to local development is often the core policy objective for urban regimes, regimes may have other purposes (see, for example, Logan, Whaley, and Crowder 1997, 606–609; Pierre 1999; Stone 1993, 18–22). Gerry Stoker and Karen Mossberger (1994) have developed a typology that distinguishes urban regimes by their primary purpose. Drawing on the work of Stone and others, Stoker and Mossberger describe three types of regimes: organic, instrumental, and symbolic. An organic regime exists primarily to maintain the city's status quo, whereas the purpose of an instrumental regime is to accomplish tangible development projects. A symbolic regime is slightly different; its purpose is to redefine the city's image.

These types of regimes differ not only in terms of purpose but also in the motivation of participants, the nature of the coalition, and the relationship of the regime to the broader environment (Stoker and Mossberger 1994, 199–200).[3] Organic regimes occur most commonly in stable, prosperous, and homogeneous areas. Members of an organic regime are motivated to participate by a sense of civic pride or shared values. As a result, organic regimes tend to exclude those regarded as "outsiders" and maintain their independence from external actors such as higher levels of government. In the U.S. context, the concept of an organic regime could best be applied to some suburban communities with well-off residents whose primary concerns are in maintaining the status quo. Such governance arrangements chiefly value efficiency and feature a pragmatic policy style and consensual politics (Pierre 1999, 388).

In contrast, instrumental regimes are found in cities seeking to promote local growth or counter economic decline. Stone's (1989, 1993) notion of a growth regime fits the instrumental regime type. Participants in instrumental regimes are motivated primarily by tangible results and coalitions—often in the form of public-private partnerships—that are held together by selective incentives. Business participants get beneficial public infrastructure and other tangible goods, while political leaders get to claim credit for new jobs, new buildings, or better transportation. Unlike organic regimes, however, greater effort is required to maintain a working political coalition because participation is motivated by access to tangible rewards rather than shared values. The need to provide tangible benefits to key participants also means that the interests of those less central to the regime will be excluded. Stoker and Mossberger (1994, 209) note that because of the need for resources to enact development projects, instrumental regimes are often dependent on outside actors such as the state or federal government.

Finally, a symbolic regime seeks to transform the image of the city. Substantial differences of interest may exist among participants in symbolic regimes, but "a common sense of purpose is achieved through the manipulation of symbols which express the rightness of the cause and its attractiveness" (Stoker and Mossberger 1994, 209). Because participation is not motivated by tangible benefits, symbolic regimes are often more inclusive than instrumental regimes. Leaders within a symbolic regime may reach out to a broad range of participants with little in common except a willingness to support the expressive goals of the regime. Unlike organic and instrumental regimes, where the deliberative process is of little interest, symbolic regimes can be process driven (Pierre 1999, 389). Yet as Stoker and Mossberger note, symbolic regimes often are transitional. A symbolic regime may emerge when key groups are "attempting to establish a new political outlook or paradigm" but may not last long given the inherent difficulties of managing a political coalition held together by symbolism (Stoker and Mossberger 1994, 205). Given their desire to change the city's image, symbolic regimes may be especially dependent on external resources.

For our purposes, the typology developed by Stoker and Mossberger is particularly useful because of its distinction between instrumental and symbolic regimes. Much of urban development politics is motivated by the desire to achieve tangible benefits. But as Stoker and Mossberger's typology indicates, urban regimes may forego the need for immediate rewards in circumstances where key players wish to transform the city's image. Symbolic regimes are not likely to last indefinitely, however, and require access to appealing symbols to evoke broad-based support. As we discuss in Chapter 3, events such as a world's fair or the Olympic games may well provide the kind of symbols necessary to change a city's image.

Instrumental regimes are the most typical ones in American cities. Thus, delivering the tangible benefits of local economic development is the primary motivation for the regime arrangement. But does the regime alone determine development outcomes in a city? The answer to this question has provoked some debate. One criticism of regime theory is that it falls into the "localist trap" (Stoker 1995, 67; see also Horan 1991; Lauria 1997). Because of its intense focus on the actions of local elites, critics charge that regime theory tends to overemphasize local action as the cause of policy outcomes and to underemphasize the effect of external conditions, such as national economic conditions or state and federal policies.

In response, advocates concede that regime theory does have a localist orientation but reject the implication that it is intended to be the sole explanation of urban policy (Stone 1998). Initially, regime theory was a response to economically based explanations of local politics, notably Paul Peterson's *City Limits* (1981). Peterson argued that the quest for economic growth at the local level could best be understood as an economic market—cities had to pursue businesses if they wanted to prosper because in the U.S. federal system, cities had few options except to attract mobile capital. In this view, the actions of cities were a response to economic incentives and not primarily the product of local politics.

Regime theorists, in contrast, argue that political choices made by local political actors are essential to local policy outcomes. "Local decision makers do not simply follow the imperatives that emanate from the national political economy; they must also interpret those imperatives, apply them to local conditions, and act on them within the constraints of the political arrangements they build and maintain" (Stone 1987, 4). Rather than ignore the impact of external economic and political factors, however, regime theory "posits that the impact of the global economy on the local community is *mediated* through local governing arrangements" (Stone 1998, 250; original emphasis).[4] So external conditions—whether changes in the national economy, federal policy, or demographic conditions—affect what happens in cities. But in the regime perspective, local political decisions also matter. If we seek explanations for why some cities prosper from an international trade deal while others suffer, why some cities are able to lessen racial segregation while others are not, or why some cities thrive when freed from federal regulation while others stagnate, regime theory instructs us to look at local politics as well as external conditions.

Regime theory, in sum, provides a framework for the study of urban politics. The essential features of regime theory stipulate that business leaders have a privileged position in local politics because of their command of economic resources. Because business leaders are affected by local political decisions, not just at the level of property taxes but by the business climate of the city as well, they attempt to shape public policies to benefit business. In order to shape an agenda and bring results, business leaders need the cooperation of elected officials. Local elected officials and local bureaucrats seize the opportunities afforded by cooperation with business leaders. Cooperation allows politicians to overcome the weakness of governing institutions and pursue substantial accomplishments, at least in the realm of development politics, and provides numerous small benefits that can be used to reward supporters or co-opt opponents. Over time, these networks of connections become so entrenched that they are the only practical mechanism for action. Thus the mutual interest of business and political leaders makes economic development central to urban governance.

The regime approach is useful because it provides a way to understand how things get done and why economic development is so central to urban politics. Regime theory also explicitly recognizes the significance of conflict. Because economic development is central to urban politics, conflict over development is central to politics in regime theory (Stone 1993; Logan and Molotch 1987; Logan, Whaley, and Crowder 1997). It may come as opposition to specific development projects from local residents or as a broader debate over the merits of development versus quality of life, but conflict between the desires of residents and the interests of business is central to politics in America's cities. Regime theory provides a powerful framework for investigating urban politics by focusing attention on the composition of the governing coalition, the substance of the dominant policy agenda, and the nature of conflict.

▓ Growth Regimes and Olympic Politics

Does regime theory help to explain why cities pursue mega-events such as the Olympic games? We argue that it does. Indeed, our thesis is that mega-events are quintessential growth regime endeavors and that the initiation of a mega-event strategy is largely inexplicable outside the context of regime politics. Why the Olympics? Playing host to a high-profile event such as the Olympic games provides an ideal platform for a local development agenda because it allows growth proponents access to the popular symbolism of international sports and makes opposition to development projects associated with those symbols more difficult.

The existence of a growth regime in a city helps explain why cities strive for economic development. The pursuit of growth by way of a mega-event signals something else as well. One factor that motivates city leaders to employ resources for economic development is the shared image among local elites of what they want their city to be: "A city's image is the backdrop against which development occurs; and image creation is frequently a goal of the economic development process" (Pagano and Bowman 1995, 67). Public justifications for an Olympic bid are presented as part of a strategy to promote tourism and, more generally, to establish the city's image as a location capable of holding a "world class" event (e.g., Hall 1996; Robertson and Guerrier 1998; Rutheiser 1997; Waitt 1999). As Pagano and Bowman (1995) point out, some cities pursue growth more aggressively because of the vision that city leaders have of the proper "orbit" for their city.

A key motivation underlying the pursuit of a mega-event, then, is the desire among the growth elite to make their city a world-class place capable of hosting an international event of the magnitude of the Olympic games. Prestigious events are desirable to growth advocates because they promise short-term tourism revenue and, more important, national and international recognition for the city in an increasingly global competition for investment capital. Hosting the Olympic games thus has great potential to justify a broad range of development activities, even if they have little relevance to a sporting event, because hosting the games is about putting the city on the world stage.

Hosting the Olympics brings worldwide attention, but it also has costs. Constructing expensive venues for elite sporting events, modifying existing transportation systems, creating or expanding public facilities for housing athletes and the media, and constructing or expanding private facilities such as hotels, resorts, parking lots, and restaurants are just some of the potential development projects. While some residents may benefit, these projects may bring substantial negative consequences for others in the form of increased traffic, loss of affordable housing and open space, or disruption of established neighborhoods.

Some scholars argue that citizen dissatisfaction with the negative consequences of growth can lead to the formation of "slow growth" or "no growth" coalitions of environmentalists, neighborhood activists, and others (Clark and Goetz 1994; DeLeon 1992; Schneider and Teske 1993). With its short duration, limited beneficiaries, and need for extensive planning, Olympic-related development may provide opportunities for opponents of the philosophy of continual growth. Thus, in addition to examining who supports Olympic mega-events, we must also attend to the sources of opposition or resistance to Olympic development.

■ Conclusion

As a result of changes in federal policy and globalization of the economy, local leaders have moved toward entrepreneurial strategies to promote growth and enhance their city's image. City leaders are not able to control the broader economic and political circumstances in which cities find themselves. They can, however, make choices about how to pursue growth that will affect the lives of residents, the prospects of local businesses, and ultimately the fortunes of the city. Such choices are rarely arrived at through meaningful democratic dialogue between citizens and local leaders. Rather, a city's political agenda is dominated by the promotion of economic growth because growth unites business and political leaders in a way that no other issue does. The pursuit of economic growth, however, can take many different paths. In the next chapter, we illuminate one of the more intriguing paths that U.S. cities have pursued—the mega-event strategy.

■ Notes

1. Baltimore embarked on an ambitious effort to revitalize the city under the leadership of an activist mayor, William Schaefer, but the results have been uneven at best (Hula 1990). Pittsburgh successfully refashioned itself from a manufacturing city into a service city through the coordinated efforts of business, government, and the nonprofit sector (Sbragia 1990). Despite a concerted effort, Buffalo continues to struggle with the legacy of economic decline (Perry 1990).

2. Logan and Molotch (1987) use the term "growth machine" rather than "regime." In the literature on urban development policy, different terms are used to describe similar empirical conditions. For example, Molotch (1976) and Logan and Molotch (1987) refer to a "growth machine"; Mollenkopf (1983) speaks of a "progrowth coalition"; Elkin (1987) describes an "entrepreneurial regime"; and Stone (1989b) discusses a "development regime." We use the terminology of regime theory here because the regime concept is more general and has been more fully developed in theoretical discussions (Stoker 1995). For further discussion on the relationship between growth machines and regimes, see Harding (1995) and Logan, Whaley, and Crowder (1997).

3. Stoker and Mossberger (1994, 199–200) identify four criteria that define regimes in addition to purpose: motivation of participants, basis for sense of common purpose, quality of coalition, and relationship with the broader environment. Their distinction between sense of purpose and quality of coalition, however, is not central to our concerns.

4. Stone (1993, 1998) uses the analogy that regime theory is like the S>O>R model in psychology. Psychologists working in the behavioral tradition realized that understanding a particular action or response (R) required more than merely knowing its immediate stimulus (S). The stimulus-response or S>R model was not supported empirically because a given stimulus could provoke a range of responses. By including the conditioning of the organism (O), psychologists could better predict responses. The S>O>R model was thus superior to the S>R model. Stone argues that regime theory is like the O—it helps explain the range of responses to a given stimulus. In Stone's terms, economic or political circumstances external to the city serve as stimuli. But we can better explain the variation in responses at the city level if we include the nature of the city's governing arrangements as a conditioning (O) factor between external events and local responses.

3

MEGA-EVENTS AND ECONOMIC DEVELOPMENT

International sports is big business. Consider, for instance, soccer's World Cup. Broadcast rights for the 2002 tournament, in which 197 nations will participate, were purchased for $960 million by a Swiss-German intermediary that will resell the broadcasts to television companies around the world (Jones 1999). Although spectators pay to watch the athletes, the competition to host these events is equally fierce. International sporting events are major tourist attractions, and their global television audience means an event can serve as a showcase for the host city or country as well.

Do sporting events, however large they might be, matter politically? The answer, in a word, is yes. They matter both because international sporting events have tremendous symbolic significance and because they influence the allocation of scarce public resources. To illustrate, the U.S. General Accounting Office (2000) reported that various agencies of the federal government have spent roughly $2 billion to help three cities stage the 1984, 1996, and 2002 Olympic games. Of this amount, Salt Lake City alone received about $1.3 billion, with Atlanta getting $609 million, and Los Angeles $75 million (all in 1999 dollars). The bottom line is, because of the Olympics, these cities got federal money to build roads, spruce up parks, and improve security—federal funds that could not go to Dallas, Newark, or Minneapolis.

In this chapter, we address the emergence of the strategy of using mega-events such as the Olympic games to promote local economic development. Hosting mega-events has become a prominent economic development strategy in the United States because of the effects of globalization, changed patterns of federal aid, and the financial success of the 1984 Olympic games. High-profile, large-scale events can provide international prestige. The Olympics, in particular, have become a sought-after event because of their positive imagery (Dyreson 1998; Espy 1979; C. Hill 1996; Mannheim 1990; Tomlinson 1996). Just seeking the games provides powerful symbols that can be used at the local level. City leaders may use the idea of hosting the games to justify encouraging a variety of development projects that might not be politically feasible if attempted in the context of everyday politics.

To establish the context for our examination of mega-events, we begin with an overview of the trend in local development policy emphasizing consumption-based activities. The focus on consumption-oriented economic development highlights activities that typically constitute this form of development, such as building convention centers, sports facilities, and entertainment complexes to draw large numbers of visitors to a city for the pursuit of pleasure, as well as to provide an impetus for further investment and development. Next we discuss the emergence of mega-events as part of an urban growth strategy, with emphasis on the Olympic games as *the* signature event. The chapter concludes with an overview of the Olympic bidding process, a prelude to the case studies of Los Angeles, Atlanta, and Salt Lake City.

■ Consumption-oriented Economic Development

The quest for economic development has long dominated the politics of urban governments. Much of the discussion of urban economic development, however, points to a major change in the orientation of development—away from the pursuit of production activities such as manufacturing and toward an emphasis on attracting consumption activities in leisure, entertainment, tourism, and sports (e.g., Eisinger 2000; Fainstein and Stokes 1998; Gladstone 1998; Hannigan 1998; Judd and Fainstein 1999; Law 1993; Mullins et al. 1999; Sorkin 1992; Zukin 1982; Zukin et al. 1998). Tourism has been described as an important indicator of the shift to a postmodern society, offering travelers vistas and venues of a romanticized past, popular culture, or the natural environment.[1] As Pearce (1988) suggests, it is the "Ulysses factor" that becomes all-important to the tourism industry: the desire to venture out, see the world, and discover one's self. Tourism is about the experience, and the range of tourist experiences includes several degrees of authenticity, from the real to the staged, in reference to both the people and the eventual destination (Pearce 1988, 176–193; see also Newman 1999; Rothman 1998; Urry 1990). One of the factors underlying success in the tourist industry is convenience, since most travelers would not enjoy the trials and tribulations of Ulysses and his motley crew. The tourism industry, like consumption-oriented economic development generally, provides a variety of staged environments to simulate an imagined reality, providing visitors with the status-boosting experiences that make them want to return (Boorstin 1971; Fainstein and Judd 1999b; Pearce 1988; Rothman 1998; Urry 1990).

Recent data indicate the level of the travel and tourism industry's growth and its importance to economic development. Nationally, tourism was the third largest private employer and the third largest segment of retail spending in dollar volume in 1997. The number of tourism-related jobs increased 30 percent between 1987 and 1997 and generated $71 billion in tax revenues for national, state, and local governments in 1997. International travelers alone spent some $73.3 billion in the United States in 1997 (U.S. Travel Data Center 1998; see also Law 1993).

Not surprisingly, such economic clout has encouraged cities to compete mightily for the opportunity to ride this wave of economic growth. The cutting edge of this type of economic growth can be seen in cities such as New York (Zukin 1982) and San Francisco (Wolfe 1999) that pioneered arts and entertainment services in their downtown areas. Most cities, however, have adopted the corporate-center strategy by building convention complexes, sports facilities, museums, shopping malls, and entertainment and gambling complexes alongside the typical government, professional, and retail-space developments. As more cities cater to this type of economic development, the image of the city becomes a central point of differentiation, a beacon that can draw visitors and investment capital amid a sea of similarly constituted consumption spaces. Thus the complex process of image building becomes a central part of consumption-oriented economic development in general, and in the mega-event strategy more specifically.

▓ The Politics of Consumption-oriented Development

Critics of consumption-oriented economic development point to the superficial "theme park" qualities that offer a sanitized, safe, and simulated environment for consumption and display (e.g., Hannigan 1998). Zukin (1991) describes several different types of consumption-oriented landscapes, including gentrified downtowns and postmodern resort colonies. In the former, exemplified by New York, Boston, and Chicago, what was touted as a way of reasserting local identity instead turned out to be the product of an international market culture, privileging middle-class consumers over low-income residents. In the latter, seen most notably in Miami, Orlando, and Los Angeles, the urban landscape is presented in fragments to heighten the visitor's fantasy or dream, hiding the growth of service sector jobs that enhance the profits of the creators of these landscapes. Sorkin (1992) decries the new American city in which public spaces have been lost and are being replaced by homogenized environments, free from the chaos of urban life.

The issues raised by these and other critics regarding urban outcomes have led to a broad critique of not only the economic and cultural effects of consumption-oriented development but also of its politics. For example, Judd (1999) uses the concept of a "tourist bubble" to illustrate these linkages. In many cities there is a well-defined boundary separating tourist spaces from the rest of the city, creating tourist reservations that are "secured, protected, and normalized environments" (Judd 1999, 36). Although land use is contested in most cities and their physical environments include areas of poverty and decay, the tourist bubble reflects a "romanticized, nostalgic sense of history and culture," with a well-crafted image of the city that displays none of this conflict (Judd 1999, 36). A key characteristic of these new consumption spaces is "the way people must visit to buy and consume within these locations the goods and services on sale there, and this is a consumption that is for fun and enjoyment, rather than for necessity" (Mullins et al. 1999, 45). Just as the competition for manufacturing led to copycat subsidy programs, consumption-oriented economic development creates seemingly standardized tourist environments consisting of convention complexes, fancy hotels, entertainment and gambling complexes, and sports facilities alongside new office towers and redeveloped waterfronts. The idea behind these developments is to provoke a certain image of the place and to provide status for those experiencing the place. Among the techniques used to achieve these aims are constructing unique visitor attractions, playing host to prestigious events, or using theme festivals to link tourism development to city marketing (Hall 1992, 1996; Paddison 1993; Short et al. 1993). To illustrate, we briefly examine three components of the tourist bubble: convention complexes, sports development, and entertainment complexes.

Convention complexes. Convention centers are seen as a way of bringing large numbers of visitors into a city's downtown. Conventions consist of business travelers and special-interest travelers, and they often mix the two (Law 1993). The development of convention complexes has been a staple of urban regeneration since the urban renewal programs of the 1950s and 1960s. The role that city and state governments play in convention development differs across the United States. In about half the states, any efforts to attract convention trade is left entirely to the cities, with no state government involvement. In the other half, state authorities are involved in an advisory or supporting capacity. Only in South Carolina does the state take the lead in promoting convention development (U.S. Travel Data Center 1999b, 135–137). But the involvement of state government can be an important mechanism for overcoming the challenges of convention complex development. One example is the state-funded Georgia World Congress Center, which opened in Atlanta in 1976. This facility energized the city's convention trade and increased development of related consumption-oriented businesses in the downtown area (Newman 1999, 194–198).

In large part, the politics of convention center development derived from the financing arrangement. In the 1950s and 1960s, financing was carried out through general obligation bonds that required a public vote (Sanders 1992, 139). The need for voter approval had two implications: voters were given a direct voice in economic development decisions, and a convention center proposal required skillful packaging to be acceptable to a majority of voters. Thus development conflicts were open to public scrutiny and resolution. By the 1980s, however, financing for convention complexes had become more specialized, for example, by creating a dedicated visitor tax as a funding mechanism. These more complex financing arrangements often involved special-purpose governments or the state government. This change has also been associated with a lack of public scrutiny and accountability in policymaking.

For example, as Sanders (1992, 144) notes, $200 million in public funds were committed to convention and stadium development in St. Louis while parks and police received very little, in part because of a shift in decision-making authority to the county and state governments. Likewise, San Diego voters rejected convention center bonds for nearly thirty-five years until a special-purpose government, the San Diego Unified Port District, proposed a convention complex on land it already owned. The convention facility, new luxury hotels, and a $10 million contribution to pay for light-rail service were financed through the port district (Sanders 1992, 148). Similarly in Denver, construction of the new Colorado Convention Center was ultimately the result of a new financing scheme that boosted hotel and car rental taxes and levied a new restaurant tax. The state also put $35 million toward acquisition of the new site, but the legislature's involvement led to a two-year delay and ended with legislation requiring local support for further state action (Sanders 1992, 151–152).

In cities without a regime to push development, the process can be even more difficult. In Kansas City, for example, two complications arose in efforts to develop a new convention center, as a result of the absence of a regime (Hoxworth and Thomas 1993). The lack of a network of cooperating economic and political leaders supporting the center meant that side payments to hesitant groups had to be made, and an extensive media campaign was needed to persuade voters of the importance of the project. In addition, given the public nature of decisionmaking, it was difficult to satisfy all the stakeholders, raising a potential problem for business interests (Hoxworth and Thomas 1993, 288). Taken together, these examples suggest that growth regimes enable the positive action necessary to pursue a convention complex, one of the staples of tourist-centered development. The pursuit of this type of development, however, may entail restructuring local politics to include a more complex role for government, particularly as entities like special-purpose governments and public-private partnerships become more important to policymaking.

Sports development. Cynics might suggest that all it takes to initiate a sports development proposal is access to a freeway system and a major media market. Indeed, two-fifths of U.S. adults are sports events travelers, most attending baseball, football, basketball, and auto-racing events (U.S. Travel Data Center 1999a, 1). A major-league team is often regarded as one of the key indicators of being a serious "player" in the competition for urban investment. The contribution of sports development, however, is negligible even in a city like Indianapolis that has a well-established sports-centered development strategy (Rosentraub et al. 1994). More generally, Baade (1996) found that sports development was correlated with neither an increase in real per capita income nor with job creation, and Baim (1994) concluded that sports stadiums are rarely a profitable endeavor for a municipality (see also Noll and Zimbalist 1997; Baade and Sanderson 1997; Rosentraub 1997). Yet sports development, particularly stadium or arena facilities for professional teams, continues at a rapid pace.[2]

Euchner (1999, 216) notes that during a three-year period in the 1990s, $7 billion was either committed or spent to build new sports facilities or refurbish existing ones. Between 1990 and 1998, 31 new sports complexes were built for teams in four major-league sports, 21 others were under construction, and 30 more were proposed. The extent of this investment is staggering, considering that each facility costs more than $100 million and it is occurring in 24 of the 60 largest American cities (U.S. Travel Data Center 1999a, 3).

In addition, over 100 cities have established sports commissions. These commissions typically are private enterprises, although some are quasi-governmental organizations (Standeven and De Knop 1999, 305). The National Association of Sports Commissions, organized in the early 1990s, serves as a clearinghouse for sports entertainment activities. Sports commissions play an important part in attracting amateur and professional sporting events, as well as sports meetings and conferences, to cities.

The cultural value of sports is reflected in how cities see themselves. The absence of a sports team and a sports identity is perceived as having a deleterious effect on a city's economic chances: "Sports must be part of [a city's] marketing image because sports is an important and defining part of life" (Rosentraub 1996, 28; see also Euchner 1993; Dyreson 1998; Pope 1997). For example, Ohio's governor warned that Cincinnati would become a minor-league city if a March 1996 voter referendum to increase local sales taxes by 0.5 percent failed and the city's professional football team moved.

The governor also pledged $110 million for the stadium complex from the state's capital budget (Kalich 1998, 215). Indianapolis was known as "Naptown" or "Indiana-no-place" before adopting its sports development strategy and is now perceived as a sports hub (Euchner 1999, 228). Rosentraub suggests that sports provides the glue to hold elements of the growth coalition together, noting that in Indianapolis the sports development strategy "did permit the city to rebuild its skyline and hold onto a portion of the growth which was to take place in the Indianapolis region" (1996, 29).

From the perspective of the team, of course, a threat to leave a city can be a valuable weapon. The National Football League's Oakland Raiders demonstrated as much in 1982, when they moved to Los Angeles and into a more lucrative stadium deal. This move changed the nature of the city-sports relationship (Euchner 1999, 220–221; Danielson 1997, 149–151). The owner of the Raiders, Al Davis, not only moved his team but won a $42 million settlement against the NFL, opening the door to a wave of sports development activities. Five NFL teams followed the Raiders' example by moving, while other teams got new stadium deals merely by threatening to move (the Raiders have since moved back to Oakland). Local governments, fearing the loss of "their team," have developed creative ways to meet team demands. These new approaches include building single-purpose facilities, establishing special tax zones, starting sports lotteries, selling personal seat licenses and rights to luxury boxes, offering guaranteed gate receipts, and introducing travel and tourism taxes. These new tools are being used in addition to the traditional mechanisms of issuing bonds and shuffling capital budgets (Kalich 1998).

Yet in America's two largest cities, love of sports and winning traditions has not meant smooth sailing for sports teams (Danielson 1997, 274). In New York's fragmented and contentious politics, business and political leaders have often disagreed on professional sports issues, resulting in the loss of four teams and a threat by the Yankees baseball team to move. In Los Angeles, the LA Memorial Coliseum Commission and public officials are constantly in conflict. With limited involvement from downtown business interests on sports issues, the LA region has been a revolving door for professional teams.

Entertainment complexes. The old-time amusement parks such as Coney Island, the gambling meccas of Las Vegas and Atlantic City, and the Disney entertainment parks represent yet another form of consumption-oriented development. Amusement, recreation, and gaming sales in the United States totaled $86 billion in 1996, up nearly 11 percent from the previous year, with much of this increase due to the rapid growth of the gaming industry (U.S. Travel Data Center 1999a, 44–45). Zukin et al. (1998) present a fascinating account of changes in the organization and use of amusement spaces in the twentieth century. Between 1895 and 1904, three amusement parks—the Steeplechase, Luna Park, and Dreamland—were developed and flourished on New York's Coney Island (Zukin et al. 1998, 635–637). In a move to differentiate them from the surrounding neighborhoods, the parks were walled in. After the subway to the West End was completed in 1920, the parks became the "Playground of the People." The surrounding area, however, remained undeveloped and the parks were not updated. In 1939, Robert Moses declared the area blighted. This designation focused subsequent policy debates on whether to retain the entertainment character of the area or build housing, with one concern being whether public housing would "reinforce Coney Island's low-class image" (Zukin et al. 1998, 637).

Las Vegas, on the other hand, showed a different pattern of consumption-oriented development. From its origins as a western gambling town, through an early transformation into a gambling and resort destination for the sophisticated set, to its emergence as a corporate destination resort, the history of Las Vegas reflects broader trends evident in tourism in the twentieth century (Rothman 1998; see also Gottdiener, Collins, and Dickens 1999). Las Vegas's transformations have coincided with the mass appeal of television and cinema and show its capability to create an image of glamour and romance (Zukin et al. 1998). In part, the image of Las Vegas can be linked to its architecture: "essential to the imagery of pleasure-zone architecture are lightness, the quality of being an oasis in a perhaps hostile context, heightened symbolism, and the ability to engulf the visitor in a new role" (Venturi, Scott Brown, and Izenour 1977, 53). But, behind the glamorous facade, a fiercely contested debate has raged between constituent parts of the southern Nevada growth coalition over whether Las Vegas should keep its "Sin City" image or become a more family-oriented "All American City" (Parker 1999).

The development of Las Vegas is unique in many ways, but it illustrates a broader point. As Zukin et al. (1998, 647) note:

> Contemporary cities are no longer built on visible and tangible
> production but on money changing hands. Urban design no longer
> delineates separate zones for work and leisure; all become one in
> the consumption of an image that is the city's primary product.

Still, perhaps the quintessential example of entertainment-driven development is Disney World. Although in many ways a success story, the creation of the Disney World park outside of Orlando is an excellent reminder of why consumption-oriented economic development should not be considered a benign endeavor. Disney World began simply enough with a secret purchase of land chosen for its proximity to major highways (Foglesong 1999, 90). In what can only be considered one of the shrewdest development deals in the twentieth century, Walt Disney was able to use Florida law to create his own "private government" (Foglesong 1999, 92). As a large landowner, the Disney company was able to create a special-purpose government that provided extraordinary control over land use, public services, and infrastructure.

This governmental status was the key to much of Disney's subsequent success because it allowed the company to carry out its development plans virtually free from interference by city, county, or state governments. "The company [created] a sort of Vatican with Mouse ears: a city-state within the larger state of Florida, privately owned yet enjoying regulatory powers reserved by law for popularly elected governments" (Foglesong 1999, 94). Ultimately, Disney's own success required restrictions on this unorthodox arrangement. Disney's impact on the public finance and public planning of surrounding counties, and the physical impact of Disney World on the regional infrastructure, eventually led the state government to include Disney within the provisions of new growth management laws. As Foglesong (1999) concludes, however, it is very difficult for locals to see growth issues in the spirit of economic partnership when the region's biggest economic actor is a transnational corporation without local or even national citizenship responsibilities.

Consumption, Image, and the Politics of Economic Development

Convention centers, sports facilities, and entertainment complexes can all be seen as components of a consumption-oriented economic development strategy. Although each component has unique features, they share a similar pattern of development activities. These developments typically begin with an expanded role for the public sector, often requiring the resources of a higher level of government or the creation of a new governmental or quasi-governmental entity. Once under way, these developments aim to attract both middle-class visitors willing to part with their money in exchange for tourist experiences and investment capital for more consumption-oriented businesses. Completing the circle is the process of residential and commercial gentrification that drives up land values in areas adjacent to the consumption zones.

The strategy of using scarce public resources for consumption-oriented development raises new political challenges and has led to a new politics of urban economic development based on image. The claim of Zukin et al. (1998, 647) that today's cities are not built on tangible production but rather on money changing hands might not be much of a stretch. Exacerbating this condition is the very real competition between cities for economic activity to regenerate older areas, build new areas, and create jobs. As these goals are pursued through consumption-based activities, the city's image becomes the new selling point: that lifestyle, that look, that *je ne sais quoi*—the desire to show a landscape of perfection (Boyer 1992).

The creation of a city's image can be a point of political contestation, however. The question of equity, always relevant in economic development, is behind this contestation. Allocating a large pool of public funds to develop a convention center, sports stadium, or theme park rather than for use by public schools, public safety, or neighborhood projects can raise questions about the legitimacy of the decision-making process. Development policy that purports to bring production-based economic activities and high-paying jobs into a city is one thing; consumption-based policy is another. In Las Vegas, for example, the underside of the tourism economy is seen in the relative sociocultural and economic difficulties it creates—low-wage jobs, lack of affordable housing, bankruptcy of small stores and markets, and the continuous fiscal strain on the public sector as it attempts to subsidize corporate gaming operations (Parker 1999, 118–121).

Far from being merely rhetoric, the desire to create a world-class or major-league image is an important element of a city's economic development strategy. As Pagano and Bowman (1995) point out, image creation has very tangible effects on local government; it provides a rationale for the allocation of scarce resources. Furthermore, consumption-based competition between cities means that image marketing will become more evident as cities search for a unique image to bring visitors and investment capital to their city (Fainstein and Judd 1999a; Holcomb 1999).

The shift to incorporate consumption-oriented activities into urban development policies is in part a reflection of larger changes in regional economies. Still, the burgeoning number of urban entertainment complexes, sports facilities, and convention centers is tangible evidence of the importance of consumption as a feature in local development policy. For some cities, such as Las Vegas or Orlando, the consumption of entertainment services by visitors is a mainstay of the urban economy. In cities like New York, Boston, or San Francisco, however, consumption services are but one element—though an increasingly important one—of the local economy. Perhaps the most striking feature of the shift toward consumption-oriented development, however, is its use as a display mechanism for the "renaissance" of cities, as in Baltimore or Detroit. Of course, any city that diverts public resources into developing consumption services must face difficult questions about the expected returns. This point is all the more significant when a city banks on creating an image and selling consumption to visitors as the key to its rebirth.

■ The Mega-event Strategy

Consumption-oriented development has become commonplace in U.S. cities. The use of a large-scale, high-profile event as a centerpiece—the mega-event strategy—should be seen as part of this pattern of urban development. The mega-event strategy is unique, however, because it depends fundamentally on bringing an external event to the city. The mega-event strategy thus entails greater risk than a typical consumption-oriented development project because it requires a city first to obtain the external event and then to stage it in such a way as to achieve the city's goals of attracting tourists and positive publicity. Even worse for a potential host city, some of the risks associated with the event, such as a boycott or scandal, cannot feasibly be anticipated by planners. Furthermore, there is always the possibility that between inception and execution the event may not be sufficiently unique or exciting to generate enough visitors or positive publicity to jump-start the city's consumption industry.

Mega-events, then, allow cities to focus economic development activities and attention for competitive gain. Mega-events are intended to attract tourist revenues and, more important, national and international media recognition for the host city. Moreover, from a local perspective, making a debut on the world stage requires looking the part, and cities can usually leverage event preparations to promote an impressive array of development opportunities.

The history of mega-events, in which myth and reality are easily substituted, is the history of modern times. In 1851, London's Crystal Palace Exposition amazed visitors with images of contemporary progress and future utopias. By the early twentieth century, world's fairs had become an urban spectacle signifying the importance of commodities and machine technology to enhanced prosperity and improved social relations. At the same time, these fairs produced some of the most spectacular architecture of the day, whether London's Crystal Palace, the Eiffel Tower in Paris, or later, Seattle's Space Needle. Berman (1982, 245) suggests that these structures were powerful symbols that embodied the myths of urban vitality while denying the reality of everyday urban life. Pairing the Olympic games with world's fairs in Paris and St. Louis early in the twentieth century signified that sport, too, could be associated with technology and social reform (Dyreson 1998, 56–57).

Hosting a mega-event such as the world's fair, the Olympic games, or a culture festival holds the potential for tremendous economic gain. The 1996 Olympic games in Atlanta are estimated to have increased tourism in the metropolitan area by nearly 10 percent over 1995, creating nearly $4.2 billion in total economic effect (Newman 1999, 342 n. 32). From a global perspective, the World Travel and Tourism Council estimated that the sports tourism industry worldwide generated $340 billion in gross output in 1994, amounting to 10 percent of global GDP (Standeven and De Knop 1999, 172). Beyond the economics, however, is the symbolic value of entering into global competition through a media-induced imagination. As national boundaries become more permeable, the flows of people, technology, and media images are more easily achieved, making competition more keen (Appadurai 1990; Sassen 1996b). The construction of a city's image is focused on drawing these flows through the city.

▨ Success and Failure with Urban Mega-events

Of course, the use of mega-events to draw attention to a city is not an exclusively contemporary phenomenon. Seattle's growth, for example, is bracketed by the Alaska-Yukon-Pacific Exposition in 1909 and the tremendously important 1962 Seattle World's Fair. Indeed, Seattle's cosmopolitan image of today, as the home to Boeing, Microsoft, and Starbucks, can be traced to the world's fair. The fair not only provided opportunities to redevelop the downtown area, it evoked a new image for the city (Gordon et al. 1991, 217). Seattle's growth regime, known as the Big Ten, was instrumental in bringing a world's fair to Seattle, even though it was one of the last significant achievements for this regime (Gordon et al. 1991, 226–227). Indeed, Seattle's Forward Thrust of the mid-1960s, led by members of the Big Ten, challenged Seattleites to take control of the city's growth by establishing a capital improvements program for roads, rapid transit, parks, and community centers. When all was said and done, Seattle voters had approved over $300 million in bonds to pay for this capital program. In sum, Seattle was able to use a mega-event as a springboard for investment in public infrastructure as well as the means for altering its previously unappealing image.

City residents are willing to be persuaded that mega-events are worthwhile investments of public resources. In addition to publicity and tourist revenues, cities may gain new facilities that can be used to provide future revenues. Yet neither the promise of a better future nor the existence of a governing regime is a guarantee the mega-event strategy will succeed. The failure of Chicago's business leaders to bring a world's fair to that city in 1992 illustrates some of the challenges (Shlay and Giloth 1987). A tightly knit group of corporate business people put the world's fair on the public agenda in Chicago via a nonprofit organization, the 1992 Fair Corporation. This organization obtained national and international approval for the designation of a site, even though this entailed nearly $1 billion in physical development and major transportation modifications (Shlay and Giloth 1987, 309). The 1992 Fair Corporation located its proposal on Chicago's South Side, promising new jobs, increased revenues, and urban redevelopment for this economically depressed area. Although the fair was included in Chicago's comprehensive plan under the administration of Mayor Jane Byrne and received support from the governor of Illinois, it never materialized.

As Shlay and Giloth (1987) note, one reason for the failure was the lack of political support for the fair from Byrne's successor, Harold Washington. In addition, the very complexity of planning the event—finding sites, involving citizens, and establishing realistic expectations about costs and benefits—helped undermine support. This problem was compounded by the lack of leadership in the 1992 Fair Corporation and the public World's Fair Authority that led to the emergence of an opposition coalition, which saw the fair as too great a public risk. As the scope of the local government's role in underwriting the costs of the fair expanded, "the psychic gratification of being competitive as a 'world class' city" became less convincing to city residents (Shlay and Giloth 1987, 319).

Assessing Mega-events

Given the record of successes and failures, how should mega-events be assessed? Although they are typically described in terms of their overall economic impact, mega-events are multidimensional and multipurpose occurrences (e.g., Cochrane, Peck, and Tickell 1996; Hall 1992, 1996; Ritchie 1984; M. Roche 1992; Rothman 1998). One of the first to recognize this, Ritchie (1984) proposed a system to classify the impacts of mega-events that included categories such as economic, physical, and sociocultural impact, as well as more speculative categories such as psychological impact.

Yet in a review of the literature on mega-events, Roche (1992) noted that most studies deal with the various impacts of mega-events in isolation and thus fail to capture the full import of the event. Roche criticized previous studies for not providing sufficient context; in particular, many studies did not include the history of urban development in the community nor did they fully consider the urban policy processes for planning and carrying out the event. In his work on the Sheffield World Student Games in 1991, Roche (1994) concludes that without strategic experience, organizational capability, and democratic legitimacy, an event is unlikely to be successful economically, socially, or politically. He notes four elements he believes will strengthen future mega-event analysis: describing the type of city; examining the nature of citizen participation in urban planning and in mega-event planning; identifying the nature of urban leadership; and identifying the urban regeneration and reimaging strategies the city may be using (Roche 1994, 14).

More recent mega-event research has reflected the contextual orientation called for by Roche and others. For example, Hall's (1996) analysis of the 2000 Sydney Olympic games' bidding process focuses squarely on urban reimaging; he examines both urban tourism and the linkage between mega-events and downtown redevelopment. In Sydney, urban redevelopment in the context of a mega-event helped to mask conflict and provided elites with an opportunity to restructure urban space to fulfill other goals. Redevelopment also resulted in the local government shifting public resources from "social welfare to imaging functions" (Hall 1996, 375). Hall concludes that mega-events serve a narrow range of interests, with imaging and marketing concerns often given prominence in policymaking to the detriment of more sustainable forms of tourism.

Similarly, Cochrane, Peck, and Tickell (1996) are highly conscious of the broader political and economic environment that informs their examination of Manchester's failed Olympic bid. Cochrane et al. grounded their analysis in the new urban politics that is concerned with globalization and state restructuring. The new urban politics of the Olympic bid involved claims-making against the central government since growth is a prerequisite for government grants, with the old politics of service cuts temporarily set aside. They conclude that, in Britain, the politics of an Olympic bid were as much about the evolving role of local government as the nature of urban growth (see also C. Hill 1994).

The Olympics as Urban Mega-event

As the experience of Manchester suggests, even failed Olympic bids can influence the nature of urban politics. Indeed, as Lenskyj (1996) argues in her comparison of bids by Sydney and Toronto, the city that loses the Olympic competition but keeps its democratic practices may be the winning city in the long run. Whatever the merits of this argument, the Olympic games have in recent decades become the most highly sought urban mega-event. The desire to host the games stems largely from the worldwide media publicity generated by them. When the games are under way, the attention of the entire planet is focused on the athletic competition.

It was not always this way. Indeed, before the 1984 summer games in Los Angeles, it had become quite difficult to sell the Olympics to potential host cities (Simson and Jennings 1992, 241). From the perspective of U.S. cities, this difficulty can be traced to two experiences that created an impression among city leaders that hosting the Olympic games would not be a rewarding experience: Denver's rejection of the 1976 winter games and the aftermath of Montreal's 1976 summer games.

In Denver, a coalition of downtown business people and supporters from the region's ski industry worked to bring the 1976 winter games to Colorado, in hopes of boosting the fortunes of the ski resorts and putting the city on the world stage (Foster 1976; Judd 1983, 174–177; Leonard and Noel 1990, 273–274; Rothman 1998, 252–278). The promises of Olympic supporters, however, often outpaced the support of area residents. In 1966, for example, even before Denver was awarded the games, the Denver Olympic Committee had to drop the town of Aspen as a potential Olympic site because of opposition from area residents. This was after the Aspen Ski Company and Aspen's mayor had offered the town as the location for alpine skiing events.

Even worse for Olympic supporters, city officials had to announce in 1972 that they could not host the games. This announcement came two years *after* the city had been awarded the games by the IOC. This startling turn of events arose at the local level as a clash over growth. In the 1960s, Colorado had become a place where the forces for growth and no-growth contested the meaning of "quality of life," and the controversy over the winter games mobilized both sides. For the boosters of growth, the winter games meant the construction of new housing, the creation of world-class sports facilities, huge profits for existing businesses, and worldwide publicity. Furthermore, for supporters the timing of the games was perfect, given the winter-sports boom sweeping the country after the success of the televised 1968 Grenoble winter Olympic games. Opponents, representing a variety of groups, saw continued development as destructive of the area's natural beauty and its lifestyle.

By early 1972, twenty thousand Coloradans had signed petitions against the 1976 winter games, which were presented to the IOC in Sapporo where the 1972 winter games were being held. At the same time, a statewide petition drive was under way to place a constitutional amendment before the voters, forbidding the legislature from spending public funds on the Olympics, and a similar petition drive was taking place in Denver to amend the city charter. When voters passed these two initiatives in November 1972, it was clear that the games lacked the necessary public support and financial backing to go ahead.

Like Denver, Montreal was awarded the 1976 games in 1970, beating out Los Angeles and Moscow. Unlike Denver, however, the Montreal games did not face strong local opposition. Rather, the dour fiscal legacy of the Montreal games was rooted, at least in part, in broader economic circumstances. As city leaders undertook grand plans to restructure parts of the city and refashion its image, the national and international economic situation deteriorated, with inflation causing a particular hardship. As a result of cost overruns, the Montreal games left the city with a debt of nearly one billion dollars (Hall 1992, 40).

The experiences of Denver and Montreal alerted other potential host cities to the risks associated with the Olympics. Ultimately, it took the combined effects of changing federal aid policies, the emergence of global economic competition, and the splashy success of the 1984 Los Angeles games to remind America's city leaders of the potential benefits of the Olympics as an urban mega-event. Of course, city leaders were not the only ones who learned from the problems that arose in the 1970s. In part as a consequence of these difficulties, both the USOC and the IOC have changed and continue to refine their selection procedures to protect the games and themselves from financial or political embarrassment.

Selecting the Olympic Host City

For U.S. cities, being designated as an Olympic host city is the culmination of a two-phase process. The first phase requires winning the USOC's designation as America's candidate city, then competing on the international level for selection by the IOC.[3] The U.S. Olympic Association, USOC's predecessor, first established a site selection procedure for the 1956 Olympics, when several U.S. cities vied for selection. Later, after disputes between rival sports organizations threatened the process, Congress passed the Amateur Sports Act of 1978, which designated the nonprofit USOC as the coordinating body for Olympic-related sporting activities in the United States (Watson 1996).

The USOC's site selection process has evolved over time, but typically it involves three steps (Wanninger 1998). First, the USOC decides whether to have a city represent the United States to the International Olympic Committee. The USOC begins the process by identifying "interested" cities, where interest includes submitting several official documents and a $100,000 bid fee. The USOC then hosts a technical seminar for interested bid cities that, among other things, introduces cities to the national governing bodies of various sports and explains the requirements for training sites, corporate services, athlete village operations, and media facilities. At the second step, a city that intends to pursue an Olympic bid must have a nonprofit bid committee in place before the city's technical qualifications can be evaluated by the USOC's Site Evaluation Task Force. Finally, members of the USOC vote on the city to be America's candidate for a specific Olympic games.

Once selected by the USOC, the U.S. city then competes against other cities from around the world for selection by the IOC. According to the IOC charter, cities are the only entities that can submit a bid to host the games. Depending on the number of candidate cities, the IOC process typically involves a preliminary examination by officials of international sporting organizations to establish that a city meets the necessary technical qualifications. The final choice is made by a secret ballot of IOC members. The entire bidding process typically unfolds over a period of several years, and host cities are usually selected seven years in advance of the games.

■ Conclusion

Consumption-oriented development has become a common feature among the development policy options of U.S. cities. Seeking out a high-profile event such as a world's fair or the Olympic games to draw visitors and attention to a city is one manifestation of the shift toward consumption-oriented development. The pursuit of mega-events, we have argued, is a particularly risky endeavor because it involves a substantial commitment of public and private resources while promising returns that are largely intangible. Still, the allure of using a large-scale, high-profile happening to jump-start a city's economic development remains strong.

Next, we examine in detail the politics of the Olympic games in Los Angeles, Atlanta, and Salt Lake City. In each of these cases, we seek to address a number of concerns. How and why did the city seek to host a mega-event, particularly the Olympic games? How were policy decisions concerning the mega-event made? What were the outcomes of hosting the mega-event? The following three chapters present case studies of the bid process and subsequent organization of the Olympic games, providing an opportunity to examine what the mega-event strategy tells us about urban politics generally.

■ Notes

1. There is no standard definition of tourism (see Page 1995, 9–19; Standeven and De Knop 1999, 9–11). We concur with the advantages of a broad definition, and so have chosen to use the definition advanced by the World Tourism Organization (1992, 2): "The activities of persons traveling to and staying in places outside their usual environment for not more than one consecutive year for leisure, business, or other purposes."

2. The obsession with professional sports may seem to be exclusively a feature of contemporary conditions in the United States. Yet it is easy to overlook the fact that municipal expenditures on athletic facilities increased sixfold in the 1920s (Pope 1997, 154).

3. Including the 2002 winter games, the United States has been an Olympic host eight times. St. Louis was the first American city to host the summer games, in 1904. Lake Placid, New York, hosted the winter games and Los Angeles hosted the summer games in 1932. In 1960, the winter games were held in Squaw Valley, California, and in 1980, the winter games returned to rural Lake Placid. The summer games in Los Angeles in 1984 and in Atlanta in 1996, and the 2002 winter games in Salt Lake City round out the U.S. experience with the Olympics.

4

LOS ANGELES AND
THE 1984 SUMMER GAMES

The 1976 summer games represented a low point in the history of the modern Olympic games. Montreal was awarded the games in 1970, beating out rivals Los Angeles and Moscow to show that a smaller city could put on an Olympic event that was completely self-financed and outside of superpower politics. Yet the clouds of an international recession, global inflation, and domestic economic problems in Canada hung over the games. The political conflict between China and Taiwan over representation in the opening ceremonies and a dispute involving the ties between New Zealand and South Africa led one commentator to conclude that the 1976 summer games were nearly canceled sixteen days before the opening ceremony (Shaiken 1988, 38). Even worse, the debt incurred by Montreal, estimated at the time to be $460 million but later calculated at closer to one billion dollars, threatened the economic viability of the games. Montreal's misfortune, however, provided a future host city with the unparalleled opportunity to negotiate with the IOC, if any city even desired to host the summer games. Los Angeles did and, in so doing, created a new paradigm for hosting mega-events.

The story of LA's 1984 summer games is really three related tales. The first, not recounted here, is the story of the international athletic competition. Although the Soviet Union and most of its Eastern bloc allies boycotted the 1984 games, the competition was keen. The second story is the struggle to win host-city designation under what can only be described as interesting circumstances. This story unfolds in the following pages, beginning with the city's bid history, continuing through the organization of the entrepreneurial

Olympics, and ending with an overview of the impact of the 1984
Olympics on LA. The third story is about urban growth politics in
the United States and how growth coalitions position their city—in
this case, by using the mega-event strategy—to increase its exposure
in an increasingly media-intensive world.

■ The City and Its Politics

Los Angeles is a booster's paradise. Throughout its history, the city
and region used the image of southern California first to attract travelers, and later capital, to the area. As it has grown, the city's economic focus has evolved from the cattle ranching boom to feed the
Gold Rush to early real estate speculation under the watchful eyes
of the Southern Pacific Railroad's political machine. In the twentieth
century, LA saw the development of a port and harbor by local business interests; the creation of a manufacturing center for defense,
aerospace, and the electronics industries fueled by federal defense
spending; and most recently, the emergence of a sophisticated, service-
based economy. Through it all, political power in LA has been
tightly interwoven with the creation and promotion of the city's
image. The pattern for growth and development of the Los Angeles
area was decentralized, resulting in a multinucleated region. Over
time, this pattern was reinforced by economic choices, social values,
and public policies.

   In the early days of California's statehood, LA was an important
agricultural center, and the region's farming image was marketed.
When it became clear that the warm, arid climate was not drawing
farmers, weather became the selling point. A railroad-induced real
estate boom lasted for a few years and was followed by a bust in the
late 1880s. One outcome was the establishment of the Los Angeles
Chamber of Commerce, which focused its attention on promoting
the region. The chamber's promotional efforts, combined with those
of the All Year Club, the Automobile Association of Southern California, and the LA Realty Board, meant that during the last days of
the nineteenth century, the Los Angeles region was the "best publicized part of the United States" (Fogelson 1967, 70; see also Starr
1990, 101). At the same time, a broader transformation in values
was under way: the purpose of life shifted from an emphasis on getting ahead economically to enjoying the comforts of everyday life.

By the early twentieth century, the chamber's promotional material reflected this shift, and instead of promoting material prosperity, it sold an easier, more varied, less complicated lifestyle (Fogelson 1967, 72). Selling the good life changed Los Angeles from a small, agricultural settlement into America's fifth largest city by the early 1930s. This shift was helped along by several large infrastructure projects designed by the newly formed, strong public bureaucracy, particularly the Department of Water and Power (Erie 1992). But as Fulton (1997, 13–14) notes, LA was marketed as the anti-city, and the promoters and developers built it to reflect a decentralized small-town lifestyle.

The influx of new residents changed the region's political culture in ways that reflected the desires of its large, transplanted midwestern population for an ordered social, economic, and political environment. Sonenshein (1993, 26) describes turn-of-the-century Los Angeles as changed from a frontier city into an economic powerhouse with a narrow civic culture. In the early 1900s, for example, LA was dominated by a white, Protestant community whose members became the civic elite through conscientious political mobilization and demonstrated electoral unity (Singleton 1979, 100–107). After a period of migration by southern whites beginning in 1910, LA also became a segregated city. Its city charters in 1911 and 1925 fragmented political power and made political control by elected officials difficult (see Schockman 1996). In this environment, LA's economic elites were able to continue to promote the city and make money in real estate development.

After World War I, for example, the five major publishers in Los Angeles started a campaign to promote LA. Mayor Meredith Snyder helped by naming one hundred community leaders to the California Fiestas Association to revive the city's Spanish heritage as a way to promote tourism. The association reorganized into the Community Development Association (CDA), a booster society consisting of the city's leading bankers, attorneys, newspaper publishers, developers, contractors, realtors, and businessmen (Riess 1981). The CDA was run by an executive committee headed by the "Prince of Realtors," William Garland, who subdivided and sold Westlake, Ocean Park, Hermosa Beach, and Beverly Hills (Starr 1990, 71). In its first meeting, a member of the executive committee suggested that Los Angeles should apply to host the Olympic games because "holding such a spectacle would direct a lot of attention to the city, improve its prestige, and bring a great deal of free publicity" (Riess 1981, 52–53). Garland left for Europe to lobby for LA only to find that the next two Olympic games had already been awarded. After returning to the United States, he was appointed to the American Olympic Committee and later became a U.S. representative for the International Olympic Committee. In 1923, Garland helped LA win the summer games. The IOC was impressed with the city's 75,000-seat arena, nearing completion, for the track and field competition (Riess 1981, 53).

The turn of the century was an important period for sports in American culture. Both professional and collegiate sports, as well as sports arenas, were becoming big business. The CDA had announced the need for a landmark arena in 1919 and had floated two plans for its funding. One was a bond issue; the second involved renting a parcel in centrally located Exposition Park, building a structure, then renting it to the city and county for a period of ten years. The rent of $475,000 per year would be used to pay off construction costs. At the end of ten years, the stadium would be turned over to the city and county, to be operated by a public agency (Riess 1981, 54). After a public vote and a court case, the stadium was built using plan two, and the Los Angeles Memorial Coliseum became the second most expensive sports facility in the country after privately financed Yankee Stadium; it was, however, the largest sports arena (Riess 1981, 56). Improvements to the coliseum for the 1932 Olympic summer games, supported by the city and county to the tune of $227,000 in the summer of 1930, also required that only LA residents could be hired to do the work. This latter requirement was important since the number of unemployed persons in LA had reached 344,000 (Belcher 1978, 3). At the end of the 1932 summer games, the CDA turned over nearly $214,000 to the city and county and the coliseum was turned over to the playgrounds commission to operate, with the city and county maintaining ownership (Riess 1981, 62). In addition, the impact of the 1932 games included sixty-two conventions held in LA, bringing $60 million in spending (Belcher 1978, 3). This was boosterism at its best.

Political power in LA's governance structure is decentralized and diffuse. In part, this legacy stems from the image of Los Angeles that was developed by promoters—the decentralization and the anti-urban bias of development resulted in a distrust of government and politics. The 1925 city charter reflected this and institutionalized a weak governing structure. The old Los Angeles was a city whose politics were dominated by a growth machine representing down-town business interests and the city's newspapers. Population growth in the post–World War II period saw a renewed emphasis on low-density development in pursuit of the good life, as the region's population tripled between the 1940s and 1970. The evolving physical and financial infrastructure permitted this development, and Los Angeles grew in a lifestyle-based region. This was aided by the Lakewood Plan in the late 1950s, which allowed cities to contract services from the county, leading to the spate of lifestyle incorporations that continues today (Davis 1990, 165–166). Exercising political power in this environment required having economic, social, and political resources and the will to use them. During Tom Bradley's tenure as mayor (1973–1993), a fragile coalition was forged that tried to empower community interests to challenge the downtown-based growth machine (Sonenshein 1993). As Bradley's agenda grew to include making Los Angeles a world-class city, the coalition's concern for community interests weakened, and the power of business interests, especially developers, ascended (Regalado 1992). The crowning moment was hosting the 1984 Olympic summer games. Although the riots in 1992 punctured LA's postmaterial, easier, more varied, less complicated lifestyle image, the economic boom of the late 1990s returned some of the luster to the city's image (see Andranovich and Riposa 1998).

■ Bidding for the Summer Games

Los Angeles hosted the 1932 Olympic summer games, and the Southern California Committee for the Olympic Games (SCCOG) was established in 1939 to bring the games back to Los Angeles. The 1932 Olympics were all that a promoter could wish for, generating an unbelievable surplus of $1 million during the Great Depression (Henry and Yeomans 1984, 454). SCCOG tried to bring the Olympics back but was unsuccessful in its competition with other U.S. cities, losing out to Detroit in 1960, 1964, 1968, and 1972 (Henry and Yeomans 1984). In 1976, the USOC selected Los Angeles as America's representative city. But the IOC, with geopolitical considerations in mind, selected Montreal over both Los Angeles and Moscow to host the 1976 summer games. The LA76 bid committee did propose two novel ideas, however, that were at the heart of the 1984 summer games' success. First, the committee proposed that the summer games could be privately financed, and second, that the host city, not the IOC, could negotiate television rights (LAOOC 1985, 7). In April 1977, SCCOG President John Argue sent Mayor Bradley a letter asking for his support in bidding for a spartan Olympic games, and Los Angeles began the bidding process once again.

Seeking the 1984 Summer Games

Several U.S. cities had announced an interest in the mid-1970s in hosting the 1984 games. Atlanta, Boston, Chicago, New Orleans, and New York each expressed an intention to bid, but all these cities suggested that federal support would be needed to bring the games back to the United States. Los Angeles organizers, however, continued to pursue their model of a privately funded Olympic games. The SCCOG jump-started its efforts with a blue-ribbon group of Los Angeles businessmen who raised $158,000 to finance the city's bid. These funds included $35,000 from Atlantic Richfield Corporation (ARCO), a major energy company headquartered in Los Angeles, to underwrite Los Angeles's presentation to the USOC in the fall of 1977 (Reich 1986). John Argue, a Los Angeles attorney and SCCOG president, noted that the overarching goal was to bring the summer games to Los Angeles at no cost to the taxpayer. An August fundraising luncheon held at Perino's restaurant was attended by over fifty businessmen, Mayor Bradley, and City Council President John Ferraro. It was also during this time, prompted by the urging of the city council, that Los Angeles's two tourism units, the fifty-six-year-old Southern California Visitors Council and the twenty-year-old Los Angeles Visitors and Convention Bureau, merged into the Greater Los Angeles Visitors and Convention Bureau. The new organization was headed by Kathy Smeby, formerly a senior vice president at Bank of America (Kilgore 1977).

The IOC, stung by the recent rebuke of the winter games at the polls in Colorado, demanded that public support for staging the games be present (LAOOC 1985, 8). The Los Angeles City Council agreed to pay $13,000 for a poll of public attitudes toward hosting the summer games, conducted by the Field Research Corporation. Following a 12–0 council vote in favor of bidding to host the summer games, the mayor announced that the 1984 Olympics, "if conducted in a spartan and businesslike manner, would bring many benefits to the city" (Baker 1977).

Still, there was an uneasy air surrounding LA's bid. In the summer of 1977, for example, the Los Angeles city administrator's office announced that without federal and state support, a deficit of $200–336 million would be incurred, depending upon whether an Olympic village and security costs were included in projected expenditures. But the city administrator and the SCCOG had very different sets of assumptions about revenues and expenditures for the summer games. While Los Angeles could rely on existing facilities for fifteen of the twenty-one Olympic sports, four of the remaining sports—rowing, swimming, shooting, and bicycling—would require facilities costing about $22 million. In addition, the costs of refurbishing the Los Angeles Coliseum and several other sites were estimated at $50 million by the city but only $15 million by SCCOG. SCCOG used Montreal's operating cost, $150 million, while the city suggested $200 million might be more accurate. The most startling difference was the projected revenues, with the city estimating $72 million and SCCOG $534 million (Soble 1977). Thus, before Los Angeles even had received the USOC's nod of approval, support by Los Angeles's public officials seemed to waver. The first stage of the bidding process revolved around building broad-based support for the LA summer games, or at least a general commitment by the people of Los Angeles, the region, and the state of California to support the bid.

The *Los Angeles Times* opined that money would be the critical factor and that the city should not host the summer games "at the expense of the local taxpayers" ("Fun and games—and money" 1977). But the *Times* editorial was optimistic in tone since Los Angeles already had most of the facilities required, unlike Montreal where construction costs alone had reached one billion dollars. The Field Research Poll showed that the public in the Los Angeles region supported the summer games at about 70 percent, unless public funds were needed. Support dipped to 60 percent if federal funds were requested, 45 percent if state funds were required, and a mere 35 percent if city or county monies were needed. Further, 47 percent of those polled agreed that the summer games would benefit Los Angeles by bringing in more jobs and 36 percent felt that the city's prestige and pride would be enhanced (LAOOC 1985). In addition, the California State Assembly Ways and Means Committee, following the lead of the state senate, unanimously passed an amendment to a bill to exempt Los Angeles from conducting an environmental impact report to host the summer games, although any new construction would still require such reports. SCCOG members John Argue and Rodney Rood met with Governor Jerry Brown to discuss the state role in the summer games.

The month of September saw a flurry of activity, including a privately funded weekend trip to Los Angeles by a USOC delegation, a declaration by Governor Brown that Los Angeles should be the site of the 1984 summer games, and a trip by a SCCOG delegation to Colorado Springs to meet with the USOC. In the end, Los Angeles received the USOC's endorsement to be the official U.S. candidate, "halting and reversing the trend of ever-increasing deficits" for the summer games (Reich 1977b).

The International Campaign, 1977–1979

After securing the USOC's endorsement, the second phase of the bidding process began: dealing with the International Olympic Committee. Despite being the sole serious bidder for the 1984 summer games, the road to win the bid was a rough one. The Los Angeles delegation that went to Monte Carlo to meet for several days with the IOC in October 1977 included the mayor's Olympic games liaison, the Los Angeles Coliseum general manager, the chief assistant city administrative officer, and an SCCOG vice president. Upon the delegation's return, Mayor Bradley suggested that he would maintain tight control over the Olympics and that not many private sector leaders would be named to the official organizing committee. In November 1977, Ernani Bernardi became the first of three city councilmen to announce that he would seek to place a charter amendment on the June 1978 primary ballot banning the expenditure of any city funds on the summer games. Bernardi noted that Lord Killanin, the IOC president, had "kind of glossed over" Olympic rules and that elected officials who were promising a spartan summer games in 1977 might not be in office in 1984 (Reich 1977a; see also Killanin 1983, 93–99). The fractiousness of the ensuing debate over public funding was best captured at a Los Angeles County supervisors' meeting following Bernardi's remarks. Supervisor Barbara Ward proposed to amend the county charter to prohibit the use of county funds, directly or indirectly, to finance the summer games (though a formal vote was not taken because two supervisors were absent from the meeting). After SCCOG Vice President McFadden told the supervisors that the county was not involved in staging the summer games, Ward responded, "then you ought to support us" (Reich 1977a).

As the level of rancor between the SCCOG and public officials rose, ARCO vice president and SCCOG member Rodney Rood outlined in a *Los Angeles Times* opinion piece where he saw the debate going (Rood 1977). The benefits of hosting the Olympics were that the summer games provided Los Angeles with a global stage to display its attractions; the games would generate sizable revenues from visitors; and there were intangibles that would enhance LA's position in history and contemporary society. The lesson from Denver's failed attempt, according to Rood, was that the organizing committee must be open and keep the community informed. The threat to put the summer games to a vote "implies that the public interest has not been zealously protected throughout the negotiations" (Rood 1977). Rood noted that in reality, the city council, the county board of supervisors, and Governor Brown had endorsed the summer games unanimously, and even the state legislature had removed some of the technical obstacles and reviewed the bid. But as the year-ending holidays approached, Montreal City Councilman Nicholas Auf der Maur appeared before the Los Angeles council's Charter and Administrative Code Committee to describe how Montreal's budget had spiraled out of control (Meagher 1977). Howard Jarvis, appearing before the city's finance committee, urged postponement of any action until his pending tax reform initiative, Proposition 13, had been voted on in the upcoming June primary. Jarvis stated that the proposition could result in a "substantial change in city revenue" if passed by the voters of California ("Jarvis Urges Delay" 1977).

In January 1978, the debate came to a head. City council president Ferraro appointed a five-member ad hoc committee to hear all matters related to the 1984 bid; the committee included three Olympics supporters, one undecided member, and one critic. Regarding this development, Mayor Bradley noted that the city's bid to the IOC expired at the end of that council session. Councilman Zev Yaroslavsky, the undecided committee member, immediately wanted to know who would be on the organizing committee, noting that no one on SCCOG had the expertise to stage and manage a major event (Reich 1978b). This led to the council's vote to participate in selecting the organizing committee. As events in Los Angeles seemed to exert a centrifugal force on bid politics, external events forced the LA participants to temporarily draw together. The Lake Placid local organizing committee raised concerns with the USOC over television revenues and the appointment of USOC members to the local committee, and this was taken as a warning in LA (Reich 1978f).

Early 1978 produced behind-the-scenes talks between the mayor and council that lasted for weeks. The talks ended with the mayor's public announcement that the proposed charter amendment was the "type of tough, no nonsense limit that would remove much of the doubt and suspicion about the City's ability to host the summer games without assuming a huge debt . . . and to let the IOC know where we stand" (Reich 1978h). This statement was the city's position in response to demands from the IOC and USOC for the development of new facilities and more control over the decisionmaking. The IOC, for example, wrote to the mayor that the "USOC and the city chosen assume complete financial responsibility for the Games" (Reich 1978d). Thus it was the locus of financial responsibility that was contested by Los Angeles in its quest to host the summer games.

By April, it was apparent that LA needed to have a local organizing committee, and SCCOG President John Argue suggested that the mayor go beyond the membership of the SCCOG to seek "broad community representation." Argue further suggested that a thirty-three-member committee be set up as a nonprofit corporation to enter into a contractual agreement with the city to put on the summer games. The purpose of this arrangement was to "insulate the committee as much as possible from city politics" (Reich 1978g). A second fund-raising luncheon was held at Perino's in late April to support the Olympic bid, organized by the presidents of ARCO and Carter-Hawley-Hale Stores, the CEO of Walt Disney Productions, and the chairmen of BankAmerica Corp. and Dart Industries. The luncheon was coordinated by Rodney Rood and Paul Sullivan, a BankAmerica executive vice president (Henry and Yeomans 1984, 456). The issue of who should have the power to appoint the local organizing committee—and whether it was independent of city control—became a critical political issue in April and May. The city council delayed its vote for a week because it had received the bid document only thirty minutes before its meeting. In addition, a councilman from LA's east side challenged the mayor's intention to name the nucleus of the organizing committee before the May meeting with the IOC in Athens because the mayor did not have a good record of appointing residents from the east side to city commissions ("The Southland" 1978). The council later voted to ask the mayor not to name the committee until the council decided how it should be established. By this time, events in Athens had taken center stage.

Negotiations with the IOC would take five months. The first LA contingent to Athens was quite large and included the mayor's Olympic liaison, Anton Calleia, and several other administration staffers, as well as members of the city council, county board of supervisors, and the SCCOG. The mayor was not scheduled to arrive in Athens until negotiations were nearly completed. The primary negotiators for LA were Anton Calleia, Sally Disco (an assistant city attorney), John Argue, and David Wolper (both representing the SCCOG). During the oral presentation, Calleia addressed two concerns held by the IOC: first, that LA's focus on cost control would still allow for optimal facilities, and second, that a referendum would not be held once the summer games were awarded. The committee's strategy followed three lines of argument: that a majority on the council had backed the Bradley administration and supported the summer games, even though media attention focused on the skeptics; that LA's cost control language was not intended to challenge the IOC's authority but to satisfy public opinion; and that the IOC had been victimized by the reputation for extravagance seen in Montreal and needed to reestablish the Olympics as a "manageable and desirable enterprise" (Reich 1978e). In the end, IOC Rule 4 proved to be a stumbling block back in Los Angeles.

Contention arose over Rule 4, which mandated that the host city and the national Olympic committee (i.e., the USOC) shoulder the "complete financial responsibility for the organization of the Games" (Baker 1977). But the LA bid noted that a nonprofit corporation was financially responsible for the games and that the City of Los Angeles was not the responsible party. Mayor Bradley, hoping to head off additional political problems, appointed John Argue to head a blue-ribbon panel to break the impasse. Members of the panel included movie producer David Wolper, Rodney Rood, and William Robertson, the executive secretary of the Los Angeles Federation of Labor. Bradley also appointed a temporary committee that included Howard Allen, of Southern California Edison and president of the LA Chamber of Commerce; Justin Dart, an SCCOG fundraiser; and Paul Ziffren, a well-known Los Angeles attorney. The mayor did notify city council president Ferraro about the temporary committee (Reich 1978a). At a news conference the following week, Argue told reporters that there was a new plan, but he refused to divulge any of its details.

With events spinning out of control in the political arena, Argue, Wolper, and Rood quietly filed papers to incorporate a private, non-profit LA Olympic Organizing Committee to go to Montreal to meet with the IOC and bring back a signed contract for the 1984 summer games. Argue noted in the news conference that at least five of the seven members of the mayor's blue-ribbon panel were going to Montreal to meet with the IOC and that no city officials would attend, stating that this would insulate the city from liability. Later, he stated that the rationale for having a private committee was that with public money comes public control (Argue 1985, 18).

By the end of June, as the council and IOC bid contract deadlines approached, contention arose over negotiating the sale of television rights, providing new facilities for the athletes, and the city's determination to resist future demands from international sports federations (Reich 1978i). By mid-July, the mayor publicly stated he would respect the council's request to withdraw LA's bid. At this point, the IOC initiated discussions and agreed to suspend Rule 4, thus absolving the City of Los Angeles from financial liability for the Olympic games (Reich 1978c). As the negotiations narrowed, the USOC board approved the plan for the LA summer games, which included a 40 percent share to the USOC of any profit from the games.[1]

The IOC formally awarded the summer games to Los Angeles in October 1978. Following the announcement, the LA City Council voted for a half-cent increase in the hotel-bed tax and a 6 percent Olympic distribution tax to cover any costs the city might incur for the games. The council skeptics then had Proposition N placed on the November 1978 ballot, fearing that their action might be overturned in a future council session. Proposition N passed, with 74 percent of the city's voters supporting it. These actions were intended to prevent any existing public monies from being used on the Olympics (Lawson 1985). Shortly after the New Year, Mayor Bradley named fifty-nine members of the newly established Los Angeles Olympic Organizing Committee (LAOOC), which was described as a "who's who of business, sports, and entertainment" in LA (Reich 1979b, II-1).

■ Managing the Games: Blending Venues and Communities

The complete sixty-one-member LAOOC met for the first time as a group in February 1979, with the mayor promising to keep the city at arm's length. Consolidation of the organizing effort began when a twenty-two-member executive committee was named in January 1979, with John Argue as temporary chair. In March, Paul Ziffren was named chairman of the LAOOC and Peter Ueberroth was named president and general manager. Ueberroth's plan for the summer games included holding everyone—corporate sponsors, government officials and agencies, and neighborhood groups and community organizations—at arm's length (Reich 1986, 125). This served the LAOOC's main objectives, which were to raise private funding, develop a cadre of volunteers to help minimize costs, and stage the sporting competition. Ueberroth's management team was small and the organizational structure was loose. The staff grew from a nucleus of eleven in 1979 to 1,700 by spring 1984. During the games, the number of paid staff grew to 12,000; 33,000 people volunteered and 36,000 people worked for companies providing services under contract with the LAOOC (Wilson 1996, 170). Ueberroth and his second in command, Harry Usher, an entertainment lawyer in Los Angeles, made most of the decisions. The LAOOC's first moves were to develop a strategic plan and to identify potential revenue sources as well as venues (LAOOC 1985, 19).

The strategic planning process indicated that the first task should be raising funds (the following discussion is based on Wilson 1996, 170–172; see also DeFrantz 1988, 58). The LAOOC sought revenues primarily from four sources: corporate sponsorships, television broadcast rights, ticket sales, and commemorative Olympic coins. The number of corporate sponsorships was limited to gain higher fees, and three different levels of participation were permitted: official sponsor, official supplier, and official licensee. Some 164 companies paid $127 million in cash, services, and products to participate, and Ueberroth received much of this in up-front payments that yielded $76 million after investment. Television broadcast rights sold to ABC Sports and foreign broadcasters raised nearly $287 million. Ticket sales brought in $156 million. Although first estimated to be $150 million, the surplus generated from the 1984 Olympics was determined in 1985 to be $225 million.

After the sale of television broadcast rights to ABC Sports, the LAOOC turned to the competition venues, most of which were selected by 1983, when attention turned to a preview of the games. The LAOOC organized international competitions in a variety of sports, known as LA83, which were sponsored by corporations and served as a dry run for the summer games. "Festive federalism," a color scheme to link the venues and help build Olympic spirit, and the star-in-motion logo were used to focus the region's attention on the summer games. To further prime the pump, the Olympics Arts Festival, the cultural component of the Olympic games, opened in June and continued through the summer games. In the months before the opening ceremonies, "venuization" took place. This was a form of decentralization in which the functional organization of technical and support staff and services at each venue site was coordinated by the venue commissioner (see LAOOC 1985, 20–22). Taken together, the organizational and operational elements that surrounded the strategic planning process became the model of the entrepreneurial Olympics.

▓ The Politics of Venue Development

The LA bid promised that existing facilities would be used for all sporting competition venues unless an existing facility did not meet international standards. In the end, four new facilities were required: a rowing course, a swim stadium, a velodrome, and a shooting facility. The LA Coliseum, important to the 1932 Olympic games, would be the site of the opening and closing ceremonies, and the dormitories on the campuses of the University of Southern California and the University of California–Los Angeles would serve as the main Olympic villages. Even with the use of existing facilities, the task of managing the sites was enormous because venues were located throughout southern California, as shown in Figure 4.1.

The LAOOC set up an extensive community relations program of twenty-one advisory committees called the Olympic Neighbors program, which was one part of its Community Action Program (LAOOC 1983). The Olympic Neighbors program, started in 1983, was seen as a booster group effort and included venue sites, Olympic villages, and practice site communities. Several locations, notably the affluent Westwood-UCLA community and the gated Coto de Caza

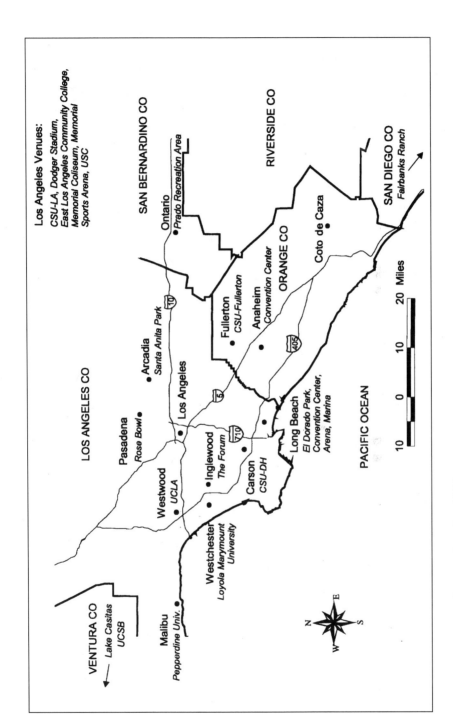

Figure 4.1 Venues for Los Angeles 1984

site in Orange County, did not wish to be part of the Olympic Neighbors program but met regularly with the LAOOC staff.

We now examine the events and activities of three venues: the
Sepulveda Basin, Exposition Park, and Westwood Village. Each of
these illustrates the private power of the LAOOC vis-à-vis the power
of neighborhood interests (see also Burbank, Heying, and Andranovich 2000). The Sepulveda Basin is in the San Fernando Valley,
an area of mostly middle-class communities that today is again seeking to secede from the City of Los Angeles. Exposition Park was and
still is a relatively poor community in south-central Los Angeles,
and Westwood is a relatively affluent west-side community surrounding the UCLA campus.

Sepulveda Basin. The Sepulveda Basin, a large recreation and open
space area in the San Fernando Valley, became the site of the first
opposition to the 1984 summer games. The Sepulveda Basin is controlled by the U.S. Army Corps of Engineers and serves as a flood
control channel during heavy winter rains. As a large open space
currently used for recreation, the basin was touted as an ideal site for
a variety of sports competitions in 1971, including archery and several water sports (Hansen 1980, 9). When this site first was identified
in 1977 as a potential location for an Olympic rowing course and
velodrome, it soon became the "second battle" of the summer games.

During 1979, Mayor Bradley developed a plan to bring federal
aid—a tactic he had used successfully during his tenure—to LA to
support the games. The need for aid stemmed in part from promises
the mayor made to the IOC in Athens to build archery, yachting,
shooting, field hockey, swimming, and cycling facilities. Since LA's
public officials vowed not to use local taxpayer funds and Governor
Brown had pledged not to use state dollars, Bradley did what had
worked in the past: he sought federal funds. Although the mayor and
council fought publicly for most of the year over many issues, they
were in general agreement about pursuing federal funds, and for the
most part, the newly formed LAOOC supported the mayor. Yet the
mayor's request did raise some concerns for the LAOOC (see Reich
1986, 126–127). Chief among these was the size of the aid package;
the request had started at $33 million in 1977, but two years later
had grown to $141 million (and the city administrator added a $43
million underground parking facility, located at the LA Coliseum).

In pursuing federal money, the mayor's first move was to
change his Olympics liaison from Anton Calleia to Ray Remy, who

had intergovernmental lobbying experience (Reich 1979a). But when LA area members of Congress demanded to know where the venues would be built and how much they were going to cost, Bradley tried to sidestep the issue, saying that the sites would be selected locally and were not yet known. Bradley's inability to be specific led some to suggest that LA's demands were dishonest, since there had been a pledge not to use public money to stage the 1984 games. Others saw this as a ploy to underwrite LA's attempts to attract the Raiders football team to the city (Hume 1979; Reich 1979c). In late 1979, President Carter rejected the mayor's request for federal aid, ending the bid to use federal funds but shifting the focus of the political debate to the San Fernando Valley, where the Sepulveda Basin is located.

When Bradley included the basin in his proposed funding plan for $141 million in federal aid in May 1979, the Coalition to Save the Sepulveda Basin emerged to challenge its designation as a venue. The coalition was made up of homeowners and environmentalists who had mobilized a year earlier to fight an effort by Hollywood Park to locate a racetrack in the basin. The coalition commissioned a survey of recreation users, conducted in shopping centers and the basin recreation areas in July 1979, which showed a lack of support for building facilities and parking areas in the basin (Orlov 1979). In response, the *Los Angeles Times* editorialized that no good purpose would be served trying to impose Olympic facilities on communities, that this was "bad government" as well as "bad sense" ("The Fight over Sites" 1979). Throughout 1980, however, the basin continued to be pitched as a site, which broadened the opposition coalition's base to include many other homeowners and some businesses. As a preliminary site visit to the basin by the representatives of the International Rowing Federation grew closer, the tactics of some opponents may have changed as well. Ueberroth was a Valley resident, and his dogs were poisoned during this time (Ueberroth 1985, 76).

In January 1981, the coalition sent Mayor Bradley a letter stating that eight polls showed local opposition to using the basin for the summer games, including one conducted by a city council member running for reelection. The letter also reminded the mayor of his earlier pledge that there would be no placement of venues in the face of substantial public opposition (Reich 1981d). The site remained viable, however. Public hearings were scheduled by the Board of Recreation and Park Commissioners to adopt a new master plan for the Sepulveda Basin, including a rowing course. Two days before the hearings, environmentalists charged the Army Corps of Engineers with trying to "distort the degree of opposition" to the proposal to build a rowing course (Reich 1981b). This followed on the heels of a Freedom of Information Act request by the Coalition to Save Sepulveda Basin that yielded a report to the corps by a consultant who examined the opinions of community leaders rather than the public at large. The rowing course was supported by businesses in the San Fernando Valley and opposed by homeowners in most communities. The board was somewhat skeptical over the $10–14 million cost and voted against including the rowing course.

Shortly after this, in September, the International Rowing Federation, responding to Mayor Bradley's request that it consider the question, ruled out the basin as the site for rowing and canoeing based on strong public opposition, and the LAOOC accepted the decision. Mayor Bradley was in the midst of the 1981 mayoral campaign, and his opponent, former mayor Sam Yorty, noted that Olympic authorities half a world away were more responsive to the people of the San Fernando Valley than was Tom Bradley (Reich 1981a). The potential siting in the Sepulveda Basin had dragged on for over four years, and the LAOOC relocated the rowing course to Lake Casitas, one of two sites in Ventura County that subsequently asked for the rowing events. In the end, the second battle of the Olympics, coupled with the city council's vote in October 1978 not to use general funds and the passage of Proposition N in November, gave the LAOOC a free hand in organizing the games.

Exposition Park. Exposition Park, which contained the USC Olympic Village, the USC Swim Stadium, the LA Sports Arena, and the LA Coliseum, was the site of the opening and closing ceremonies and therefore strategically important to the summer games. In the early 1980s, Exposition Park was a predominantly poor area that was 45 percent black, 38 percent Latino, and 17 percent white (Clayton 1981). At that time, the community was still smarting from the expansion of USC in 1967, an expansion that resulted in the loss of hundreds of units of housing. These had not been replaced and were a source of conflict in the LA City Council's Hoover Expansion plans in 1981, which would expand the southern boundary of the park south of Martin Luther King Boulevard, an area of single-family houses and apartments (Boyarsky 1983, 3). Community fears regarding the 1984 summer games included a lack of employment opportunities, security and crime issues, and further impact on the local housing supply. A number of discussions were held in the early 1980s between the University Neighborhood Relations Commission and the University Parish Group, an interdenominational group of churches and small businesses in the USC area. A key issue that may have contributed to the LAOOC Exposition Park strategy was raised during these meetings: the summer games were perceived as a "private games" with a structural insensitivity to the community because public officials were not involved. Indeed, some local officials stated that this might be a perfect opportunity for the Reagan administration's enterprise zones program (Clayton 1981).

The Exposition Park community was of particular interest to the LAOOC because of its strategic importance to the success of the summer games; the LAOOC conducted an analysis of the Olympics' impact on the area and then developed its community relations plan. The impact analysis identified traffic congestion and street closures as the greatest negative effect and job opportunities and parking revenues (so-called front-lawn revenues) as the greatest positive effect. Jobs, albeit temporary in nature, would be created for nearly four thousand people, the majority in concessions and cleanup and the remainder in housekeeping, food service, and maintenance in the USC Olympic Village. The impact analysis also included the following three points: a pledge to "not leave a major positive or permanent manifestation behind us based on our current plans"; regular communication that could alleviate community animosity; and consideration of temporary benefits at least equivalent to the effects of dislocation (LAOOC 1984a, 1).

The community relations program plan contained several guidelines and operating assumptions (LAOOC 1984b). First, the relationship with the community should be based on personal, one-to-one contact and should be run out of an office in the neighborhood. Second, the objective of the program should be to provide accurate information to the community and deal with concerns on a case-by-case basis. Further, the LAOOC should support existing community programs, organizations, and leadership, strengthening these groups rather than creating new, temporary groups. Fourth, while the LAOOC should try to enhance community employment opportunities, it should be a catalyst rather than simply a funding source. Finally, the last two guidelines summarized the LAOOC's interests in the Exposition Park community. "We will not propose a major physical contribution or

'payoff' as part of the community plan. We will not pledge to alleviate all of the problems created by the Olympics on a direct problem-
solution basis, but will project the belief that the overall impact will
be a positive one" (LAOOC 1984b).

The plan also identified several areas of concern. The Olympic
Neighbors program was seen as a way to create a sense of pride in
the community and to foster participation in the Olympic effort, but
more emphasis was needed on opportunities for "troublesome kids."
Youth programs needed to address the closure of the USC swim facility and a neighborhood pool that provided summer recreation opportunities for five hundred to a thousand neighborhood kids daily
(LAOOC 1984a). Finally, the plan emphasized the need to develop
an "interface with local politicians."

The key issues in the venue development plan for Exposition
Park, then, focused on such concerns. Community relations, however, were relegated to the category of "non-operating issues"
(LAOOC 1983, 61). The LAOOC's strategy for Exposition Park illustrated this approach. The strategy consisted of seven points: (1)
create a positive feeling by providing accurate information about
employment and involvement opportunities to the community; (2)
cooperate with political leaders, community programs, sponsors, and
others to create a community pride and improvement program, including participation in decorating, special projects, and other activities; (3) involve the LA Community Redevelopment Agency, Summer Youth Employment program, and other government departments
"to allocate funding resources to specific projects and supplemental
employment opportunities"; (4) assist LA City Recreation and Parks
Department in planning to provide alternative recreational and community activities "to alleviate real and potential problems relative to
closure of the LA Swim Stadium and the Exposition Park Recreation
Center"; (5) coordinate these efforts with other LAOOC community
relations program activities; (6) coordinate with the LAOOC government relations department to keep appropriate political and administrative leaders informed and to enhance their participation; and (7)
ensure that the Exposition Park community contact center was
staffed by "multi-racial, bilingual staff."

The LAOOC overcame weak neighborhood resistance by carefully
developing a strategy that brought city departments into the Olympic
equation to provide program support that the LAOOC was not willing to fund. In June 1983, the Eighth District Olympic Neighborhood

Advisory Committee was formed with the help of city council member Robert Farrell (LAOOC 1983, folder 17). The issues discussed in monthly meetings at USC in 1983 and 1984 were employment opportunities, vending opportunities, and youth activities. The LAOOC did open an office in Exposition Park in April 1984, and it provided a new gym floor in the Challenger Boys Club and youth activity programs in twenty-two recreation centers in the South LA area, as well as sponsoring a cleanup campaign to get ready for the summer games. In all, nearly $1.8 million in improvements went into Exposition Park, but these were in the form of Olympic needs: new irrigation and lighting systems, new restrooms, roadway repairs, parking lot repairs, landscaping, recreational equipment, and new signs (Perelman 1985, 71–73; LA Chamber of Commerce n.d.). Additional investment went into coliseum repairs; some of this was in the form of a proposed enticement to bring the NFL Oakland Raiders to LA and was to be repaid to the LAOOC (Weinstein 1980). The new McDonald's Swim Stadium at USC cost $4 million and was funded entirely by the six thousand participating McDonald's franchises in the United States. Serving the Olympic Village at USC was the new Frank L. King Olympic Dining Hall, supported by $3 million from the LAOOC; one million of this was credited as partial payment for renting the campus (LAOOC 1985, 93). As the Exposition Park experience shows, the desire to conduct the summer games in a businesslike manner was reflected in LAOOC planning and practice. The LAOOC directly supported business and institutional interests that coincided with its interests in this strategically important community, but it addressed community concerns only indirectly.

Westwood-UCLA. Like Exposition Park, UCLA was a necessary piece of the 1984 mega-event infrastructure. The university has excellent athletic facilities but, unlike Exposition Park, is located near several of LA's wealthier neighborhoods. By the 1970s, homeowners' associations had become powerful players in local Los Angeles politics (Davis 1990).

This area's Olympic task force, established by LA city council member Zev Yaroslavsky, consisted of five homeowners' associations (Bel Air, Beverly Hills, Brentwood Park, Holmby-Westwood, Westwood Hills), the West Los Angeles Chamber of Commerce, the Westwood Merchants Association, and the UCLA Student Olympics Committee. This group did not participate in the Olympic Neighbors program but did meet quarterly with LAOOC staff to discuss security, transportation, the Olympic Village, and staffing issues (LAOOC 1983, folder 17, Addendum A).

In general, there were three sets of contrasting views toward the games. The homeowners' associations reflected the views of their members who feared traffic and parking problems as well as "wanderers." The merchants' associations took a cautious stance before the summer games. The university on the other hand was generally enthusiastic about the games. Together, these views reflected the type of support for the summer Olympics in this part of Los Angeles (see Fairbank, Canapary, and Maullin 1983). As the summer games grew closer, business was slower than usual in the UCLA area, and the West LA Chamber of Commerce staged a laser light show at night on the side of the Federal Building to develop visitor interest in the community (Stewart 1984).

The LAOOC worked closely with UCLA (the university president sat on the executive committee), and UCLA received $11.2 million in payments for use of the university's facilities, including $6 million for the Olympic Village facilities alone (Reich 1984). UCLA also benefited from a new building constructed on campus to house the administration of the games. Campus projects supported at least in part by Olympic payments included: construction of the new tennis stadium; development of the Wooden Center; remodeling the J. P. Morgan Athletic Center; expansion of the athletic services building; refurbishment of several campus theaters; development of a plaza and the Bruin Walk, remodeling the student union; rebuilding the swimming pool at the Sunset Canyon Recreation Center; and the renovation and expansion of four cafeterias (UCLA Chancellor's Memorandum 1984; Reich 1984). The LAOOC also carpeted residence halls, widened an access road, and installed a new practice track at Drake Stadium at its own expense.

The homeowners' associations, area merchants, and the university were supportive of the summer games, but they were concerned about the attitudes of the LAOOC representatives with whom they met. In large part, this was the result of the arm's-length approach taken by the LAOOC, which included repeating "there's nothing to worry about" in community meetings. The director of the West Los Angeles Chamber of Commerce expressed her exasperation in a newspaper interview by responding, "There's plenty to worry about" (Orlov 1980).

■ Impact of the 1984 Summer Games

After the closing ceremony in the fall of 1984, the Greater Los Angeles Visitors and Convention Bureau presented a new marketing strategy based on the success of the Olympic games. The positive image of Los Angeles seen by millions of television viewers worldwide stimulated an aggressive marketing campaign that included advertising for convention business in trade journals, radio, and Sunday newspapers and a doubling of trips to familiarize travel agents and tourism officials with the area (Rivera 1984). In addition, the bureau began to push for an expansion of the LA Convention Center, then a paltry 350,000 square feet.

The direct economic impact of the games on the regional economy was estimated to be more than one billion dollars (Barker 1984). This included $330 million in lodging and meals by visitors and another $30 million by locals. An additional $100 million was to be spent on media and telecommunication upgrades to enhance the broadcasting and reporting of the games. Staging the Olympics was estimated at $465 million (including the costs of the Olympic Villages), and Olympic-related spending and cultural events were projected to add $150 million.

In its post-Olympics impact analysis, Economic Research Associates (1986) found these estimates to be fairly accurate. Visitors spent $420 million on lodging and meals while locals spent $26 million, and media-related investment added $96 million. LAOOC costs were $420 million, and operating the Olympic Villages added another $30 million. Sponsors and suppliers provided nearly $44 million in goods and services, and cultural activities added another $9 million. In addition, local government revenues received an Olympic boost of $47.2 million ($32.8 million to the City of Los Angeles alone), and California received nearly $49 million, all of this from sales, income, and occupancy taxes and the City of LA's fees (Economic Research Associates 1986, 21).

Although the summer games were staged in existing facilities, the legacy of the 1984 Olympics included building five new facilities and refurbishing some existing venues (see Table 4.1). Private funds were used to construct an Olympic velodrome ($3 million from Southland Corporation, parent of the 7-11 chain), an Olympic diving and swimming stadium ($4 million from six thousand McDonald's franchises), and a shooting range (Fuji Film). New training tracks were constructed at several area colleges and high schools. A new $3.2 million hockey field was built, courtesy of a local non-profit foundation (LAOOC 1985, 83). The LA Coliseum received refurbishing, both of the track (by ARCO) and the spectator areas ($5 million from the LAOOC and $12 million more from private funding; LAOOC 1985, 68).

UCLA and USC did very well as a result of the summer games. UCLA received a newly constructed building used to administer the operations of the games and then turned over to the university. Both UCLA and USC upgraded their permanent facilities by serving as Olympic Villages, and UCLA built a new tennis stadium. Beyond the universities, Los Angeles International Airport accelerated construction of its upper deck to ease the trip in and out of the airport, and LA received faster installation of the latest fiber-optic telecommunication technology (Economic Research Associates 1984, 46).

Of course, not all business interests profited as handsomely. The LA region is a great entertainment mecca, and several of its biggest stars suffered during the summer of 1984. Disneyland, Universal Studios, and Six Flags Magic Mountain reported lower than normal attendance during that summer, although the extent of the impact was related to the parks' dependence on out-of-area visitors (Economic Research Associates 1984, 55–56). Within the region's Olympic communities, the economic effects were uneven. For example, Long Beach hosted four Olympic venues and saw little displacement of its tourism; in fact, it had an increase in foreign visitors.

Perhaps overlooked in an overview of the summer games' impact were two long-term benefits to the region. First, the Olympics Arts Festival added nearly $9.2 million to the economic impact of the summer games and helped LA to be seen as "an exciting cultural center" (Barker 1984, 3). The staging of the mammoth festival at various locations around the region was highly successful given its short planning period, although there was the well-publicized cancellation of an eight-hour opera called *The CIVIL warS* (see Levitt 1990, 215, 220–222). The support for arts festivals in LA continues, although none of the subsequent festivals has achieved the attendance levels of the Olympic Arts Festival. The second benefit was the creation of the Amateur Athletic Foundation of Los Angeles, with a $93 million endowment to continue the support of amateur athletic competition and training as well as public education in the region (Economic Research Associates 1984).

Table 4.1 Attributes of Venues for the 1984 Games

Location	Venue	Events	Attributes
Los Angeles County			
Los Angeles	LA Coliseum	Athletics	Refurbished
	LA Sports Arena	Boxing	Refurbished
	USC	Swimming	New: private
	USC	Olympic village	Refurbished
	East LA Community Coll.	Hockey	Refurbished
	California State Univ., LA	Judo	Refurbished
	Dodger Stadium	Baseball	Existing
Westwood	UCLA	Olympic Village	Refurbished
	UCLA	Gymnastics, tennis	Refurbished
	UCLA	Administration building	New: LAOOC
Malibu	Pepperdine University	Water polo	Existing
Westchester	Loyola Marymount Univ.	Weightlifting	Existing
Long Beach	El Dorado Park	Archery	Refurbished
	Convention Center	Fencing	Existing
	Long Beach Arena	Volleyball	Existing
	Long Beach Marina	Yachting	Existing
Inglewood	Forum	Basketball, handball	Existing
Carson	California State Univ., DH	Cycling	New: private
Arcadia	Santa Anita Park	Equestrian	Existing
Pasadena	Rose Bowl	Football	Refurbished
Orange County			
Fullerton	California State Univ., Ful.	Handball	Existing
Anaheim	Convention Center	Wrestling	Existing
Coto de Caza	Modern Pentathlon	Existing	
Ventura County			
Lake Casitas	Lake Casitas	Rowing, canoeing	New: private
Santa Barbara County			
Santa Barbara	UCSB	Olympic Village	Refurbished
San Bernardino County			
Chino Hills	El Prado Recreation Area	Shooting	New: private
San Diego County			
Fairbanks Ranch	Fairbanks Ranch	Equestrian	Existing

Source: Compiled by the authors.

Notes: Attributes indicate whether a facility was new or existing with minimal modifications for the games. Private funds were from corporate sponsors; refurbishments included LAOOC funds, foundation funds, and/or corporate donations.

■ Conclusion: Whose Dream?

Los Angeles Mayor Bradley enjoyed a stable governing coalition in the city, close ties to national Democratic politics, and a slim one-vote majority on the city council in favor of the Olympic games. LA's aspirations, as articulated by the mayor, to become a world-class city played a large part in seeking to host the Olympic games. But these aspirations also were reflected in the mayor's downtown redevelopment program, described by one observer as "downtown sprawl" characterized by "speculative commercial development" (Davis 1987). The latter characterization also attests to the relatively closed nature of economic development decisionmaking, with coalition members making all the major moves, including speaking up for neighborhoods and other interests. Cracks in the coalition's facade did appear throughout the Olympic bidding process, however. Much of the conflict centered on the city council, as supporters sought to maintain a pro-Olympic majority. The conflict was pronounced at times, including an open warning to city council skeptics by the mayor's chief protocol officer on her way to the May 1978 IOC meeting in Athens. The LA business community had wanted the summer games for twenty years, and skeptics who were talking about obstructionist tactics were "playing a dangerous game" with their political supporters, she warned (Reich 1978e). In the end, a council vote and a city charter amendment vote removed the games from city control and gave the LAOOC a free hand in organizing the summer games. Bradley's hope to benefit from the games was dashed when President Carter did not honor the mayor's request for federal funds.

The summer games did impact the many communities and cities with Olympic venues. Exposition Park, located in south-central LA, was the focus of much attention in the LAOOC's organizing plans because of its strategic importance to the 1984 Olympics. These efforts included establishing the Olympic Neighbors program in 1983, using the Olympic Encounter program to introduce area youth to Olympic athletes, and an Olympic Neighbors training session, which provided orientation to community residents working or volunteering for the summer games.

In keeping with the region's past, most of the communities hosting Olympic venues tended to be boosters for the games. For example, in the well-to-do Orange County community of Coto de Caza, residents were both "pleased and appalled" that their management association agreed to host four events in the modern pentathlon for publicity. But neighborhood barbecues and a dry run with the junior pentathlon seemed to ease the concerns of most residents; "they could have consulted us" appeared to be the tenor of residents' complaints (Dolan 1984b). In Arcadia, a million-dollar sprucing-up was shared by the LAOOC and the Santa Anita racetrack. Used to the horse-racing crowds, residents were taking the coming Olympic games in stride (Boyarsky 1984). Chino Hills, in San Bernardino County, saw the Olympic games as a chance to gain some positive publicity. The Chino Valley, then home to 200,000 cows and 45,000 people, is well known to freeway commuters regardless of which way the wind is blowing. As a representative of the Chino Chamber of Commerce said, "We want to lure fans to restaurants, the museum, and the cheese factory; Chino really is an international city" (Dolan 1984a).

Mayor Bradley's position that the summer games would bring many benefits to the city if conducted in a spartan and businesslike manner became the mission of the LAOOC. The city's capacity to influence the staging of the games was most evident during the bidding process; however, the city's pledge not to use public funds, the widely spread venue sites, and the relaxing of the IOC's Rule 4 diminished the city's role in organizing the games. The summer games were organized around three objectives: raising private funding, developing a cadre of volunteers to help minimize costs, and staging the sporting competition. The single most important priority in the three years leading up to the staging of the Olympic games was raising revenues, and the LAOOC looked everywhere to maximize its revenue. From television rights to commemorative coins and from not reimbursing the Southern California Rapid Transit District for mass transit services to not buying volunteers lunch, the LAOOC took a tough bargaining position that continually focused on reducing the costs of staging the games. While the arm's-length relationship between the LAOOC and the city was unique in the staging of the Olympics, LAOOC's model of entrepreneurship, particularly the LAOOC's direct negotiation of television rights and approach to corporate sponsorship, earned the 1984 Olympics the moniker of the "capitalist games" (Nixon 1988).[2] Ueberroth's second in command, Harry Usher, pointed out in an interview after the games: "It was a perfect match. He was the perfect man for the job at the right time in our society . . . Peter is the 80s. He almost embodies what the 80s are about and I'm not saying it's good or bad, it's factual" (Usher 1985, 16).

The LA games were boycotted by the Soviet Union and others but were highly acclaimed nonetheless for the spectacular entertainment, fierce competition, and the intangibles of a glorious two weeks in Los Angeles with no smog, no traffic hassles, and no terrorism. These factors all contributed to the feeling that the games were great for the city. The $225 million surplus that the LAOOC generated contributed to the sense that LA was the place to get things done. It also put the luster back on the Olympics as the mega-event of choice for cities wishing to achieve world-class status.

■ Notes

1. The contract between the LAOOC and the USOC gave the USOC representation on the executive committee of the LAOOC's board and a 40 percent share of any profits. The contracts were negotiated over many months and signed in early March 1979. Reich reports that the USOC wielded little control over the LAOOC, however, and that the "partnership was a sham" (1986, 132).

2. The LAOOC model has been adopted by the IOC in its corporate sponsorship program, which has turned the IOC into a global sports entertainment powerhouse (see Abrahamson and Wharton 2000; Larson and Park 1993).

■■ 5 ■■

ATLANTA AND
THE 1996 SUMMER GAMES

The success of the Los Angeles games put the Olympics in a new light for city leaders across the nation. Atlanta, a city whose leaders were concerned with its image and always looking for promising opportunities, pursued this appealing new development strategy and landed the 1996 Centennial Olympic games. In this chapter we investigate Atlanta's experience, focusing on the relationship between the Olympics and the politics of urban revitalization. The chapter begins with an overview of image-building politics in Atlanta, then turns to a detailed examination of the process of bidding for and organizing the Centennial Olympic games. It concludes with an assessment of Atlanta's Olympic legacy.

■ The City and Its Politics

Atlanta, the self-proclaimed capital of the New South, has been a city united by its desire for economic growth and driven by its penchant for self-promotion. Lacking any natural or geographically defining features, Atlanta owes its existence to the building of the Western and Atlantic Railroad's southeastern terminus. The railroad anchored the fledgling city between rivers that flowed to the Gulf and the Atlantic and allowed it to secure freight that was moving from the South to the West or the Northeast (Doyle 1990, 33). Irish rail workers established a town near the railroad juncture. Variously referred to as Terminus or Marthasville, the town was incorporated in 1847 and renamed Atlanta. The name was "invented by local promoters to suggest its role as gateway to the Atlantic" (Doyle 1990, 33). This early experiment with image building would become Atlanta's defining characteristic.

Atlanta's centrality in trade and transportation allowed it to become one of the important cities of the Old South and subsequently a logistical center of the Confederacy. During the Civil War, a Union army captured Atlanta and torched it, leaving most of the city in charred ruins (Doyle 1990, 32). Atlanta's rebirth and phoenixlike rise from the ashes of war have provided it with an origin myth more auspicious than the banal stories of a transport hub.

The destruction of Atlanta and its subsequent rise to glory as the capital of the New South form the core of what might be considered Atlantan culture. The willingness of the city's elite to tear down the markers of the past in order to revise the city's projected future could be read as a recapitulation of its second founding. Atlanta's preoccupation with its rebuilding, and the boosterism such a preoccupation engenders, is visible in the events that in part have driven the city's success.

Eager to become the capital of an economically revitalized New South, Atlanta embarked on a series of three image-building events in 1881, 1887, and 1895. The first event was the 1881 International Cotton Exposition, which offered Atlanta the opportunity to begin integrating itself economically and culturally with the nation. According to Newman (1999, 34), the importance of the 1881 exposition was the presentation of "the 'Atlanta Spirit,' the ability of business leaders to organize an event to promote the city." The second event was the 1887 Piedmont Exposition, the goal of which was the "modernization and industrialization of Southern agriculture" (Rutheiser 1996, 25). The third event was the 1895 Cotton States and International Exposition. In addition to the mandatory focus on the southern articulation of modernity, the exposition incorporated a woman's building and a Negro building in an attempt to show a new face toward gender and race issues (Rutheiser 1996, 27).

The proclivity for image building defines the "Atlanta Spirit" and remains a pervasive ethos of the city's business elites. What is unique about Atlanta's boosterism is the extent to which the city has been so thoroughly defined by its trade and commercial energy and by its lack of countervailing cultural or physical attributes.

While boosterism defines Atlanta's ethos, its politics are characterized by an informal governance regime dominated by white business leaders and an aspiring black political leadership. Floyd Hunter was one of the first scholars to identify the interplay of these two elements in the governance structure of Atlanta. In *Community Power Structures* (1953), Hunter showed that the origin of new policy in Atlanta could be attributed more to informal discussions among elites than to formally rendered pluralistic politics. Hunter extended his thesis to Atlanta's black elite structure, identifying the importance of regular lunches at the Hungry Club in the historically black YMCA. At these lunches, black and white elites could build consensus around issues of growth that joined them and negotiate issues of race that divided them.

At the time Hunter conducted his study, William B. Hartsfield was Atlanta's mayor. Hartsfield enjoyed considerable support from business leaders for his resistance to patronage, ability to modernize city government, and willingness to consult with them before making decisions. This close working relationship allowed business elites and city government to achieve their common goal of redeveloping the central business district. During his tenure, Hartsfield faced two emerging trends that would be significant for future Atlanta politics: the rise of a politically active black middle class and increasing white flight to the suburbs. Both these trends predicted a stronger role for blacks in Atlanta's formal governing structures. Hartsfield's response to the need for more inclusiveness in city government was largely symbolic. According to Stone (1989b, 46), "What Hartsfield offered was mainly racial moderation in campaign speeches and public utterances."

Hartsfield's successor, Ivan Allen, Jr., continued the tradition of racial moderation. Allen, a leader in the business community before becoming mayor, successfully engaged a biracial civic coalition in his effort to desegregate schools and other facilities. His desire to make Atlanta a city with national stature, however, led him to construct the Atlanta Fulton County Stadium on land that had been cleared by urban renewal. Although successful in attracting professional sports teams, the destruction of functional black neighborhoods such as Summerhill for this and other civic projects created a disturbing legacy that still resonates in Atlanta politics.

Over time, the rise of a black middle class coupled with white flight to the suburbs changed the electoral demographics of Atlanta. This became evident with the 1973 election of Maynard Jackson to the office of mayor. The effect was that "electorally, the white business elite was reduced to junior partner in the biracial coalition"

(Stone 1989b, 81). Since Jackson's election, Atlanta has consistently and overwhelmingly maintained a strong African American presence in city politics. The informal power of Atlanta's business elites, however, has not diminished. It is in the context of its history and politics that we now consider Atlanta's successful quest to stage the 1996 Olympic games.

■ Seeking the Games

A single entrepreneur, William "Billy" Payne, initiated Atlanta's bid for the 1996 Olympics. His quest to bring the Olympics to Atlanta is reported to have begun one February morning in 1987. Sitting in his office following a successful church fund-raising campaign, Payne sought a more substantial leadership challenge. According to the now mythic tale, he scribbled a note "1996 Olympics" (Johnson 1990, 36). While his ability to promote a mega-event was untested, Payne did have some important credentials. He was a successful real estate lawyer, a former defensive end at the University of Georgia, and a member of its Alumni Foundation Board. While not one of the city's elite, he did have friends to open doors to the powerful (ACOG 1997, 6).

One of Payne's first contacts was his friend Peter Candler, a Coca-Cola heir. Candler liked the idea and together they formed the Georgia Amateur Athletic Foundation (GAAF) as a platform for their efforts. Payne's public forays were initially unsuccessful. Appearing on a local talk radio show, he was mocked; the *Atlanta Journal Constitution* was unsupportive; and Mayor Andrew Young could not find time to meet with him. In spite of the rough early going, Candler and Payne persisted. Candler contacted an old friend, Horace Sibley, a senior partner in King and Spalding, one of the city's oldest and most distinguished corporate law firms. Together they secured a hearing with Coca-Cola president Don Keogh. Getting Coca-Cola support was critical to an Olympic campaign because ten years earlier it had suppressed a similar effort to bid on the 1984 Olympics (Johnson 1990, 37–38).

Payne was graciously received by Keogh but left without a commitment of funding. In response to Payne's plea that Atlanta was Coca-Cola's backyard, Keogh is said to have remarked, "Billy, the whole world is our backyard" (Allen 1996, 236). Even though Payne did not secure immediate financial help, he was given a blessing to proceed, and his enthusiasm for the project began to attract a coterie of volunteers, such as Ginger Watkins, Linda Stephenson, and Cindy Fowler. Prominent socialites, they brought years of event-planning experience to the organization. Payne also attracted three other critical players, Charlie Shaffer and Charlie Battle, partners at King and Spalding, and John Patrick Crecine, president of Georgia Tech. Payne's most important early convert, however, was Andrew Young. A skeptic at first, Young was finally swayed when Payne assured him that the Olympics could be staged without any serious expenditures of city money. Young's commitment of support was soon transformed into a full-time position with GAAF. In his second term as mayor, Young stepped down to run in the Democratic gubernatorial primary. Defeated in a grueling campaign, Young was free to devote himself full-time to the Olympic campaign.

The first task of the fledgling group was to secure from the USOC the right to represent the United States in international bidding. The GAAF bid team initially faced four other cities, but as the final vote neared, only Atlanta and Minneapolis–St. Paul remained. In winning the bid, the GAAF team demonstrated the persuasiveness of southern sociability. While the straightforward midwesterners entertained USOC officials in hotel banquet rooms, Atlanta's coterie of socialites rented a mansion, hired butlers, and entertained USOC officials with strolling violinists (Allen 1996, 237).

With the nod from the USOC, money and support were more forthcoming. Atlanta's new mayor, Maynard Jackson, found money in Atlanta's tight budget to help underwrite the bid. Georgia Tech produced a virtual reality tour of Atlanta and its Olympic venues that helped solidify its claim to technological sophistication. Atlanta's corporations found free office space for GAAF and offered corporate jets to help the bid team visit members of the IOC in their home countries. A delegation from GAAF also visited the 1988 Olympics in Seoul, Korea. In Seoul, Payne and Young made their first presentation to the IOC executive board and met IOC President Juan Antonio Samaranch.

After the Seoul games, the Atlanta team created a new organizational structure, the Atlanta Organizing Committee (AOC), to legitimate their efforts and broaden their base of support. The AOC was directed by a fourteen-member executive committee. Billy Payne was selected president and CEO, Andrew Young was named chair, and Gerald Bartels, president of the Atlanta Chamber of Commerce, became secretary. An advisory council, representing a broad coalition of private interests from throughout Georgia, supported the executive committee (ACOG 1997, 9).

Atlanta faced diverse competition in the international bidding. Athens was the sentimental favorite for the centennial celebration of the modern Olympics, but Belgrade, Manchester, Toronto, and Melbourne also sought the games (Maloney 1996, 194). Atlanta's bid had to overcome some negative consequences of the Los Angeles Olympics. Having been staged only six years earlier, there was a sense among some IOC members that it was too soon to return to the United States. LA proved the Olympics could be profitable, but some members of the IOC were still annoyed that so little of the $225 million surplus had reached the IOC. To overcome these negative perceptions, Atlanta's bid emphasized its substantial advantages. Being in the eastern time zone, Olympic broadcasts would reach the largest prime-time television audience. To counteract concerns about profits, the AOC offered to share surplus revenues (Maloney 1996, 194–195). Atlanta went out of its way to promote its distinct regional character and its record in civil rights. Andrew Young played a key role in persuading international delegates. As a close associate of Martin Luther King, Jr., and former ambassador to the United Nations, Young found a receptive audience for his message of progressive Atlanta and its heritage of human rights.

While Atlanta's symbolic strengths were important, Olympic promoters argued it was the technical strength of Atlanta's bid that was most persuasive in the end. With CNN headquartered in the city, it offered state-of-the-art telecommunications and media services. Atlanta's transportation infrastructure included Hartsfield International Airport, one of the busiest in the world, and MARTA, a high-speed rail system linking the airport to the city center and to the majority of proposed Olympic venues. And Atlanta was a convention-tested city, already chosen to host the Super Bowl and national political conventions (AOC 1990, 12–34).

The IOC met in Tokyo in September 1990 to make the final choice of host city for the 1996 Centennial Olympic games. Although Athens was the sentimental favorite, it was clear the vote would be close. When the vote was finally taken, Athens edged Atlanta only in the first round. Atlanta gained votes in each of the next four rounds, and by the fifth it was victorious (AOC 1990, 35–36).

■ Organizing the Games

Having won the bid, the Atlanta team began the difficult task of organizing the games and constructing venues. In the end, nearly $3
billion would be expended on seventeen new or renovated facilities,
a process that would involve Olympic planners in Atlanta's unique
politics of place, race, and development. The first task of the AOC
was to create a new operating structure to oversee contracts, policies, and investments. One possibility was to have the City of Atlanta take responsibility. Georgia's constitution, however, specifically prohibited the city from accepting certain IOC obligations.
Another option was to utilize the Metropolitan Atlanta Olympic
Games Authority (MAOGA), a semiautonomous governmental body
established by the Georgia legislature in 1989 to enable the bid
process in lieu of the city (ACOG 1997, 18). MAOGA had been
granted considerable public powers and would have been an appropriate vehicle for such a public event. But MAOGA's board was
composed almost exclusively of public officials. The members of the
AOC preferred an organizational structure where decisionmaking
could be closely controlled and operations would be less subject to
public oversight. To this end, they incorporated the Atlanta Committee for the Olympic Games (ACOG) as a nonprofit civic organization with a thirty-one-member governing board. The board included
Mayor Jackson, delegates from the USOC and IOC, holdover members from AOC, and others drawn from Atlanta's civic and business
elites. Operations were delegated to a nine-member executive committee with Billy Payne serving as president and CEO. Andrew
Young and Robert Holder, Jr., were selected as co-chairs of ACOG
(ACOG 1997, 18–19).

The relationship between the city, MAOGA, and ACOG was
stated in a Tri-Party agreement. In the agreement, ACOG accepted financial responsibility for any games-related liabilities and MAOGA
was given "responsibilities to review ACOG construction contracts in
excess of $250,000, approve venue changes within the city limits,
and enter into any intergovernmental contracts on ACOG's behalf"
(ACOG 1997, 18). For its part, the City of Atlanta created the Office
of Olympic Coordination that facilitated service agreements between
ACOG and city departments. Surprisingly, ACOG funded both the
city's Office of Olympic Coordination and MAOGA. The Tri-Party
agreement relieved the city of any financial obligation for Olympic

debt but also demonstrated that it would be a weak third party in Olympic planning. Although MAOGA seemed to provide a level of public accountability, it was financially dependent on ACOG and had little direct control if ACOG violated the public trust. Finally, the terms of the Tri-Party agreement and ACOG's independent status made it clear that real decision-making authority would reside with ACOG (Fish 1992; Roughton 1992a).

■ City Government: A Weak Partner

Mayor Jackson expected the city to be a major player in Olympic development. He hoped the games would leverage the resources to restore Atlanta's crumbling infrastructure and revitalize its distressed neighborhoods. The city's efforts, however, did not meet these aspirations. In comparison to ACOG, the city was reactive, undercapitalized, and unable to mount a coordinated effort to match ACOG's initiatives. In the final analysis, city government played a supporting role at best in organizing the games and saw its efforts to use the games for neighborhood revitalization co-opted by ACOG and redirected to support a business development agenda.

The Corporation for Olympic Development in Atlanta (CODA) was the centerpiece of the city's efforts. For Mayor Jackson, the creation of CODA was a response to the challenge he referred to as "the twin peaks of Atlanta's Mount Olympus" (Roughton 1991a, F-3). Jackson saw the city's goals as, first, to stage the best Olympic games ever, and second, to use the games to "uplift the people of Atlanta and fight poverty in the process" (Roughton 1991a, F-3). Jackson's desire to uplift the people of Atlanta focused on redeveloping the fifteen neighborhoods within the "Olympic Ring," an imaginary circle radiating out from downtown Atlanta that encompassed most of the city's Olympic venues. By all accounts, CODA faced a challenging task. Initiated two years after winning the bid, the organization was late getting started and had no dedicated source of funding. The Olympic Ring neighborhoods, ravaged by disinvestment, were among the poorest and most physically neglected in the city. Estimates for the cost of redevelopment were routinely stated at between $500 million and $1 billion.

The most serious roadblocks to concerted action, however, were differences in outlook among political, neighborhood, and business leaders. Mayor Jackson envisioned CODA as a way to generate public and private funds for "bricks and mortar" projects like sewers, bridges, and streets (Hill and Roughton 1992). People in the neighborhoods focused on immediate needs, especially housing and jobs. Business leaders articulated neighborhood development in terms of urban landscaping, city parks, and pedestrian corridors. The *Atlanta Journal Constitution* appeared to play a mediating role by highlighting both infrastructure and neighborhood needs, but in effect it framed the issue consistent with business interests. The mission of CODA was most often described as "making the city presentable" for the games. Similarly, Olympic Ring neighborhoods were characterized as "outside the fences" (Roughton 1992b, H-6), terminology that reinforced the concept that "venues" were distinct from "community."

The reluctance of the business community to cooperate on a grand vision for the neighborhoods was apparent at the outset. Even two months after CODA was created, Mayor Jackson was unable to find a business leader willing to co-chair the organization. Only after Billy Payne interceded did John Aderhold, chairman of the Georgia World Congress Center, agree to serve. Civic and political leaders also resisted tax proposals intended to provide CODA with a dedicated source of funds. Payne criticized a proposal by Mayor Jackson to tax tickets, fearing its potential to cut into ACOG revenues. The *Atlanta Journal Constitution* declared Jackson's proposal for a one-penny increase in sales tax to be politically unacceptable ("Picking up the check" 1993). Ultimately, the state legislature refused to place any tax referendums on the ballot.

This legislative defeat was followed by an organizational setback. Less than four months after taking the job, Shirley Franklin resigned as CODA president to return to ACOG as a senior policy advisor. Franklin's replacement was Clara Axam, a pragmatic administration insider with deep roots in the African American community (Hill 1993d). The leadership transition took place as commitments and funding opportunities were already determining the trajectory of CODA's efforts. In February, CODA commissioned $600,000 worth of schematic designs for parks, plazas, and pedestrian corridors. By July, $15 million in federal funds became available for the pedestrian corridors intended to connect Olympic facilities on Atlanta University Center campuses with MARTA stations. The National Park Service offered an additional $12 million for rehabilitation of the Martin Luther King, Jr., Center and historic district. Atlanta's Woodruff

Foundation provided $6 million for the redevelopment of Woodruff Park in downtown Atlanta. By fall 1993, Clara Axam announced that CODA would move forward on these "immediate opportunity areas" if matching funds could be found (Hill 1993c, C-4). By plan or default, it was clear that the "immediate opportunity areas" were closely matched to the business and ACOG agenda favoring downtown urban landscaping and high-visibility tourist and Olympic corridors.

The fall and winter of 1993–1994 were difficult for CODA. Administrative costs and design commissions had nearly exhausted its start-up funds, and no dedicated source of funding had yet been secured. Business and philanthropic organizations remained on the sidelines, focusing on downtown projects they had initiated, such as the Woodruff Park renovation, and political leaders continued to waffle in setting priorities (Roughton 1993b). For its part, CODA blundered into an unnecessary confrontation with the neighborhoods by seeking city council approval to have some of them declared "slum areas." The designation was requested to give CODA special city powers to act on code violations and expedite condemnation procedures. But the neighborhoods, with long memories of urban renewal displacements, protested both the symbolism of the designation and its potential to hurt existing residents who had little ability to make required changes (Hill 1993a).

Mayor Jackson was also struggling as he neared the end of his term. Personally, heart bypass surgery had thrown him off stride politically and emotionally. Publicly, there was no shortage of negative news. In June, two hotel workers died after being washed into a huge hole in Midtown created by heavy rains and a failed sewer line. The structural problems of the city's ninety-year-old trunk lines were compounded by the city's inadequate treatment facilities that forced it to pay daily fines of thousands of dollars. Deferred maintenance of the transportation infrastructure was also critical. The Georgia Department of Transportation had declared five of the city's major viaducts unsafe for MARTA buses to cross (Rutheiser 1996, 254).

Mayor Jackson seemed increasingly unable to energize the public or Atlanta's elite to address civic problems. CODA was widely criticized as a failure. Jackson's efforts to leverage Olympic funding were being blocked by a recalcitrant state legislature, squeezed by a perennially inadequate city budget, and hemmed in by a tight-fisted ACOG. And with Atlanta's unbroken string of failed bond measures going back twenty-five years, the mayor publicly admitted that a bond measure stood little chance of passing in the November 1993 election. In the face of these unexpected personal events and intractable public problems, Jackson decided not to seek reelection in 1993.

Ten months later, in July 1994, the political sands had shifted dramatically. A new business-friendly mayor was in office, city voters overwhelmingly supported the sale of $150 million in general obligations bonds, and the city council approved the sale of $225 million in revenue bonds. Together these events represented a significant reversal of public resistance and official neglect of city needs. The two bonds were not without cost to citizens, however. The $225 million revenue bond designated for upgrading the city's water system would double water rates over a three-year period. The $150 million general obligation bond would, over twenty years, be redeemed by tax revenues perhaps diverted from other city services. Fortunately for the city and ACOG, the Olympics provided ideal political cover to disguise these financial impacts.

The surprising turnaround in public and private support resulted from the confluence of events beginning with the election of Bill Campbell as Atlanta's mayor in November 1993. Campbell, an African American from upscale Inmann Park, had forged close alliances with Atlanta's business community during his tenure on the city council. One of Campbell's first acts as mayor was to hold a summit with business leaders to sell them on a restructured CODA more sensitive to their interests (Fox 1994). Unexpected events opened other windows for policy action. In January, a major water main broke in downtown Atlanta, forcing Campbell to impose mandatory water rationing for two days. The water shortage provided the media with an opportunity to revisit the sewer collapse and the viaduct failures and to evoke the specter of an Olympic embarrassment (Harris 1994).

With these dramatic events fresh in voters' minds, the time seemed right to move quickly on the bond. Mayor Campbell got approval for a mid-March special election, but a technical challenge by tax protesters forced a delay (Blackmon and Pendered 1994). The misstep proved fortuitous. Only two weeks after the canceled election, Coca-Cola chairman Robert Goizueta, in a rare appearance before the Commerce Club, called on business leaders to take a leadership role in supporting initiatives to help the city prepare for the Olympics. Noting that the games could leave Atlanta with a social and financial burden and "embarrass us in front of the world,"

Goizueta made it clear that civic leaders must get behind Olympic actions (Turner 1994, C-1). He especially chided business leaders for failing to support the bond issue adequately.

The bond referendum was rescheduled for July 1994, and within two months Campbell had assembled a $360,000 war chest for the campaign. Of that, $200,000 came from the chamber of commerce, with other large donations from investment banks (Pendered 1994). The resulting paid media blitz, as well as constant reminders in news coverage of the deadly Midtown sinkhole, worked to guarantee overwhelming support for the measure (Blackmon 1994).

The passage of the $150 million bond issue meant that the city could proceed on its most pressing infrastructure projects and be reasonably prepared for the Olympics. For CODA it meant $38 million, not an enormous sum given the need but adequate to provide matching funds for federal grants. Along with access to new bond funds, CODA's private fundraising was energized when G. Joseph Prendergast, president of Wachovia Bank of Georgia, replaced John Aderhold as co-chair of the organization (Saporta 1994). Aderhold had faced a business community suspicious of CODA's social mission and unspecified goals. Prendergast faced a very different environment. CODA's new agenda was favorable to downtown interests and focused on visible Olympic corridors. This new agenda represented CODA's pragmatic response to federal dollars, the selective interests of private funders, and wording of the bond issue.

In total, Prendergast raised $16 million in private funds. This money plus the $38 million from bond funds and $22 million in federal grants brought the total to $76 million. By the summer of 1995, all major construction projects were under way, and by the opening of the Olympics, they were substantially complete. In the end, CODA upgraded twelve major pedestrian corridors and five parks and plazas. It widened sidewalks, buried power lines, added curb cuts, and constructed medians. Streetscapes were enhanced with fluted lights, furniture, trees, and public art. Along the corridors, history panels and way-finding markers informed and directed Olympic visitors. Twenty-four new public art projects were installed, including those in a $1.2 million Folk Art Park (Turner 1996b).

Of the $76 million in CODA funds, roughly 46 percent was spent to improve streets and parks in the downtown business area, 31 percent went to pedestrian corridors leading to Olympic venues, and 14 percent to other markets, parks, and art. Only about 9 percent of the total was expended specifically for neighborhood streets. No money was spent on housing.

As Clara Axam neared the end of her term, the *Atlanta Journal Constitution* was lavish in its praise, describing her work and CODA as one of the important success stories behind the Olympics (Turner 1996b). In explaining the failure to address real problems in the neighborhoods, the *Atlanta Journal Constitution* rationalized, "The expectations of neighborhood groups that their communities would be revolutionized by the Olympics were not met, of course, because they weren't realistic" ("Atlanta neighborhoods need CODA successor" 1996, A-10). CODA closed its books in June 1997.

Selling the Games: Extending Private Power

The contrast between ACOG's successful exercise of private power and the limitations of city government initiatives was also played out in the process of marketing the games. ACOG's ability to generate revenue from broadcast rights, sponsorships, and tickets contrasted sharply with the city's parallel attempt to capitalize on its Olympic affiliation. The difference in resources and power became evident when the city's plan ran into conflict with ACOG's marketing efforts. During this conflict, ACOG successfully asserted its commercial rights over the city's territorial prerogatives. And where ACOG was successful in developing its revenue stream, the city's returns were marginal at best.

The amount of money that any U.S. host city can generate in the post–Los Angeles era depends on its arrangements with the IOC and the USOC, as well as the generosity of corporate sponsors and the sale of broadcast rights and merchandise. As Table 5.1 shows, the sale of broadcast rights at $568 million was the largest source of revenue for ACOG. Ticket sales generated $427 million and the combined revenues from national sponsorships, and licenses brought in a similar amount. ACOG's share from international sponsorships marketed by the IOC was $81 million. Lesser amounts were derived from the leasing of media facilities, merchandise sales, and interest. In all, ACOG's marketing efforts netted $1.72 billion (Turner 1997).

The promise of revenues to stage the games belies the risk and hard work behind the scenes. One of ACOG's first tasks after winning the bid was to develop an equitable arrangement with the USOC.

Table 5.1   Revenue Sources for the 1996 Atlanta Olympic Games

Source	Amount (millions)
TV Broadcast Rights	$ 568
Ticket Sales	$ 427
National Sponsorships and Licensing	$ 426
International Sponsorships	$ 81
Media Facilities	$ 63
Merchandising	$ 34
Interest Income	$ 19
Other Revenues	$ 102
Total	$1,720

Source: Compiled by authors.

They formed a precedent-setting joint marketing venture, required under newly adopted IOC guidelines, that eliminated the problems of previous Olympics where the host city and national committee ran separate and sometimes conflicting marketing programs (Maloney 1996, 198). The partners set a goal of finding ten to twelve national sponsors willing to contribute $40 million each. ACOG scored an early success by signing on NationsBank for a full sponsorship. Of equal importance was NationsBank's offer of a $300 million line of credit to sustain ACOG during its early stages when cash flow was low and uncertainty high.

The story of NationsBank's support is revealing for what it tells about personal relationships, corporate goals, and Olympic symbolism. In 1991, NationsBank, headquartered in Charlotte, North Carolina, had just been created by a merger of C&S/Sovran in Atlanta and NCNB in Charlotte. According to Hugh McColl, Jr., the bank's CEO, his offer to support the Olympic effort came during a courtesy visit with Mayor Andrew Young following the merger (Turner 1992a). Young, co-chair of ACOG, asked McColl to meet with a few Olympic supporters, including Billy Payne; NationsBank's support was offered and accepted at the meeting.

For McColl the offer made good sense. It would heal some rifts created by the loss of a venerable Atlanta institution and make important friends in a city that is one of the economic engines of the South. It would also preempt rivals and help NationsBank establish a presence on the national scene. The Olympic tie-in would link NationsBank's promotional efforts to a highly regarded cultural symbol.

Finally, the substantial number of event tickets and hotel suites provided to Olympic sponsors would give NationsBank an opportunity to reward corporate executives. The games would engage them in a larger-than-life spectacle whose messages of competition, teamwork, and success reinforced corporate values (Turner 1992a).

The expected cascade of other sponsors did not follow the quick success with NationsBank. The $40 million cost may have seemed high to corporations that had paid only $4 million to be national sponsors less than a decade earlier. The problem of corporate reticence prompted ACOG to revise its marketing plan and offer a lesser level of sponsorship at the $20–25 million range. The strategy was successful, and ACOG eventually exceeded its revenue projections using the two-tier model (Turner 1993).

While the cost issue was successfully negotiated, the issue of maintaining sponsorship prerogatives proved more problematic. The problem stemmed from the practice of "ambush marketing." For example, American Express ran a series of advertisements during the 1992 winter games that implied an Olympic affiliation even though the company was not an official sponsor. The problem of ambush marketing ultimately drew the IOC and ACOG into direct confrontation with city hall's attempts to capitalize on the games by leasing public spaces and trading on its Olympic affiliation (Turner 1992b).

The city's marketing effort was managed by Munson Steed III, a young entrepreneur with political ties to Mayor Campbell. In 1994, when the newly elected mayor was searching for creative promotional ideas, Steed came forward with a plan that appealed to Campbell. The mayor, using his influence as chair of the Atlanta Economic Development Commission (AEDC), helped Steed secure a $30,000 consulting contract to develop his plan into a comprehensive city marketing program for the games.

Steed wrote his company into the plan as the sole agent for the city, projecting $80–90 million revenues from leasing public areas to vendors and selling advertising space. Steed proposed a no-risk deal to guarantee the city an initial $2.5 million for the marketing contract and sliding-scale returns on any money over that. Campbell fast-tracked the bidding process and secured Steed's confirmation from a largely quiescent AEDC.

Steed's implementation of the marketing plan drew immediate resistance. His proposal to lease up to one thousand vendor carts and tents at prices up to $20,000 per site was challenged in court by existing vendors. His attempt to lease Piedmont Park to a festival company was stopped by elite members of the Piedmont Park Conservancy. Steed also blundered by trying to strong-arm Olympic sponsors such as Kodak and Coca-Cola by suggesting that he might open bidding to their competitors if they did not meet his terms for leases and marketing rights. The IOC and ACOG were irate that the city would permit this type of marketing.

Surprisingly, Steed's boldness was welcomed in city hall because it strengthened the city's hand in its negotiations with ACOG for reimbursement for city services such as police overtime. ACOG finally agreed to pay $8 million for services while the city agreed to a no-ambush policy and a reduction in the number of vendor sites from a thousand to four hundred (Whitt 1996b). Although the settlement reduced Steed's expectations, it enhanced his ability to obtain commitments. Coca-Cola, Kodak, and others signed contracts for carts and the right to be official city sponsors. Even ACOG paid $500,000 to lease most of the five thousand street-pole banners in the Olympic Ring (Harris 1996a).

Steed continued to strike controversial deals. He negotiated a $400,000 fee from a Connecticut company for the right to place four thousand advertisement-laden barricades along city sidewalks. When the company tried to deploy them before the games, ACOG officials threatened to remove them as a violation of the "clean venue" agreement banning advertising along marathon routes. As a result, fewer than three thousand were deployed, and the company sued Steed for misrepresentation (Whitt 1996a).

All of these controversies were a prelude to the troubles that faced vendors at the games. By all accounts, the games were a financial disaster for a significant number of vendors who had paid a high price for their sites and services. In the post-Olympic shakeout, nearly one-third of the vendors joined a lawsuit against Steed and the city charging that spaces were leased to more than one vendor, services were not provided, carts were not delivered, and sites were blocked by fences or other vendors (Whitt and Turner 1996).

As to the aesthetic impact, Richard Pound, chair of the IOC oversight commission, severely criticized the barricades, tents, and proliferation of advertising banners for destroying the "look of the games." Pound, a persistent critic of the city's marketing efforts, emphasized that future Olympic cities would not repeat Atlanta's carnival atmosphere: "We will tell them don't even think about doing something like this!" (Harris 1996b, S-1).

City government's foray into Olympic marketing was an attempt to grab the brass ring after being relegated to a background role in organizing the games. The political fallout for Mayor Campbell was substantial. Irate vendors testified at hearings, and the city council passed resolutions to stop payment to Steed and audit his company's operations. In the end, however, Steed delivered on his commitment. The council audit showed that the city received the $2.5 million it had been guaranteed ("Vending tarnished Atlanta" 1997). Although this sum met Steed's obligation to the city, it was nothing in comparison to the $80–90 million he had projected or the more than $1 billion ACOG raised.

■ The Politics of Venue Development

The revenue from marketing the games gave ACOG great latitude in determining where resources would be expended and whose development goals would be achieved. The development goals ACOG chose to pursue were marked largely by its need to construct Olympic venues and stage an exciting competition. But in numerous cases, including the Olympic Stadium and Centennial Olympic Park, ACOG crafted plans that furthered the redevelopment interests of business elites. In contrast, the resource-poor city government and urban neighborhoods were unable to assert their territorial rights or significantly shift ACOG's agenda. The politics of venue development illustrates the power of ACOG and business interests to overcome resistance.

Atlanta's bid emphasized compact and accessible venues. Most events were to be held at two locations, the Olympic Ring in central Atlanta and Stone Mountain Park on the perimeter of the city (AOC 1990, 24, 59). Figure 5.1 shows the Olympic Ring, a three-mile area radiating out from the city center that symbolically encircled three-fourths of all venues. Northwest of downtown lies the campus of the Georgia Institute of Technology, the eventual site of the Olympic Village. Georgia Tech would also host boxing in Alexander Memorial Coliseum, and swimming, diving, and water polo events in a new $24 million Aquatic Center built with Olympic funds.

South of the Georgia Tech campus was the roughly twenty-five-square-block area of Techwood, which at the time of the bid was occupied by the twelve-hundred-unit Techwood/Clark Howell public housing complex. Below Techwood was a triangular-shaped area of warehouses, small businesses, and homeless shelters that would eventually become Centennial Olympic Park. Neither of these areas was mentioned in the bid book, but as Olympic planning moved from glossy renderings to bricks and mortar, these areas became critical and contentious locations for Olympic development.

As the site for the opening and closing ceremonies, track and field competition, and the soccer finals, the Olympic Stadium was the centerpiece of Olympic activities. With a $209 million price tag, the stadium was also the most expensive of all Olympic facilities. After the Olympics, the new stadium was extensively renovated to house the Atlanta Braves baseball team and renamed Turner Stadium after Ted Turner, the team's owner.

As Table 5.2 shows, other Olympic sports were spread throughout the metro region and state. Outside of the Olympic Ring approximately 20 miles east of downtown Atlanta is Stone Mountain Park, the site for archery, cycling, tennis, and pentathlon events. Olympic plans called for a new permanent velodrome to be built for cycling competition but cost factors forced ACOG to go with a temporary facility designed to be removed after the games.

Outside the Atlanta metro area, yachting was held at Savannah on the Georgia coast and women's softball in Columbus. The University of Georgia in Athens hosted rhythmic gymnastics, plus volleyball preliminaries and soccer semifinals. Whitewater canoeing, held on the Ocoee River near Ducktown, Tennessee, was one of two out-of-state venues. The other was soccer, where preliminary rounds were held in four southeastern cities in an effort to broaden the base for ticket sales.

The politics of venue development can be understood in a number of ways. One way is to contrast those venues whose development took place within the boundaries of large institutions with those whose development impacted areas outside of institutional boundaries. Generally speaking, larger institutions such as Georgia Tech, Stone Mountain Park, and the Atlanta University Center campuses were receptive to Olympic proposals and formed partnerships with Olympic planners. In contrast, those facilities that affected surrounding communities but were not part of an institution, such as the Olympic Stadium and Centennial Olympic Park, created opposition and resistance. A second divide might be drawn between suburban venues outside the Olympic Ring and downtown venues within it. This also marks the divide between success and failure in terms of influencing venue development.

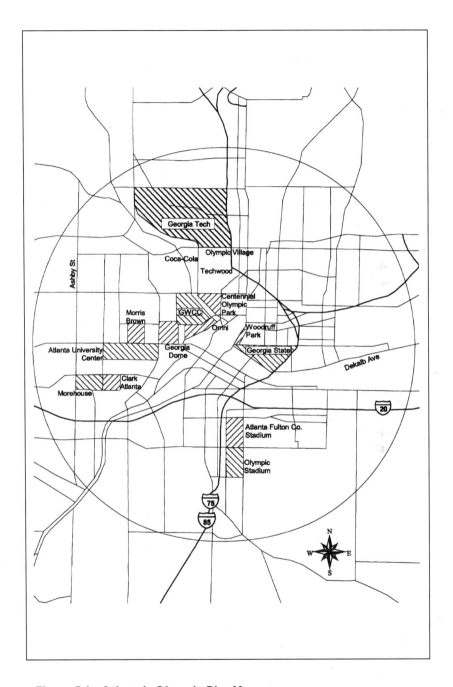

Figure 5.1   Atlanta's Olympic Ring Venues

Table 5.2 Attributes of Venues for the 1996 Games

Location	Venue	Event	Attributes
Atlanta—Olympic Ring	Olympic Stadium	Opening and closing ceremonies, track and field, soccer	New
Atlanta—Olympic Ring	Atlanta Fulton County Stadium	Baseball	Existing
Atlanta—Olympic Ring	Aquatic Center, Georgia Tech	Diving, swimming, synchronized swimming, water polo	New
Atlanta—Olympic Ring	Alexander Coliseum, Georgia Tech	Boxing	Renovated
Atlanta—Olympic Ring	GSU Sports Arena, Georgia State	Badminton	Renovated
Atlanta—Olympic Ring	Herndon Stadium, Morris Brown College	Field hockey	New
Atlanta—Olympic Ring	Panther Stadium, Clark Atlanta Univ.	Field hockey	Expanded
Atlanta—Olympic Ring	Olympic Gymnasium, Morehouse College	Basketball	New
Atlanta—Olympic Ring	Georgia Dome	Gymnastics	Existing
Atlanta—Olympic Ring	Omni	Volleyball	Existing
Atlanta—Olympic Ring	Georgia World Congress Center	Fencing, judo, team handball, table tennis, weightlifting, wrestling	Existing
Stone Mountain Park—Metro	Archery Field	Archery	Existing
Stone Mountain Park—Metro	Velodrome	Cycling	New
Stone Mountain Park—Metro	Various sites	Pentathlon	Existing
Stone Mountain Park—Metro	International Tennis Center	Tennis	New
Clayton County—Metro	Clayton County International Park	Beach volleyball	New
Hall County—Metro	Lake Lanier Rowing Center	Rowing, sprint kayaking	New
South Fulton County—Metro	Wolf Creek Shooting Range	Shooting	New
Conyers-Rockdale Co.—Metro	Georgia International Horse Park	Equestrian	New
Columbus, Georgia	South Commons Softball Complex	Women's softball	Expanded
Savannah, Georgia	Marina, Atlantic Ocean	Yachting	Renovated
Athens, Georgia	Georgia Coliseum, U. of Georgia	Volleyball	Existing
	Georgia Coliseum Annex, U. of Georgia	Rhythmic gymnastics	New
	Sanford Stadium, U. of Georgia	Soccer	Existing
Various southeastern cities	Various sites	Soccer	Existing
Ducktown, Tennessee	Ocoee River	Whitewater canoeing, kayaking	New

Source: Compiled by authors.

We begin with the two examples of suburban resistance, both successful perhaps because they reflected the interests of the well-connected and better-off white citizens, but also because they involved noncritical projects that were of less concern to downtown interests. Then we discuss points of resistance within the Olympic Ring. These were less successful probably because the resisters were African American and poor but also because the disputed areas were more essential to the redevelopment desires of business elites. Finally, we consider peripheral Olympic projects such as the renovation of Woodruff Park, where antihomeless design elements became part of a new Olympic order to secure the downtown for tourists and upscale residents.

▧ Blackburn Park and Cobb County

Blackburn Park seemed like a natural site for Olympic tennis. Located in suburban Dunwoody, the Blackburn complex sported thirty-one tennis courts and three stadiums. The Olympic bid proposed to expand the main stadium and to remodel the two smaller ones (AOC 1990, 66). Blackburn Park was ACOG's first attempt at implementing its Olympic plan. Residents in the affluent, predominantly white suburb were not impressed with ACOG's plans even if Billy Payne, a local resident and one of their own, proposed them. Residents feared the traffic and disruption and let their dissatisfaction be known. With little notice, ACOG moved the venue to Stone Mountain and constructed a new facility there at a cost of $24 million (Newman 1999, 257).

ACOG's plan to bring the preliminary rounds of Olympic volleyball to suburban Cobb County were stopped at the cultural moat of the Chattahoochee River. Cobb County's resistance was unplanned but firmly rooted in its anti-urban and deeply conservative political culture. The particular decision that prompted the conflict with ACOG occurred in the summer of 1993. Public concern about a local play that featured homosexual characters caused the Cobb County commissioners to withdraw financial support from the theater and to issue a resolution condemning "the gay lifestyle." Picked up by national media, the actions provoked protests by gay activists and a threatened boycott of the Olympics. ACOG's attempt to salvage the situation was adamantly resisted. Fearing the prospects of tarnishing its carefully crafted civil rights image, ACOG quickly moved the volleyball preliminaries to the University of Georgia in Athens (Maloney 1996, 196; Rutheiser 1996, 244).

■ Olympic Stadium

Within days of Atlanta winning the Centennial games, concerns about the siting and construction of the proposed Olympic Stadium were already surfacing. Leaders from the poor and predominantly black neighborhoods surrounding the stadium site—Vine City, Mechanicsville, Peoplestown, and especially Summerhill—voiced their objections and suggested alternative locations for the construction.

ACOG's plan for the stadium called for construction of an 85,000-seat Olympic Stadium in the parking lot south of the Atlanta Fulton County Stadium. Following the Olympics, about one-third of the seating in the new stadium would be removed, and the remaining structure would become the new home of Ted Turner's baseball team. Atlanta Fulton County Stadium, home to the Braves since its construction in 1961, would be demolished and the area resurfaced for parking.

The stadium project was nicely packaged for everyone who mattered. Turner had been making veiled threats to move the Braves to the suburbs if a new stadium was not built. For the city and county, the new stadium would keep the Braves in town, securing one of the big draws for the convention trade. Since most of the construction would be financed by Olympic funds, the new stadium seemed a golden opportunity, even if local governments would eventually bear some of the infrastructure and maintenance costs. For Turner, the new stadium was also a winner. It would have the baseball-friendly design that the old stadium lacked, and it would be fitted with revenue-generating skyboxes (Rutheiser 1996, 250–253).

While the advantages for local government and corporate powers seemed obvious, leaders in the African American neighborhoods that would bear the brunt of construction and displacement were less convinced of the stadium's benefits. They had good reason to be skeptical. Summerhill, a historically black community of over sixteen thousand residents in 1965, had been reduced to about twenty-five hundred by the 1990s. Strangled first by construction of the interstate highways, then decimated by the stadium construction in the early 1960s, Summerhill was hit again in the late 1980s when the I-75 downtown connector was put through. Neighborhood leaders remembered the failed promises for relocation assistance and the legacy of abandonment as the neighborhood was cut off from the downtown by the maze of freeways and inhospitable paved surfaces (Foskett 1993a). Residents were well aware of the one hundred–plus days and nights when their neighborhoods would be clogged with stadium traffic searching for overflow parking on vacant lots. While Summerhill was the most seriously affected community, the Vine City neighborhood northwest of the stadium area had its own scars. The Georgia Dome had recently been carved from the interior of Vine City to create the covered playing field for the Atlanta Falcons football team (Booker and Durcanin 1990).

Two people stand out among those who most stridently resisted the stadium: Ethel Mae Mathews, lifetime resident of Summerhill, local activist, and organizer of Atlanta Neighborhoods United for Fairness (ANUFF); and Columbus Ward, Vine City resident and chair of Neighborhood Planning Unit V, a neighborhood advisory board to Atlanta's planning department under the city's 1973 charter. Mathews and other members of ANUFF reminded ACOG and the city of the failures of the past and noted how quickly ACOG responded to the concerns of the wealthy residents in Blackburn Park (Roughton 1990b). During the three years leading up to the decision to build the stadium, ANUFF protesters marched to Billy Payne's Dunwoody home, to his office, to the IBM Tower where the Olympic planners had offices, and to a tent city encampment at the stadium site to witness against the ceremonial groundbreaking (Foskett 1993b; Laccetti 1991). Columbus Ward used his position as chair of the planning unit to criticize ACOG and city planning officials for their insensitivity to the displacement that would take place for temporary and permanent parking. Ward reminded them of the recent battle over the Georgia Dome and reasoned that the neighborhoods had already paid dearly. He argued for compensation to be paid to the neighborhoods for the inconvenience and loss. Ward also employed confrontational tactics. When Leon Eplan, director of city planning for Atlanta, came to a meeting to present the post-Olympic parking plans, Ward refused to let him present his proposal, noting that the decisions had already been made and Eplan's only reason for coming was to seek legitimacy by speaking to neighborhood residents (Hiskey 1993).

More moderate resistance was offered by Douglas Dean, a former state legislator and director of Summerhill Neighborhood Inc.
(SNI), a planning consultant group. Dean was a vocal but concilia-
tory critic working within the system to extract what concessions he
could to help redevelop the neighborhood. It was Dean's SNI group
that worked with the Urban Land Institute when it came to the area
prior to the Olympic bid and developed a proposal for mixed-use redevelopment of Summerhill. And it was Dean who was willing to
accept some displacement in return for support of the redevelopment
plan (Roughton 1991b).

ACOG and business leaders attempted to frame the community
opposition as futile and obstructionist. At one of the first neighborhood meetings, John Leak from Central Atlanta Progress, an elite
business group, predicted the stadium would be built and that residents would be better off to go along and make the best of it: "We
have to realize that when a certain movement occurs in the community with the support of a certain level of leadership, some things are
going to happen, some things are going to change. The world is big-
ger than any of us individuals" (Roughton 1990a, A-1). With a bit
more misdirection, this was also the line that the *Atlanta Journal
Constitution* promoted in editorials about stadium opposition. The
paper accused ANUFF and the neighborhoods of NIMBYism and
lack of public spirit and praised Douglas Dean for his wise and con-
structive partnership with ACOG ("ANUF is too much" 1990).

While grassroots activists were being stonewalled, there was one
final battle over the stadium that demonstrated elite black resistance
could produce results. Five days before the vote was to be taken by
the Fulton County commissioners to approve the $209 million sta-
dium package, Commissioner Martin Luther King III stunned ACOG
by describing it as a white elitist club. In doing so, he challenged
their right to invoke the memory of his slain father in their promotion of Atlanta's human rights heritage. Since King had been uncom-
mitted on the stadium proposal, the charge of elitism was unexpected. Though caught off guard, Payne and ACOG were quick to
respond. Payne suggested a meeting with King to discuss the possibility of top executive hires. ACOG's public relations machine justi-
fiably pointed to their substantial accomplishments, noting that 37
percent of all hires were minority and 58 percent women, and in the
managerial ranks, 31 percent were minority and 11 percent women
(Roughton 1993a). But King recognized that ACOG was vulnerable

at the highest ranks, where even the visible presence of Andrew Young did not dispel the reality that ACOG was run by a predominantly white and well-connected Dunwoody crowd.

The final decision on the stadium took place on March 11, 1993. Negotiations were difficult, but the final vote was 6–1 in favor, with King siding with the majority. King's unexpected critique of ACOG had been effective. In a sidebar to the deal, he was able to increase ACOG's financial commitment to venues at the historically black Atlanta University Center campuses from $40 million to $50 million. Payne agreed to hire a top black executive who would report directly to him and appoint eight additional black officials to top posts. For their part, the Atlanta Braves also made concessions on maintenance responsibilities and agreed that debts would not be the responsibility of local government (Foskett 1993c; Foskett and Roughton 1993).

While the location and design of the stadium were not significantly changed from the original plan, the neighborhoods could claim some victories. The deal reduced the total number of parking spaces from ten thousand to nine thousand and included an agreement that 8.2 percent of gross revenues from stadium parking would be set aside for neighborhood projects. There was displacement, however. Peoplestown, immediately south of the Olympic Stadium, lost a block of land for a parking lot; and Mechanicsville, just to the west, lost several blocks of structures, including a church, commercial buildings, and two apartment houses. Douglas Dean and Summerhill perhaps fared best, receiving a $300,000 pledge to support neighborhood redevelopment and $150,000 for a neighborhood job training program (Foskett and Roughton 1993). Perhaps more important, ACOG eventually rented the townhomes in Dean's newly built Greenlea Commons, paying $20,000 each to house corporate sponsors during the games. This money helped reduce the purchase price for low-income buyers. After the games, Greenlea Commons became an anchor for neighborhood revitalization (Hill 1995).

Ted Turner and the Atlanta Braves did very well. After the games, the Braves invested another $35 million in the stadium to add attractions, including restaurants, a hall of fame, and interactive game areas (Hiskey 1997). The new stadium, combined with a new agreement that gave the Braves complete control of revenues and a twenty-five-year lease, helped double the value of the franchise (Unger 1996).

▨ Centennial Olympic Park

To the broad-stroke Olympic planners, the triangular sixty-plus acres needed for Centennial Olympic Park were occupied by an underproductive assortment of small businesses, light manufacturing, and marginal housing. If their plans were realized, this area would become one of the largest public open spaces created in any modern U.S. city. While the boundaries of the area were loosely configured, some obvious features marked its perimeters as the plan took shape. The northern side of the triangle was bounded by the Techwood/Clark Howell public housing complex. The most prominent feature along its southwest edge was the Georgia World Congress Center (GWCC), and Spring Street marked the eastern side of the triangle. The area was strategically located for conventioneers and tourists; it was within walking distance of downtown, Atlanta's Underground, and the Peachtree Center and Hotel complex. Included within the orbit of its amenities would be the corporate headquarters of Coca-Cola, CNN, the *Atlanta Journal Constitution,* and the chamber of commerce (Rutheiser 1996, 259–260).

It is difficult to know when the idea for the park was first discussed. No mention of it is found in the official Olympic bid. One scholar has the project emerging from a luncheon between Billy Payne and Robert Goizueta, chairman of Coca-Cola (Newman 1999, 272–273). Regardless of when, it is obvious that the park descended from a considerable lineage of previous plans for redeveloping the area. A plan in the 1970s proposed a central park green space bordering a one hundred–story hotel. The 1986 Central Area Study II, sponsored by the downtown business association, Central Atlanta Progress, envisioned a commercial retail zone nestled within surrounding highrise apartments and townhouses. Among the reasons none of these plans materialized were difficulties of assembling the land and financing. Perhaps as important was the difficulty of isolating the redeveloped area from the black urban poor of the Techwood/Clark Howell public housing complex that bordered its northern edge. So important was the problem of securing the area for conventioneers and downtown professionals that one plan proposed separating Techwood/Clark Howell from the redeveloped area by a moat, or a "water feature," as it was euphemistically described in the plan (Rutheiser 1996, 260).

ACOG was able to overcome the difficulties that had frustrated other developers by bringing together parties with the necessary clout, assembling the financing, and skillfully coordinating the park proposal with other Olympic projects. Most important, ACOG used the Olympics to generate the momentum to make things happen. The Techwood/Clark Howell "problem" was solved by packaging ACOG's Olympic Village project with HUD Hope VI redevelopment financing. As a result, the twelve hundred units of public housing were leveled in 1993 and later replaced with nine hundred units of new mixed-income housing (Keating and Flores 2000). The financing and ownership of the park as it eventually emerged were accomplished through a public-private partnership between the State of Georgia and ACOG. The Georgia World Congress Center, a quasi-public state authority, was given the power to condemn the properties and assemble the land. ACOG financed the project and controlled design and development. Pointedly absent from the arrangement were both the City of Atlanta and CODA, its nonprofit authority charged with revitalizing neighborhoods within the Olympic Ring (Newman 1999, 273).

Typical of ACOG, the development of the plan was secretive, and neither the city nor the neighborhoods were consulted. Faced with an end run by the governor and the GWCC and obvious support from business elites, Mayor Bill Campbell gave his approval (Rutheiser 1996, 260). Neighborhood activists were vocal opponents but largely ineffective. Columbus Ward, president of Neighborhood Planning Unit V, complained that the proposed $100 million funding would divert money away from neighborhood development. Douglas Dean, Summerhill activist, charged ACOG with contradicting its policy to fund only Olympic venues, a policy ACOG had used to reject demands for neighborhood redevelopment (Hill 1993b). The most effective resistance was mounted by the one hundred–plus property owners who were able to carry their arguments to court. But the *Atlanta Journal Constitution,* a potential beneficiary of the development, did its part to devalue the resistance, charging the owners with making unreasonable demands and hindering development of a project that would benefit the Olympics and future Atlantans.

In its original design, the park was to cover the entire sixty acres and cost $100 million, but limited revenues caused it to be downsized to twenty-two acres and projected funding to be reduced to $50 million. Of this amount, $25 million would come from the Woodruff Foundation, $10 million from the chamber of commerce, and $15 million was to be raised by ACOG through a cooperative arrangement with Atlanta-based Home Depot, which agreed to sell 750,000 engraved brick pavers. The northern parcel of the original project area was ultimately purchased by Coca-Cola, which developed a $20 million interactive Olympic attraction to complement the Centennial Olympic Park (Rutheiser 1996, 262–265).

With the exception of ACOG, all the funders delivered on their pledges. The failure of Home Depot to promote the brick pavers adequately forced ACOG back to a familiar strategy of seeking corporate sponsorship. For a mere $10 million, ACOG allowed AT&T to construct a Global Olympic Village on park land. The AT&T Village included a second story where Olympians and their families could find respite from the games. The lower, public portion included an eighty-five-hundred-seat amphitheater with live entertainment and a giant video screen displaying Olympic activities. Two other corporate sponsors also paid to be in the park. Swatch, the official Olympic timekeeper, erected an eighteen-foot "Swatch O'clock" and Anheuser-Busch installed a high-tech beer garden (Quesenberry 1996, 6–7).

The park was a major attraction during the games but was closed the year after for a $17 million renovation. Plans for the post-Olympic period suggest that substantial benefits of the park will be realized by the city, the quasi-public authorities, and the private interests whose agendas have long included the redevelopment of this area. The GWCC, which owns and maintains the park, secured a palatial green space for its front yard. For the city, the increases in land value surrounding the park have probably offset the removal of the twenty-two acres from its tax rolls. Some fortunate landowners profited handsomely from increased values. One was Inman Allen, son of Ivan Allen, Jr., former mayor and member of the exclusive Woodruff Foundation board that provided seed money for the park. Inman Allen was the largest landowner in the area before the park was developed (Salter 1994). Another insider who did well was Ralph Jernigan, a member of the Olympic bid team. Jernigan and a partner purchased land adjacent to the park before it was developed. Their land eventually became the site of the 321-unit Embassy Suites Hotel, a $100 million office and commercial complex (Salter 1999).

Coca-Cola quietly assembled a large parcel along the northern edge of the park, with plans to expand its headquarters. Turner Broadcasting, CNN's parent company, has made the most substantial investments. Turner completed a $27 million remake of the CNN Center and the Omni Hotel and opened the Philips Arena, a $217 million replacement of the Omni Coliseum; the arena is home to the Thrashers and Hawks, Turner's professional hockey and basketball teams. Turner credited the creation of Centennial Olympic Park with his decision not to build a new stadium in the suburbs (Turner 1999e). He also has announced plans to spend $1.2 billion to construct two new downtown office towers next to his corporate headquarters (Robinson 2000).

▦ Techwood/Clark Howell

Redevelopment of the Techwood/Clark Howell public housing community was one of the keys to securing the Centennial Park area for future use. Lying on the coveted land between Georgia Tech, Coca-Cola headquarters, and Coca-Cola's north Centennial Park parcel, the vintage public housing complex had long created a physical and psychological barrier to the type of upscale development envisioned for the area. When the housing complex was desegregated in the early 1970s, Paul Austin, then president of Coca-Cola, expressed fear of rising crime and proposed tearing down the complex and replacing it with higher-income housing. The plan received the backing of Central Atlanta Progress, but Mayor Jackson, Atlanta's first black mayor, rejected it when he took office in 1974 (Allen 1996, 186).

The Olympics refocused attention on the public housing community. The plan to construct the Olympic Village in close proximity to Techwood evoked long-standing concerns of race and class, now couched in the terminology of Atlanta's international aspirations. Georgia Tech President John Crecine stated bluntly what many in the business community were thinking: "Number one, there is one of the finest international corporations [Coca-Cola]. Two, here is one of the world's finest technological institutions [Georgia Tech]. And here is one of the world's best cesspools [Techwood]. It doesn't play well" (Dickerson 1991, A-14).

The pressure to "do something" about Techwood/Clark Howell drew a series of unsolicited plans in 1991. Georgia Tech made several proposals to public housing residents, including one for a private buyout. County Commissioner Marvin Arrington startled many people with his suggestion that Techwood/Clark Howell be leveled and replaced with mixed-income housing. Mayor Jackson, fearing further end runs, created a Techwood task force to consider the future of the public housing community (Keating and Flores 2000, 288–289).

Three redevelopment plans emerged between 1991 and 1995. The first was a product of the PATH group, a consulting firm hired by Jackson's Techwood task force. The PATH proposal outlined a vaguely defined mixed-income community, demolition of Clark Howell, and renovation of Techwood. The plan was approved by residents in a hotly contested election, but the vote was highly suspect. The consultants had allowed residents of two senior high-rises to vote, thereby diluting the weight of Techwood/Clark Howell residents to 60 percent of the total, even though the high-rises would not have been affected by the redevelopment. The consultants also misled residents with suggestions they would be eligible for private replacement housing when only a small number actually would qualify. And they withheld information from a resident survey until after the vote but publicly suggested that the majority of residents favored relocation. Following the vote, the PATH plan was submitted to HUD for approval. HUD rejected the plan, citing a lack of adequate financing, overreliance on HUD funding, and failure to plan for sufficient replacement housing.

A second plan was submitted to HUD a year later and was accepted. The revised plan was developed for the Atlanta Housing Authority (AHA) by Richard Bradfield, an Atlanta architect experienced in public housing issues. Bradfield was sensitive to concerns of residents and stated his belief that they wanted to preserve their community. His plan proposed rehabilitation of Techwood and Clark Howell with minimal loss of units and minimal displacement of residents (Keating and Flores 2000, 290–297). HUD's acceptance of the plan allowed AHA Director Earl Philips to begin packaging funding for the project. This process coincided with an offer by ACOG and the state to purchase 114 units of Clark Howell bordering the Georgia Tech campus as a site for Olympic Village housing and an additional student dormitory. The AHA director was sympathetic to the plan since the suggested price seemed more than adequate to fund replacement housing as required by federal law. After some finessing of the financing, the deal was made. The plan called for construction to begin in summer 1994. ACOG promised $47 million and the state agreed to sell $194 million in revenue bonds for the balance (ACOG 1997, 325; Harris 1993).

Before the Bradfield plan could be implemented, however, political events intervened. In 1994, Bill Campbell replaced Jackson as mayor. While on the city council, Campbell had developed a close working relationship with downtown business interests. His election precipitated the resignation of Earl Philips as director of AHA. Philips was replaced by Renee Glover, a corporate attorney and political advisor to Campbell. At the national level, the election of a Republican congressional majority accelerated HUD's shift toward privatization of public housing. In particular, this resulted in changes in HUD's Hope VI program, including a relaxation of federal requirements for replacement housing and permission for complete demolition of struggling public housing projects (Keating and Flores 2000, 298–299).

This shift was welcome news for Glover, who made it clear that she believed public housing was fundamentally flawed and that Techwood/Clark Howell must be integrated into plans for downtown redevelopment. To this end, she revised the original PATH proposal to produce a new plan calling for leveling the twelve hundred units of Techwood/Clark Howell and replacing them with nine hundred units of mixed income. The new proposal required another vote by tenants, but the process had essentially become meaningless. Under Philips and later Glover, the AHA had pursued a policy of depopulating the public housing complex by removing residents for nonpayment of rent and other techniques. By the time of the vote on Glover's plan, fewer than 10 percent of the units were occupied. The final vote was 60–9 in favor (Keating and Flores 2000, 298–299). In March 1995, HUD approved the plan and provided $42 million toward the $100 million project. Construction of the first phase of the mixed-income Centennial Place began in the summer of 1995, with the fifth and final phase to be completed in 2001.

By design, Centennial Place targets the less needy, with 60 percent of the units reserved for renters who pay at or near market rates. For those who receive substantial public housing subsidies, AHA is enforcing new standards requiring employment and a clean credit record. As a result, fewer than 8 percent of the original residents of Techwood/Clark Howell have found housing at Centennial Place. About 62 percent have found replacement housing; however, many of these are in Section 8 units in which tenancy is less secure and quality is often worse than public housing. Renee Glover makes no excuses for AHA's new direction, stating that providing housing for the jobless or homeless is better handled by organizations that cater to "special needs" populations (Towns 1998).

Although news coverage focused on the Techwood project, the larger story of public housing "revitalization" in Atlanta may have been missed. Under the banner of AHA-designated "Olympic Legacy Communities," large numbers of public housing units are being permanently lost or made unavailable to low-income tenants (Reid 1996). In its initial renovations, the AHA established a pattern of reducing the total number of units by about 20 percent and making only one-third of the renovated units available to the lowest-income residents. Extending this to Olympic Legacy projects, completed or presently under way, results in the following estimate of the number of units lost: Techwood/Clark Howell, 894; Harris Homes, 728; John Eagan Homes, 419; East Lake Meadows, 453; John Hope Homes, 420; Carver Homes, 446; and Perry Homes, 859. These estimates total 4,170 lost units. If each unit housed an average of four people, the Olympic Legacy programs could displace as many as 16,680 low-income residents.

While Renee Glover and the AHA have been showcased as national models for housing reform, others have offered a more cynical appraisal of what has been accomplished. The Reverend Tim McDonald, former head of Atlanta's Concerned Black Clergy, described the Techwood redevelopment as a hoax perpetrated by the Atlanta business community who had always coveted the area. McDonald argued that the Olympics were used to gain political and community support for the displacements, and he noted there was no way to discover who had been displaced because there was no tracking of residents (Quesenberry 1996, 8).

Woodruff Park and Homeless Displacement

Olympic construction was a convenient excuse to displace uncounted numbers of homeless Atlantans. For example, the construction of Centennial Olympic Park and the Olympic Village forced the closing of at least one single-room occupancy residency and three homeless shelters. By one estimate, this alone displaced more than 10 percent of the city's homeless. The renovation of Woodruff Park, a favorite gathering place for the homeless, was symbolic of the new

Olympic order that favored tourists over residents. Studded with decorative fountains and a cascading waterfall, the place invited strollers but not stayers. The sleep-proof benches, intermittent sprinklers, and lack of public restrooms sent the message to homeless citizens that their claim to a place in the city was further marginalized (Rutheiser 1996, 263–264).

With the help of Task Force for the Homeless, Atlanta's displaced citizens resisted their marginalization. Their most notable action occurred at the ceremonial groundbreaking for Woodruff Park. Protesting the park's inhospitable design and the preference of Olympic planners to fund high-profile projects rather than human needs, the protesters surrounded the podium and drowned out the speakers (Hiskey 1994). Despite the protests, Olympic planners, business, and city government remained united in using the Olympics to further their long-held agenda of securing the downtown area for "respectable" citizens and tourist consumption.

This agenda was legitimized by a spate of new city ordinances that criminalized homeless behavior. With these new ordinances, it became illegal to enter vacant buildings, beg aggressively, or even to remain in a parking lot if one did not have a car there. The new loitering law was used forcefully at Hartsfield Airport where "suspicious looking people" were asked to show their tickets to establish their right to be there. Intimidation reached a low point with Fulton County's "Homeless Bound" program. Homeless citizens were offered one-way tickets out of town if they would sign a statement that they would not return (Quesenberry 1996, 8–11).

Removing the poor and unkempt reflected the Olympic planners' need to present a wholesome product for visitor and viewer consumption. The desire to project an image of the city that was as world class, youthful, and energetic as the Olympics became a justification for substantial resident displacement. In the next section, we explore the "success" of Atlanta's efforts to create and maintain this image at the expense of its marginalized citizens.

■ Atlanta's Olympic Image

For Atlanta, hosting the Olympics was an opportunity to claim world-class status. But was it successful? On the positive side, 2.5 billion viewers worldwide now associate Atlanta with an inspiring and spectacular event, a rare achievement among cities. Atlanta was also criticized, especially by members of the international press. ACOG irritated them by bungling their accommodations and transportation. And Atlanta's commercial zest and undistinguished venues seemed tacky in comparison to Barcelona's cultural and architectural heritage. Press reports citing Atlanta's "tin pot organization" and "small town commercialism" were typical (Gratton 1999, 123; Rybczynski 1996, 146).

Atlanta was more successful at home. From the time of the winning bid through the post-games period, residents of the Atlanta metro area consistently gave Olympic planners very high marks. At the national level, a majority of respondents to one survey said the Olympics gave them a more favorable impression of Atlanta (Newman 1999, 275, 281).

Surprisingly, Atlanta survived a tragic event that could have negated its well-honed image as a city of hospitality and political moderation. Early in the morning of July 27, a bomb exploded in Centennial Olympic Park. The blast killed two people and injured 111. In the aftermath, questions arose concerning Atlanta's security preparations and the safety of the games. Commentators suggested the bombing would forever mar the Centennial games. Atlanta leaders, especially Andrew Young, quickly reframed the criticism by praising Atlanta's decision to provide a free and accessible public space. Young condemned what appeared to be the work of terrorists and challenged Olympic visitors to defy intimidation by celebrating the games and reclaiming the park for the people. The games continued, and when the park reopened, Olympic visitors returned in large numbers, apparently affirming Young's vision (Soto 1996). The general public also seemed to exonerate Atlanta. When respondents to a national poll were asked if Atlanta had done enough to prevent the tragedy, 79 percent agreed that it had (Turner 1996a).

In the long run, Atlanta's image was perhaps hurt more by internal corruption than external events. Two years after the Atlanta games, allegations surfaced of widespread corruption in the bidding process for the 2002 winter games. The Salt Lake City scandal brought media attention to other Olympic bids, including Atlanta's. The *Atlanta Journal Constitution* pursued the investigation in Atlanta, at first reluctantly but later aggressively (Turner 1999g). Initially, Payne refused all access to the fourteen hundred boxes of Olympic records by arguing that the material was the property of the

ATLANTA 115

Georgia Amateur Athletic Foundation (GAAF), the private organization that had been the springboard for the Olympic bid. Technically,
Payne could make this case since ACOG had quietly transferred
ownership of the documents to GAAF a year after the games ended.
But the use of public funds in ACOG and GAAF operations left
Payne open to legal challenges from the *Atlanta Journal Constitution* and the Georgia attorney general. Increased public pressure
from these sources forced the release of some documents and produced some embarrassing revelations. Ultimately, the threat of a
subpoena by the U.S. House subcommittee investigating the allegations pried open all the records.

The bid material revealed a pattern similar in form and scale to
that disclosed in Salt Lake City, including payments of college tuition, shopping sprees, donations of sports equipment, and excessive
reimbursement for delegate travel. The bid committee's aggressive
pandering included compiling extensive dossiers on IOC members
describing their taste in gifts, susceptibility to bribes, and sexual
preferences. These revelations elicited no admissions of wrongdoing
from Billy Payne or Andrew Young. Payne claimed they were initially naive but learned to play by the rules as they understood them.
Young suggested that many gifts were simply humanitarian aid to
countries that lacked resources (Turner 1999a, 1999b, 1999c).

In the end, the investigation revealed much about the limitations
of public-private partnerships and how organizations and individuals
play and win the insiders' game. King and Spalding, Atlanta's premier corporate law firm, was the consummate organizational insider.
Partners Charlie Battle, Charlie Shaffer, and Horace Sibley were
three of the original nine members of Atlanta's bid team; the wife of
another partner was also on the team. These four, plus Billy Payne
and Andrew Young, also controlled the GAAF board. Horace Sibley's
family ties on the boards of Coca-Cola and the Woodruff Foundation
enabled Payne to gain a sympathetic hearing for his proposals. King
and Spalding was amply rewarded for its efforts. As the primary legal
representative of GAAF and later ACOG, the law firm received over
$19 million for legal work (Campbell 1999b; Turner 1999f).

Billy Payne also mastered the insider game for his benefit. One
year after the games concluded, ACOG transferred its archives and
several million dollars to GAAF. GAAF, in turn, paid Billy Payne
$975,000 for a dozen boxes of personal Olympic memorabilia (Camp-
bell 1999a). Payne was also involved in real estate speculation while

organizing the games. He and his partners made a profit of nearly one million dollars after they sold land very close to the Olympic horse park in Conyers, a site ACOG selected over nearly a dozen competitors (Turner 1999d).

The Olympic bribery investigation also highlighted the structural limitations of public-private partnerships. As a private, nonprofit organization, ACOG was primarily accountable to MAOGA, a semi-public organization that was empowered both to oversee ACOG and to enter intergovernmental agreements on its behalf. This arrangement enabled Payne and others to use the public partnership for private ends. At every occasion, ACOG leaders claimed the mantle of public purpose, when necessary they used public powers, and when possible they leveraged public dollars. When challenged, however, ACOG leaders vigorously asserted the prerogatives of a private organization to make decisions without public oversight and to withhold records from public view.

■ Conclusion: Atlanta's Olympic Legacy

For the neighborhoods of Atlanta expecting the Olympics to produce a windfall of redevelopment, the legacy has been limited. Most of CODA's $76 million budget was used for urban landscaping in the downtown area and along Olympic corridors. Less than 10 percent found its way into the poorest Olympic neighborhoods. The Olympics was instrumental in helping Atlanta receive an empowerment-zone designation and $250 million in federal grants and incentives for economic development. But the impact on the neighborhoods before the Olympics was minimal, and the outcome of post-Olympic development is uncertain. The current agenda favors large-scale projects consistent with development interests and includes few small-scale community and human capital efforts.

The federal government has been an active participant in the Olympic development. Table 5.3 shows some of the more significant expenditures. The federal government contributed nearly one billion dollars, a considerable sum for an Olympics touted as costless to taxpayers. Federal contributions to CODA and Atlanta's designation as a federal empowerment zone accounted for $272 million. The empowerment zone included thirty central city neighborhoods, half within the Olympic Ring. Unfortunately, it was slow to start, at first

Table 5.3 Atlanta's Olympic Legacy (spending in millions of dollars)

Facility	ACOG	Private	Local	State	Federal	Total
Olympic (Turner) Stadium	209	35				244
Olympic Village/university housing	47			194		241
Centennial Olympic Park	15	45		7		67
Georgia Tech Aquatic Center	21			3		24
Atlanta University Center						
Stadiums	37					37
Basketball arena	11					11
Other facilities	3					3
Stone Mountain						
Tennis Center	22					22
Velodrome	6*					6*
Lake Lanier Rowing Center	10					10
Georgia International Horse Park	28	50	20			98
Ocoee Whitewater Kayaking					21	21
Savannah Yachting Marina	4					4
Wolf Creek Shooting Complex	17					17
Hartsfield Airport			455			455
Infrastructure			337		371	708
Safety and security	8		7	22	86	123
Atlanta Housing Authority						
Centennial Place (Techwood)		58			42	100
Olympic Legacy communities		191			204	395
CODA						
Pedestrian corridors, parks		10	38		10	58
MLK, Jr., Historical Site					12	12
Woodruff Park		6				6
Empowerment zone					250	250
Total	432	395	857	226	996	2,906

Source: Compiled by authors.
Note: The velodrome was not a permanent facility, so spending on it is not included in the totals.

poorly managed, then mired in controversy (Gittell et al. 1998, 542, 546–547). Another $371 million in federal money went to road, transit, and sewer construction. While these projects might have been funded even without the Olympics, it is clear they came sooner because of the games. Other expenditures, however, were specific to the Olympics. These included $21 million for construction and operation of the whitewater Olympic venue and $86 million for safety and security services (U.S. General Accounting Office 1999, 5–8).

The U.S. Department of Housing and Urban Development helped finance a dramatic change in the landscape of public housing in Atlanta. Starting with the razing of Techwood/Clark Howell and its replacement by a mixed-income gated community, HUD has supported the similar conversion of over fifty-seven hundred units of public housing. When all the "Olympic Legacy" housing projects are completed, an estimated $500 million will have been expended, with federal and private dollars spent in roughly equal amounts. Although the physical improvements are substantial, the human cost has been the displacement of an estimated sixteen thousand of the city's lowest-income residents.

The Olympics were instrumental in generating local support for infrastructure bond measures totaling $375 million. With state and federal matching funds, Atlanta is beginning to reverse years of disinvestment in its streets, sewer, and water systems. The bond issues have not been without cost to consumers who now pay double the water rates they did before the games. The Olympics also hastened the city's investment of $455 million in Hartsfield Airport, primarily to fund a new international concourse (Ray 1995, 4).

The games left other visible marks on Atlanta (French and Disher 1997). The $244 million investment in Olympic (now Turner) Stadium encouraged the Atlanta Braves to stay in the city. The $42 million provided by ACOG to construct the Olympic Village became the catalyst for the state to invest another $194 million for university dormitories. Georgia Tech retains parts of its $24 million Aquatic Center. Private universities also shared Olympic largess. Atlanta University Center campuses now have new sporting facilities worth over $50 million (Char and Holmes 1995, 57). The $6 million renovation of Woodruff Park and the $67 million investment in Centennial Olympic Park remain as a legacy of the games. Centennial Olympic Park has stimulated considerable office and loft construction on its perimeter.

Outside the city, the $22 million tennis complex remains at Stone Mountain State Park, but the velodrome has been removed. The Georgia International Horse Park in suburban Conyers has evolved into a $98 million complex. Unfortunately, this highly speculative venture forced Conyers to sell its water system to pay its debt. But with much of the debt repaid, park operations are moving into the black and generating peripheral development activity (Nurse 1999).

ACOG also left a substantial record of affirmative action employment and affirmative action purchasing. Although other activities generated concern, ACOG's record on this issue is sound. And there is little dispute that the Olympics produced a substantial tourist, employment, and construction windfall for the region. Of ACOG's $1.7 billion in revenues, roughly a third was spent on construction. Overall, the region was expected to receive a $5 billion economic boost, an amount roughly equivalent to the impact of twenty Super Bowls (Char and Holmes 1995, 52–57).

These staggering numbers, however, provide little consolation to those who did not benefit from the 1996 summer games. Mayor Jackson's Olympic dream was to scale the twin peaks of Mount Olympus by staging the best games ever and uplifting the people of Atlanta. In the end, however, the politics of image building and downtown revitalization displaced neighborhood redevelopment, as well as the needs and dreams of central city residents.

■■ 6 ■■

SALT LAKE CITY AND
THE 2002 WINTER GAMES

We have now seen how the Los Angeles Olympics created an entrepreneurial model by separating organizational control of the games
from local politics and aggressively seeking corporate sponsors. In
contrast to Los Angeles, extensive redevelopment became a focal
point of Atlanta's Olympics, resulting in renewed conflicts over the
costs and benefits to be derived from staging the games.

In this chapter, we use the 2002 winter games in Salt Lake City
to investigate how the dream of Olympic-driven revitalization plays
out in a smaller city hosting a smaller Olympic games. We start with
a brief overview of politics in Salt Lake City, then turn to the bid
process and organization of the games. Although the cities and sporting events may be quite different, the political themes are strikingly
similar.

■ The City and Its Politics

From its founding by Mormon pioneers in 1847, Salt Lake City has
maintained its historical identification with the Mormon Church
while serving as the capital city of Utah and becoming a regional
trade and service center. The city is located in a valley bound on the
west by the Great Salt Lake and the Oquirrh Mountains and on the
east by the Wasatch Front Range of the Rocky Mountains. As a consequence of these physical features, intensive urban development
has occurred along a narrow corridor of the Wasatch Front running
from the cities of Ogden in the north to Provo in the south. The four

Wasatch Front counties—Weber, Davis, Salt Lake, and Utah—hold
more than three-quarters of the state's population. The proximity of
the mountains, with their abundant snow and numerous ski resorts,
to the amenities of the city provides Salt Lake with a physically advantageous location for holding a large winter sports event.

Salt Lake City is a mid-sized city in the rapidly growing and ur-
banizing Mountain West (Weatherby and Witt 1994). Like a number
of core cities within expanding metropolitan areas, Salt Lake City
has struggled to maintain population in the face of suburban growth.
As Table 6.1 shows, between 1950 and 1990, Salt Lake City lost
more than twenty-two thousand people, or 12 percent of its population, while its southern suburb, the city of Sandy, grew dramatically.
Since 1990, however, Salt Lake City has experienced an increase in
population that has nearly restored the city to its 1970 size, while the
suburban communities of Sandy and West Valley City continue to
grow rapidly. Overall, Salt Lake City lost population as a result of
both migration to the suburbs and general economic decline between
1950 and 1990. In the 1990s, the city and its suburbs witnessed population growth driven by a high internal birthrate and migration into
the state.

Economically, Salt Lake City is anchored by the presence of
state government, higher education, the headquarters of the Church
of Jesus Christ of Latter-day Saints (LDS), as well as private sector
businesses. Along with the standard collection of large hotels and

Table 6.1   Population of Salt Lake City and Two Major Suburbs

Year	Salt Lake	Sandy	West Valley
1950	182,121	2,095	—
1960	189,454	3,322	—
1970	175,885	6,438	—
1980	163,034	52,210	72,378
1990	159,936	75,058	86,976
1992	162,671	81,588	88,730
1994	165,519	90,959	90,991
1996	169,278	96,602	95,007
1998	174,348	99,186	99,372

Source: U.S. Bureau of the Census.

Note: Population figures for 1950 to 1990 are from the decennial census. Post-1990
figures are the Census Bureau's population estimates for July 1 of the year indicated.
Figures for West Valley City were not available prior to 1980, because it was not an
incorporated city.

corporate buildings, downtown Salt Lake City is heavily influenced by the presence of the LDS Church. The church is a major property owner in the city, its headquarters bring hundreds of employees into downtown each workday, it has interests in local businesses including insurance and media, and the church's Temple Square is the city's prime tourist attraction. Even with substantial growth of the metro area and greater diversity in the city, the LDS Church continues to be the most important institution shaping both the city's image and its built environment.

As the state's capital and largest city, the politics of Salt Lake City can never be entirely disentangled from state politics. Utah is a conservative and Republican state. Indeed, studies using public opinion data to summarize the ideological and partisan orientations of citizens by state have identified Utah as the most conservative and most Republican state on average (Erikson, Wright, and McIver 1993, 14–19; Wright et al. 2000, 41). Not surprisingly, Republicans have controlled the state legislature, the governorship, and the state's congressional delegation since the mid-1980s.

Salt Lake City is an exception to the broader pattern of partisan politics in Utah because the city is nearly evenly split among people who identify themselves as Democrats, Republicans, and independents.[1] As a result, the congressional district that includes Salt Lake City and its closest suburbs is not a safe seat for either Democrats or Republicans and is nearly always hotly contested. Results for the city's highest elective office, the mayoralty, show a different pattern. Although formally a nonpartisan office, in practice Democrats have controlled the office since the city adopted a mayor-council system in 1979.

Aside from electoral politics, where does power reside in Salt Lake City? Writing in 1960, a local political scientist described the city's power structure as a "triumvirate" consisting of the LDS Church, the chamber of commerce, and the city's leading newspaper, the *Salt Lake Tribune* (Williams 1960, 1). Of course, times have changed, particularly with respect to the influence of the *Tribune,* which is no longer locally owned and only one voice in a highly competitive media market. The role of the LDS Church in local politics has also changed. Church leaders have consciously attempted to distance the church from most matters of day-to-day politics, choosing instead to encourage members to be active participants in the political process.

Although it would no longer be accurate to speak of city politics
in terms of a triumvirate, nevertheless this description still has a ring
of truth to it. In particular, in contemporary Salt Lake City both
business and the LDS Church enjoy what in regime theory is termed
"systemic power" (Stone 1980; Stoker 1995, 64–65). Business, though
certainly not a unified whole, can exercise substantial local political
power because it is well organized (through groups such as the
chamber of commerce), has significant resources, and encounters little opposition from organized labor. Williams's (1960, 5) description, "Salt Lake City is a business town—not a labor town," still fits.
As in many other cities, the concerns of business tend to dominate
the local political agenda because businesses have the desire and
sufficient resources to shape public policy directly.

The LDS Church, on the other hand, is able to exercise power
without having to engage in overt forms of political activity such as
lobbying (Hrebenar, Cherry, and Greene 1987, 114–115). The church
has overt interest in local policy because of its sizable real estate and
business holdings. Perhaps more important, the church has a "presence" in local politics that does not stem from any direct interest or
instruction from church leadership. This presence exists because
many people active in local and state politics are also committed
members of the LDS Church. "Whether the church is or is not particularly interested in a given policy is not the question. The point is
that decisions are often made in Utah as though the church [were]
concerned" (Hrebenar, Cherry, and Greene 1987, 115). Although
members of the church's hierarchy are careful to observe the princi-
ple of political neutrality, a widespread awareness and acceptance of
the church's views among political and business leaders mean important decisions that run counter to the church's interest seldom occur
and most political activities undertaken have at least the tacit acceptance of the church.

At times, differences between Mormons and non-Mormons have
served as the main political cleavage within the city. This tension
has been less evident in recent decades. In part, the softening of this
division reflects the growth of the metro area and the growth of the
LDS Church from a predominantly Utah-based organization to a
worldwide religion. With its expansion, church leaders have become
increasingly concerned with the church's national and international
image, illustrated by such actions as the president of the church
appearing on the CBS news show *60 Minutes*. As with the church,

political leaders in Salt Lake have been intent on enhancing the
city's image as a wholesome and business-friendly place. The desire
to propel its reputation beyond the Mountain West has been one of
the reasons why city leaders have repeatedly embraced the goal of
becoming an Olympic city.

■ Seeking the Games:
The Roots of Salt Lake City's Olympic Bids

Salt Lake City has had a long history of seeking the Olympic games,
including unsuccessful bids for the 1972, 1976, 1992, and 1998 winter games. Over the course of these bids, the city's approach evolved
into a highly sophisticated campaign.

The earliest organized attempt to attract the Olympics to Utah
began in 1965. The idea to bid for the 1972 winter games originated
with three influential individuals: Utah's governor, Calvin Rampton;
the publisher of the *Salt Lake Tribune,* John Gallivan; and the executive vice president of the Salt Lake Chamber of Commerce, Maxwell
Rich. Governor Rampton established a small committee to seek the
endorsement of the USOC and, if successful, to pursue an IOC bid
as well. The governor's committee consisted of seven people, most
of whom were from businesses in Salt Lake City's downtown. The
group's intent was not necessarily to win the games for Salt Lake
but to attract attention to the area's emerging ski industry. As John
Gallivan recalled about this early effort, "We weren't all that convinced we could really host [the Olympics] . . . we were more interested in drawing attention and publicity for our ski industry"
("Olympic torch" 1995, H-8).

Although Salt Lake City was chosen by the USOC, the IOC
gave the 1972 games to Sapporo, Japan. Shortly thereafter, Salt Lake
City again sought USOC endorsement to compete for the 1976 games,
but Denver was selected instead. Although awarded the 1976 games
by the IOC, Denver did not host the games because in 1972 voters in
the city and statewide passed initiatives that effectively prevented
spending tax money on the games (Foster 1976; Leonard and Noel
1990, 273–274). After the announcement that Denver would not host
the games, city officials convinced the USOC to name Salt Lake as
the U.S. replacement. The IOC, however, chose Innsbruck, Austria,
to replace Denver.

Despite these frustrations, Salt Lake's leaders did not abandon the idea of hosting the games. During a prolonged economic slowdown in the mid-1980s, the idea of using the Olympics to boost Utah's tourism industry was rekindled. In April 1984, the mayor of Salt Lake City and the governor of Utah formed a committee to investigate the feasibility of hosting the Olympics.

Although the committee was brought together by the mayor and the governor, the driving force behind the bid committee was the local ski industry. In contrast to the city's previous Olympic bid endeavors, this committee was not composed of representatives from downtown businesses but was made up primarily of people from area ski resorts, the ski association, and government agencies.[2] The committee's composition reflected the growing importance of skiing and tourism to Utah's economy. Between 1965 and 1985, the ski industry had expanded and changed. In 1965, there were approximately 388,000 total skier visits to local resorts, and 88 percent of these were by Utah residents. By 1985, the number of skier visits had increased to 2.4 million, with the more lucrative destination skiers accounting for 53 percent (Governor's Office of Planning and Budget 1999, 1). In the afterglow of the 1984 Los Angeles games, the Olympics were seen as a way to attract attention to Utah skiing and justify the expansion and development of area ski resorts.

These hopes for Olympic glory were quickly dashed. In 1985, the city of Anchorage was chosen by the USOC as America's Olympic competitor for both the 1992 and the 1994 winter games. Salt Lake's renewed interest in the Olympics was unsuccessful, but it shaped subsequent events in important ways. First, the 1985 bid raised the specter of opposition. Environmentalists became concerned when, as part of the bid process, a feasibility study was commissioned that indicated resort owners intended to use the Olympics to expand the size and accessibility of their resorts. The expansion plans alarmed environmentalists and some local government officials, because the resorts were located in two canyons, Big Cottonwood and Little Cottonwood Canyons, that were relatively undeveloped and were sources of drinking water for Salt Lake City. Environmental concerns over the two canyons led to changes in the proposed Olympic venues in later bids and thus altered the coalitions of both Olympic supporters and opponents.

A second legacy of the 1985 bid was that it brought two future Olympic entrepreneurs, Thomas K. Welch and David R. Johnson, into the picture. Welch was an attorney for a local grocery chain when he was recruited by the mayor and the head of the chamber of commerce to help prepare the city's bid. Afterwards, Welch remained active in the business of sports promotion and over time became the city's best-known Olympic promoter. Welch served as chairman for Better Utah Inc., a nonprofit organization that sought to attract amateur sporting events to Utah. The executive director of Better Utah was David Johnson. Johnson ran another sports promotion organization, the Utah Sports Foundation, that came into existence when the state of Utah privatized its sports promotion office. In the interim between the city's Olympic bid in 1985 and a renewed effort in 1988, these two organizations run by Welch and Johnson were primarily responsible for efforts to attract amateur sporting events to the city and state.

In November 1988, the USOC announced that it was reopening the bidding process for the 1998 winter games. Anchorage was the USOC's choice for the 1992 and 1994 competitions and logically should have been the front-runner for 1998 as well. The USOC reopened the competition, however, because it wanted to modify its selection agreement with cities; the committee wanted cities to commit to build Olympic-quality winter sports facilities as a condition of their selection. Such a commitment would mean more training facilities in the United States, but it also meant that a city would have to begin constructing Olympic venues before knowing the outcome of the IOC process.[3] Despite this potential burden, Salt Lake City was eager to get back into the Olympic bidding business.

Only days after the USOC announcement, Mayor Palmer DePaulis announced that Salt Lake City would again seek the USOC's endorsement. The timing of the USOC announcement was awkward for the city because it came in the midst of a controversy over the use of funds by Better Utah. A month before the USOC decision, city officials had announced an audit of Better Utah to determine whether $20,000 in city funds had indeed been used for the promotion of sports. The city audit was triggered by a state audit of the Utah Sports Foundation after questions had been raised about the privatization of the state's sports promotion office.

Neither audit ultimately produced evidence of wrongdoing, but the dispute raised serious questions about the involvement of Welch and Johnson in the city's bid. As Mayor DePaulis stated about Johnson's management at Better Utah: "His bookkeeping was sloppy,

messy, and he gave us bad figures. That's why I called it a breach of
trust, and that's why I don't want to do business with him" (Weeks
1988a, E-1). The mayor's desire to control the bid process was expressed the next day by his chief of staff who said, "If the city pur-
sues [an Olympic bid], it will do it under the auspices of Salt Lake
City, not a private sports foundation. . . . The city would clearly be
in charge of that effort" (Fitzpatrick 1988, B-1).

Environmental issues and conflicts between city officials and
private sports promotion entrepreneurs were important elements of
the context within which another Olympic bid was undertaken in
Salt Lake City. The bid effort unfolded in three stages: the establishment of a formal bid organization, a campaign for public funding,
and the international bid campaign.

The Road to 2002: Establishing the Bid Committee

The bid committee formed in 1988 to pursue the 1998 winter games
can best be described as a "grand coalition" of actors from the public and private sectors. The announcement of a new committee was
made by Mayor DePaulis along with David W. Adams, the state's director of the Department of Community and Economic Development, and Olympic entrepreneur Thomas Welch. In contrast to the
1985 committee, which was dominated by people from the ski industry, the 1988 committee included people from a range of businesses and governments to broaden the base of support for a bid. As
it was reported at the time: "To help build regional support, the Salt
Lake Winter Games Organizing Committee includes . . . county
commissioners of Weber and Summit counties, and the mayors of
Ogden, Park City, and Alta. The Mayor said the committee will also
include environmentalists and others" (Weeks 1988b, B-1).

Fifty-six members were named to the original committee, with
twenty-eight of these having primary ties to business and twenty-two
coming from government. Members were organized into seven subcommittees, with the executive and finance committees being the
most important. Among the businesses represented on the full committee were banking and finance, media, the ski industry, travel
agencies, developers, and attorneys. The executive committee had
fourteen members, nine from local businesses that included the
city's two largest banks, the owner of a large development firm, the

head of an insurance company (who was later elected governor), the owner of a local travel agency and air charter service, an attorney for a local television station, and a partner in one of the city's premier law firms. Despite the ongoing dispute over city funds, Thomas Welch was named to head the bid committee and chair the executive committee.

Government representatives on the full committee included Salt Lake's mayor, four members of the city council, and the directors of development services, economic development, and the airport authority. The state's lieutenant governor, director of economic development, and two members of the legislature also sat on the committee. The mayors of four other area cities were included, as were commissioners from three Wasatch Front counties. Elected officials, however, were less evident on the key executive and finance committees, which had only one elected official each.

There was considerable debate initially about how the committee should be funded. Preliminary estimates put the cost of the USOC stage of the bid at approximately $200,000. The debate concerned whether public money should be used to finance the bid or whether money should be raised from private sources. Although office space and staff were provided by his office, Mayor DePaulis argued that no public money should be spent until after the USOC decision. The state's lieutenant governor countered that cities and counties should provide the bulk of the money. This debate was effectively silenced when members of the bid's finance committee announced they were confident all the necessary funds could be raised from private sources (Evensen 1989).

For the most part, resources for the bid were provided by businesses. Between November 1988 and May 1989, the committee raised and spent about $250,000. Of that amount, businesses contributed roughly $205,000 in cash and $34,000 in-kind (mostly lodging and airline tickets), with the only significant money from a government agency being $15,000 spent by the Salt Lake Airport Authority from airline user fees (Rice 1989).

Once the bid process got under way, government officials were less central to bid activities than were local business people. City officials were well represented on the bid committee, but it quickly became apparent that city officials had neither the resources nor the willingness to run an Olympic bid organization. Mayor DePaulis revealed his limited enthusiasm for the undertaking in a statement after the committee's first meeting: "I really don't see myself as a cheer-leader for the Olympics" (Rice 1988, B-1).

Despite the intentions of some city officials to maintain public control over a bid bearing the city's name, the committee that organized Salt Lake City's bid nicely illustrates the reality of regime politics. The endorsement of elected officials was necessary to provide formal authority, but public officials lacked the resources to control the process. The resources to undertake the bid were provided by local businesses and, as such, representatives of the local business establishment filled the key positions and made decisions about how resources would be used.

The Push for Public Money

The bid organization achieved two major successes. The first was to convince the state legislature to provide public funding to support the Olympics. Olympic promoters lobbied the legislature to fund construction of Olympic venues, specifically a bobsled and luge run, ski jump, and speed-skating oval that would be required if Salt Lake City were to be selected by the USOC. A bill introduced by House Speaker Nolan Karras, who sat on the bid committee, passed easily.

The legislation authorized the earmarking of one sixty-fourth of one cent of sales tax money designated for Utah towns and cities and a corresponding one sixty-fourth from state sales tax revenues to be placed in a fund for Olympic construction starting in January 1990. The legislation did not authorize a tax increase but allowed a diversion of sales tax revenues that would otherwise have gone to state and local government. It was estimated that the diversion would provide about $4 million annually to create a pool of about $59 million, but the legislature stipulated that a referendum must be held prior to the diversion taking effect. The legislation also created the Utah Sports Authority (USA), an entity authorized to build and operate public sports facilities, and the Utah Sports Advisory Committee (USAC) to advise the legislature and governor on use of this public money.

The bid committee's second success came in June 1989, when the USOC selected Salt Lake City to compete for the 1998 games and, if need be, the 2002 games. Given the USOC's desire for additional athletic facilities, passage of legislation to establish a construction fund was undoubtedly an important consideration in the selection process.

After the city's selection by the USOC, the state legislature met in special session to provide for a November referendum on the funding question. The referendum campaign became the focal point for supporters and opponents of the Olympic bid. The campaign for the Olympic referendum was headed by a nonprofit organization known as Olympics for Utah, Incorporated (OUI). Though formally a separate organization, OUI was closely associated with the bid committee. The president of the bid committee announced the formation of OUI, many bid committee members were active in OUI, and the estimated $250,000 spent by OUI was provided by the same businesses and individuals who were funding the bid.

The pro-Olympic view was supported by many prominent elected officials, including the governor, speaker of the Utah house, and the mayor of Salt Lake City. Proponents advanced pragmatic and symbolic arguments for voting yes on the referendum: (1) the use of public money was not a tax increase but a diversion of sales tax revenue that amounted to less than $3 per person per year; (2) the use of tax money would build sports facilities that would be used whether or not the IOC chose Salt Lake because it would make Utah a training ground for winter sports; (3) the direct and indirect economic benefits of hosting the Olympics could total $900 million and benefit the entire state; (4) environmental objections had been met by agreeing not to build venues in Big or Little Cottonwood Canyons; and (5) hosting the Olympics would provide a "lasting legacy" for Utahns.[4]

Opponents were not nearly so well organized or funded as the pro-Olympic side. In general, opposition was strongest from people who disliked using public funds for the Olympics, with some support from environmentalists concerned about the potential for Olympic-related development. A group calling itself Utahns for Responsible Public Spending (URPS) was established in September 1989, and it became the chief source of organized opposition to public funding. The group included some who opposed the Olympic bid in general, but it mostly sought to appeal to people who opposed public financing of the Olympics (Pace 1995). The group raised less than $4,000 and so had limited access to paid advertising.

Opponents concentrated on the use of tax money, though they raised questions about the environment as well. The concerns most commonly expressed by opponents included: (1) the diversion of sales tax was equivalent to a tax increase because that money would not be available for other uses; (2) the economic projections of the bid committee were overly optimistic; (3) Olympic facilities would benefit only a few elite athletes and would require substantial public subsidies in the future; and (4) city or state government must guarantee to pay any deficits resulting from the games, according to IOC rules, but the host city could not earn a profit.

The Olympic referendum was technically nonbinding, since the funding mechanism had been passed by the legislature, but elected officials pledged not to implement the funding plan if the referendum did not pass. After a spirited campaign, it passed 57 percent to 43 percent. Its passage gave a boost to Olympic supporters, despite the unexpectedly large no vote, because it provided money for construction of venues and because it helped proponents claim widespread public support for the games. Although the money was controlled by a state board and not the bid committee, its purpose was clearly to help attract the Olympic games to Salt Lake City.

Campaigning for the Games, 1989–1995

With the USOC selection secured, bid supporters needed to raise substantial resources to lobby the IOC. The bid committee began by reorganizing its structure from a grand coalition to a corporate model. The original committee was impractically large, but its size helped ensure that all the relevant actors from business and government entities were represented. Once local support was established and the USOC decision made, the committee's focus shifted to the IOC. This international lobbying effort still needed local support, but raising money and meeting with IOC members became higher priorities. Thus the purpose of reorganizing was to limit the size of the executive committee in order to improve its ability to implement a lobbying strategy and to increase the organization's ability to raise funds.

The reorganization created a board of trustees and a small executive committee. The executive committee had seven members and was headed by Thomas Welch, who was named chairman and CEO (Wilkinson 1989). A new position of chief administrative officer was added, and each member of the executive committee was the head of a subcommittee. The three key subcommittees were for fundraising, public relations, and "international relations" (i.e., lobbying IOC members). The executive committee was responsible for day-to-day operations and the board of trustees was to set policy. The board of trustees had fifty-five members, but the full board was expected to meet infrequently and members were not expected to take part in most committee activities.

The board of trustees was, however, central to the goal of raising money. In essence, appointments to the board were rewards for large donations or fund-raising ability. With the shift to the IOC phase, the bid committee made a concerted effort to target corporations because of the need for large sums of money. It was at this point that Fred Ball of the Salt Lake Area Chamber of Commerce took over the committee's fund-raising operation. Ball used his connections with business leaders to raise money and encouraged the committee to reward contributors with places on the board of trustees. One of Ball's most productive fundraisers was Frank Joklik, CEO of Kennecott Copper, who was subsequently named chairman of the board of trustees. With the heavy emphasis on fundraising, a new group of business leaders representing large corporations appeared as members of the board.

Of the approximately $13 million raised to finance bids for the 1998 and 2002 games, nearly $12 million came directly from corporations or business-based philanthropic donors (Keahey 1995; "Private dollars, public dream" 1995). In comparison, Salt Lake City budgeted approximately $250,000 to support the bid between 1988 and 1995 (Gust-Jenson 1994). Among the largest contributors to the Olympic committee were corporations with close business ties to Utah, including First Security Bank, Zion's Bank, Kennecott Copper, Utah Power, Questar, Sinclair Oil, Deer Valley Resort, Geneva Steel, Hercules, US West, and Franklin Quest. Some of these businesses, particularly the banks and resorts, had been involved from the first, but large corporations such as Kennecott, Geneva, and US West only became prominent as the need for resources increased. Business groups, such as the Salt Lake and Park City chambers of commerce and the Salt Lake Travel and Convention Bureau, also contributed substantially to the committee's efforts. Businesses controlled by the LDS Church contributed both cash and in-kind donations to the Olympic committee. National companies with Utah interests, such as Delta Airlines, helped primarily through in-kind contributions. The Eccles Foundation, a philanthropic organization founded by a prominent Utah banking family, was an important source of local support.

The move to reorganize the bid committee affected the role of government, as development agency officials who had been involved in getting the bid under way were replaced by business leaders. In 1988, the bid committee included the director of Salt Lake City's Development Services, the director of the city's Division of Community and Economic Development, a staff member from the city's Local Business Advocacy Office, and the state's director of the Department of Community and Economic Development. The city paid the salary of the director of Development Services, Craig Peterson, while he worked full-time as the committee's administrative director. After the reorganization, Peterson was the only one of the development agency personnel left. Several displaced economic development bureaucrats found positions on the Utah Sports Authority board. As it entered into IOC competition, positions on the bid committee's board of trustees were filled almost exclusively by business leaders.

Salt Lake's bid organization was successful raising money and lobbying IOC members. With the city's infrastructure and with many Olympic venues built or under construction, Salt Lake City was considered to have a strong technical bid. Despite these advantages, however, the city lost to Nagano, Japan, by four votes in June 1991.

The loss to Nagano was a disappointment to bid supporters. This setback, however, had surprisingly little effect on the bid organization. Shortly after the loss to Nagano, the mayor and the governor held discussions with bid committee officials and announced that a new bid for the 2002 games would be launched immediately. This announcement made it clear there would be no shake-up of the Olympic team; the structure of the committee and its key players remained the same. Tom Welch stayed as head of the executive committee, and David Johnson continued to handle IOC lobbying as vice president for international relations. Frank Joklik, a board member and successful fundraiser for the previous bid, was named chairman of the board of trustees. Political support for the bid was serendipitously enhanced when Deedee Corradini, a businesswoman and early bid committee member, was elected mayor of Salt Lake in 1991, and Michael Leavitt, another bid committee member, was elected governor in 1992.

The period after the loss to Nagano in 1991 until the city's selection by the IOC in 1995 was a time of frenetic activity at the international level but of relative quiescence at home. The bid committee had the local logistics, including venue locations, public funding, political endorsements, and public support, largely in place as a result of having gone through the previous IOC competition. Further, the city already had the USOC's endorsement to bid for the 2002 games. Thus the committee's primary task was to lobby IOC members for their votes in the next selection decision in 1995.

In retrospect, the activities of bid committee members during the years leading up to the IOC selection decision in June 1995 formed the substance of the bribery scandal that came to light in 1998 and 1999. The actions of Salt Lake bid committee members were a reaction to the 1991 loss to Nagano. Salt Lake bid officials believed their bid was technically superior to other cities in the competition, but they felt the city lost because Nagano bid officials had done more to appeal to individual IOC members. The Japanese bid was believed to have won support among IOC members when, for example, a substantial contribution was made by a Japanese business to the Olympic museum in Switzerland, a pet project of IOC President Samaranch (Evensen 1998). The lesson Salt Lake bid officials took from this experience was that they needed to cultivate stronger personal relationships with IOC members and officials in key athletic organizations in order to win.

During this period of intense international lobbying, there was relatively little Olympic-related activity within the city. Public debate over the merits of bidding for the games had largely been muted by the referendum vote and the fact that much of the ongoing bid activity took place out of public view.

As the IOC deadline approached, however, Olympic organizers found themselves trying to stanch an erosion of public support at home. Debate over the value of the Olympics was renewed when an influential Salt Lake businessman, Jon M. Huntsman, criticized the bid committee for not dealing realistically with financial risk. In a speech to a Salt Lake civic club, Huntsman stated that the committee was "sugarcoating" the financial projections and not adequately informing the public of the potential for debt (Fidel 1994, A-1). Huntsman's speech criticizing the boosterism of Olympic supporters repeated themes that critics had raised during the referendum campaign. But this criticism took on new respectability coming from an enormously successful businessman and pillar of the local establishment. Unfortunately for the bid committee, their public relations efforts to contain the damage hurt as much as they helped. The responses by bid committee officials to Huntsman's objections were superficial and emphasized the importance of associating the city and state with the

Olympic image (L. Roche 1994a). In response, Huntsman challenged the premise that the games brought economic growth or improved the city's image (L. Roche 1994b).

Huntsman's statements triggered media stories about "growing
opposition" to the Olympic bid at home. As Table 6.2 shows, opinion polls continued to find a majority of people supporting the bid,
but the number of people opposed did increase in 1994 and 1995. The
bid committee had focused its attention nearly exclusively on woo-
ing IOC delegates, but after Huntsman's speech, bid officials began
attending to local issues again. Not all the bid committee's actions
were well advised, however. An extreme example occurred when bid
officials appeared to pressure a state education committee to drop
the Olympics as a debate topic for elementary school students for
fear of raising doubts about the bid (Autman 1994). Of course, such
actions reinforced the negative media attention. Even the normally

Table 6.2 Public Opinion on the Salt Lake City Olympics (in percentages)

	Strongly Favor	Somewhat Favor	Somewhat Oppose	Strongly Oppose	Don't Know	N
Feb. 1989[a]	53	23	5	15	4	601
Nov. 1989[b]	48	19	9	17	7	604
Oct. 1993[c]	42	31	9	13	6	605
Nov. 1994[d]	32	24	12	20	12	605
Mar. 1995[c]	37	22	12	25	5	603
Jun. 1995[c]	40	20	10	22	9	601
Mar. 1996[c]	45	20	10	18	8	608
Jul. 1996[c]	39	25	10	16	10	617
Aug. 1996[c]	30	31	9	19	11	602
Jul. 1997[e]	41	21	12	23	8	305
Sep. 1997[e]	23	30	15	18	14	404
Jan. 1998[e]	34	27	11	23	5	603
Mar. 1998[e]	43	24	11	18	4	600
Jan. 1999[c]	39	23	9	22	7	423
Feb. 1999[c]	38	22	8	25	6	401
Jul. 1999[c]	35	25	9	22	9	411
Dec. 1999[c]	39	25	9	21	5	405

Source: Polls conducted by Dan Jones and Associates for KSL/*Deseret News.* Data
provided courtesy of Dan Jones.
Notes: Question wording:
a. "Would you favor or oppose Salt Lake City hosting the 1998 Winter Olympics?";
b. "Based on these items, do you favor or oppose Utah continuing its efforts to host the
Winter Olympic Games?"; c. "Do you favor or oppose Salt Lake City hosting the 2002
Winter Olympic Games?"; d. "First of all, do you favor or oppose Salt Lake City being
picked to host the 2002 Winter Olympic Games?"; e. "Do you favor or oppose Utah
hosting the 2002 Winter Olympics?"

supportive *Salt Lake Tribune* editorialized against "Olympics Paranoia" (1994). In response, the bid committee organized a new public relations effort designed to shore up local support.

The bid committee's actions in the period leading up to IOC selection illustrate the nature of the Olympic bidding process. Rather than a serious rebuttal to the charge of sugarcoating the financial projections, the bid committee chose to stifle public debate. The reason for this tactic appears to have been that the committee was well aware its financial figures were optimistic, but they had been crafted to meet the expectations of international competition. The bid committee's budget projections were not intended to represent the reality of putting on the games but were intended first and foremost to make the city look good to the IOC and international athletic federations. Having put such effort into lobbying IOC members, the bid committee did not want to engage in a debate at home that they could not win and that might appear to international observers as a lack of political support for hosting the games. In short, Salt Lake City residents seeking reassurance that the games would be beneficial were no longer the bid committee's audience; the selection decision was in the hands of IOC members, and their votes were all that counted at that point.

■ Organizing the Games:
The Politics of Coordination and Conflict

By June 1995, Salt Lake City was one of four finalists to host the games, along with Quebec City (Canada), Sion (Switzerland), and Osterlund (Sweden). The bid committee's years of work paid off when members of the IOC overwhelmingly chose Salt Lake City to hold the 2002 winter games. The results of the secret ballot election revealed an easy first-round win. Of the ninety valid votes cast, Salt Lake City got fifty-five, Sion and Osterlund each got fourteen, and Quebec City received seven.

The Organizational Structure

Having finally won the coveted games, Salt Lake now had to move from the rosy scenario set out in the bid to the reality of holding the games. Two elected officials took the lead in creating an organizational structure: the mayor of Salt Lake City and the governor of Utah. The mayor was a key player because the city was the governmental entity that had signed the agreement with the IOC to host the games. The governor's role, however, was a function of money. As a result of the public money used to construct Olympic venues, the governor already had power to appoint members of the Utah Sports Authority board. Further, in a 1991 agreement between the city, state, and bid committee, the state had agreed to indemnify the city against any financial liability from the games (Fowler 1999, 18–19). In return, the city agreed not to claim control over revenues generated by the games.[5]

Shortly after the IOC selection, the key organizations for the "Salt Lake City Olympics" were: (1) the Salt Lake Olympic Organizing Committee (SLOC), a private, nonprofit organization; (2) the Utah Sports Authority, a state board that had been established to build and operate certain Olympic venues; (3) the Utah Sports Advisory Committee, an oversight committee made up of members of the state legislature and representatives of local governments; and (4) the Utah Athletic Foundation (UAF), an organization created to manage some of the publicly built Olympic facilities after the games.

Formally, the bid committee ceased to exist after the city's selection by the IOC and the creation of an Olympic organizing committee. In reality, the bid committee was merely transformed into the organizing committee. The structure of the new organizing committee matched that of the bid committee, and the top personnel remained the same. As with the bid committee, the SLOC consisted of a board of trustees to set policy and an executive staff to carry it out. Initially, the board of trustees had thirty-one members: twenty members from Utah, three from the USOC, two IOC members, one from the Winter National Sports Council, and five athletes.

Among the Utah members named to the board, fourteen of the twenty had served on the bid committee, including the chairman, Frank Joklik. Members of the SLOC executive were also holdovers from the bid committee. Thomas Welch was named president and chief executive officer, and three of the four vice presidents of the organizing committee had worked on the bid committee.

According to the SLOC's bylaws, the Utah members and the athletes were to be jointly appointed by the governor and the mayor of Salt Lake City. This power-sharing arrangement between the mayor and the governor functioned smoothly for the most part. When the

Salt Lake City Council tried to influence appointments to the organizing committee, however, the governor reacted strongly. The dispute began before the IOC selection, when a coalition of community groups calling itself Impact 2002 and Beyond publicly expressed fear that the Olympics would exacerbate the shortage of affordable housing. Members of the bid committee met with coalition leaders and agreed that the housing issue needed attention. In response to the concerns raised by Impact 2002, the city council passed a unanimous resolution pledging to examine growth issues and to create a community planning committee if Salt Lake was selected.

Shortly after the IOC decision, members of Impact 2002 met separately with Mayor Corradini, Governor Leavitt, and members of the newly established organizing committee. Coalition members pointed out that members of the SLOC were overwhelmingly wealthy white men, and they provided a list of candidates who might help diversify the views of the committee. Mayor Corradini was sympathetic to the coalition's concerns. Governor Leavitt, on the other hand, rejected the group's demands. He argued that the task of the organizing committee was not to be representative but to conduct the games and that there were not enough places on the board of trustees to accommodate all groups that might demand representation.

The Salt Lake City Council, based on an advisory opinion from the city attorney, asserted that it had "advice and consent" power over appointments because the organizing committee was technically a city commission. The council then endorsed Mayor Corradini's decision to nominate Maria Garciaz, the director of a nonprofit housing service agency, to the organizing committee. Governor Leavitt withheld his consent, effectively preventing the appointment, until the state legislature came into session. Leavitt convinced the legislature to "clarify" the law so that the city council could not claim power over Olympic committee appointments. Subsequently, Leavitt and Corradini agreed to expand the board of trustees and appointed Garciaz along with several other new members.

In addition to the SLOC, three state organizations were involved in Olympic preparations. The most important of these, the Utah Sports Authority, was created by legislation in 1989 to build and manage several major Olympic venues, including a speed-skating oval, ski jump, and bobsled track. Members of the USA board are appointed by the governor, in accordance with a formula intended to provide representation to local governments and other interests. A second organization, the Utah Sports Advisory Committee, was created along with the USA in an effort to provide legislative over-sight, though as an advisory board it never played a crucial part in Olympic planning.[6]

The Utah Athletic Foundation was created in 1995 to assume ownership and operation of some of the publicly built Olympic facilities after the games. In accordance with state law, the Utah Sports Authority sold the public Olympic venues to the SLOC for $99 million. Of that amount, $59 million was to be returned to the state and cities for repayment of the sales tax diversion, and the remaining $40 million provided a "legacy fund" to operate the venues. Membership on the UAF board is interlocked with membership on the SLOC and USA boards. Of the seventeen UAF board members, ten also serve on the SLOC and three on the USA. According to the chairman of the USA, membership on these boards was intentionally designed to overlap to encourage members to take a long-term view of the success of the games and the public venues (Gorrell 1995).

In sum, despite public funding for key venues, preparations for the games in Salt Lake were conducted in a fairly closed environment, with limited opportunities for public involvement. The lion's share of the planning responsibilities for conducting the games fell to the organizing committee, which was essentially run by the same group who conducted the bid. Oversight of executive operations was to be provided by the board of trustees appointed by the mayor and the governor. Yet the trustees were largely the same group of people who had been appointed to the bid committee's board because of their prowess at raising money. Even after its expansion, the board in 1998 included the CEO of a large development company, the CEO of the state's largest bank, a senior vice president of a major utility company, the CEO of another utility company, the chairman of the board of a large oil company with holdings in a Salt Lake City hotel and ski resort, the CEOs of a major steel company and a major lumber company, and the president and past president of two state universities. In short, the Salt Lake organizing committee looked much like the bid committee, and both reflected the powers that be within the city's growth regime.

Venues and Olympic Development

Although not of the same magnitude as a summer Olympics, organizing a modern winter games is a substantial undertaking. Not only must the host city provide locations for events ranging from down-hill skiing to curling, it must also supply lodging and security for elite athletes, facilities for media from around the world, as well as rooms and transportation for visitors. Hosting the winter Olympics and Paralympics is no small endeavor.[7]

The winter games are a complex undertaking politically as well. Even though Salt Lake City is the nominal host and key aspects of the games are conducted within the city, the games in fact are spread across a number of sites and government jurisdictions outside the city (see Figure 6.1). As Table 6.3 shows, the 2002 winter games involve public and private facilities spread across several counties and cities. The location of facilities reflects the requirements of sporting events as well as the political advantages to local organizers of spreading the costs and benefits. It should be noted, however, that Salt Lake City's bid was considered particularly desirable because of its compact location.

Some proposed Olympic facilities, such as the Delta Center, were well-established sites that have attracted little public concern. Other venues were positively sought after. For example, Salt Lake and West Valley City competed intensely to build a facility that could be used for Olympic hockey events and become home to a professional hockey team. The competition, eventually won by West Valley City, was spurred by the promise of Olympic construction funds and the potential for ongoing revenues from a professional sports team.

Other venues, however, have been more controversial. To the extent that there has been organized opposition to Olympic activity from citizens in Utah, it has been sparked by plans for particular Olympic venues (Burbank, Heying, and Andranovich 2000, 348–352). One venue that created controversy over its location was the speed-skating oval. Although the cost of constructing the oval was to be paid for by the Olympic construction fund, neighbors in two areas of Salt Lake City objected to its proposed location. Initially, Mayor Palmer DePaulis wanted the oval situated in an area near the University of Utah campus. University officials objected because the location interfered with plans for a parking lot, and residents of a middle-class neighborhood adjacent to the proposed site objected for fear of increased traffic and noise. The cost of mitigating residents' concerns, combined with difficulties in obtaining land, led DePaulis to withdraw his proposal. The next mayor, Deedee Corradini, favored putting the skating oval downtown. Corradini saw the speed-skating

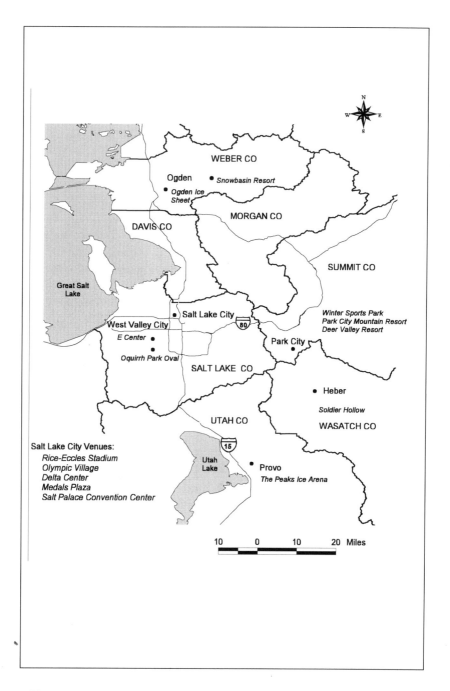

Figure 6.1 Venues for Salt Lake City 2002

Table 6.3 Attributes of Venues for the 2002 Games

Location	Venue	Events	Attributes
Salt Lake County			
Salt Lake City	Oquirrh Park Oval	Speed skating	New: USA, SLOC funds
	Rice-Eccles Stadium	Opening/closing ceremonies	Expanded: University, SLOC funds
	University of Utah	Olympic Village	New: University, SLOC funds
	Delta Center	Figure skating	Existing: Privately owned
	Medals Plaza	Award ceremonies	Temporary: Private donation
	Salt Palace	Media center	Existing: Publicly owned
West Valley City	E Center	Hockey	New: City, USA, SLOC funds
Summit County			
Park City	Winter Sports Park	Ski jump, bobsled, luge	New: USA, SLOC funds
	Park City Mountain Resort	Alpine skiing, snowboarding	Existing: Privately owned
	Deer Valley Resort	Alpine skiing, freestyle	Existing: Privately owned
Utah County			
Provo	Peaks Ice Arena	Hockey	New: SLOC, city, county, USA, private funds
Wasatch County	Soldier Hollow in Wasatch Mountain State Park	Cross-county, biathlon	New: SLOC, state funds
Weber County			
Ogden	Snowbasin Resort	Downhill skiing	Expanded: Private, SLOC funds
	Ice Sheet at Ogden	Curling	New: City, county, USA, SLOC funds

Source: Compiled by the authors.

Notes: Attributes indicate whether the facility was newly built, expanded, or an existing facility requiring minimal modifications for the games. Funding sources indicate the major source of funds to build or modify the venue and include public money provided through the Utah Sports Authority (USA), private money provided by the Salt Lake Olympic Organizing Committee (SLOC), as well as funds provided by specific government entities or private businesses.

oval, combined with a new baseball field and the Delta Center, as part of a "sports corridor" in downtown Salt Lake. Her proposal, however, ran into resistance from area residents, advocates for low-income housing, and a group of religious leaders who called the proposal a "speculative recreation scheme" (Jorgenson 1992, B-3). Although the city council voted for the site and it won approval from the Utah Sports Authority, Corradini withdrew her proposal because of continuing opposition. Ultimately, the skating oval was located at a recreation center in Salt Lake County.

Controversy also erupted over an effort by the SLOC to move the location of the cross-country skiing site. The original site proposed for the cross-country events was a golf course on city-owned land located east of the city (Salt Lake Bid Committee 1994). After winning the bid, however, the organizing committee announced that the site was unsuitable for technical reasons and that its preferred location was an area of undeveloped land also owned by the city. Activists from several environmental groups, including the Sierra Club and a local organization called the Citizens Committee to Save Our Canyons, saw the move as an attempt by the SLOC to renege on its promise to minimize the environmental impact. The proposed location raised concerns among city officials as well, because the area was part of the city's watershed. City officials insisted the new location could be considered only if no permanent facilities were left after competition. National and international skiing and biathlon organizations quickly objected to the city's conditions, citing bid committee promises that the games would leave a legacy of facilities for training future Olympic athletes.

After considerable controversy, all sides agreed that a new site selection committee, consisting of athletes, Olympic organizers, and environmentalists, would search for new locations. The selection committee was able to agree on a new location on state park land not far from Park City, which was acceptable on environmental and technical grounds. Although the new site was praised by nearly everyone involved, the question of a continuing legacy was left unresolved. The postgames operation of the speed-skating oval, bobsled track, and ski jump were to be funded by the $40 million legacy fund. The cross-country venue at Soldier Hollow, however, was not included. In an effort to keep the site operating after the games, proponents established a nonprofit organization to operate the venue during the winter and so share the operating costs with the state's Division of Parks and Recreation (Beattie 2000, 18–19).

Olympic organizers and environmentalists were able to find a satisfactory solution in the case of the cross-country venue. In other circumstances, however, Olympic organizers asserted considerable political muscle to overcome objections from environmental groups. Environmentalists led by the Citizens Committee to Save Our Canyons strongly opposed expanding Snowbasin, the ski resort designated to hold the downhill events. The resort is located north of Salt Lake near Ogden and is owned by Earl Holding, who was a member of the SLOC board of trustees and the owner of a large hotel in downtown Salt Lake City. The plan to expand the resort required a land swap with the U.S. Forest Service and construction of a new road to the resort. After members of Save Our Canyons filed a federal lawsuit over the environmental impact of the expansion, Olympic organizers turned to Utah's congressional delegation for help. Utah's members of Congress worked to pass legislation that ensured the land swap took place and earmarked federal funds to pay for the road construction. Thus when opponents threatened to slow development at a crucial venue, Olympic organizers were able to call on powerful allies for help.

Controversy also arose over the site of a plaza in downtown Salt Lake to serve as a venue for the ceremonial awarding of Olympic medals. This debate illustrated the tensions between Olympic organizers and city officials. In August 1999, SLOC officials announced they had accepted a donation from the LDS Church that included the use of a downtown city block and approximately $5 million to transform it into a ceremonial plaza. Although Olympic planners had always wanted to hold the awards ceremonies downtown, they had no money budgeted for such a facility. Thus SLOC officials approached the church about donating use of the land, known as Block 85, and the resources to turn a parking lot into a temporary venue. Although the church's donation was welcome news at the SLOC, city officials were unhappy because they had not been informed about the decision ahead of time and because they favored another location. City officials wanted SLOC to provide money for a plaza located on city property near the historic city and county building, where they hoped to establish a permanent Olympic legacy. Some city officials expressed concerns about traffic congestion at the Block 85 site and hinted that SLOC might run into difficulties getting the necessary city permits for that site. Ultimately, however, Block 85 won out because city officials could not match the church's offer and could not force SLOC to budget money for a plaza. Although the resolution of this issue depended on money, the location was important symbolically as well. At the city's preferred location, the backdrop for the televised ceremonies would have been the city and county building. At Block 85, the television backdrop will be the LDS Temple and Temple Square (Walsh 2000).

Despite the controversy, development of these venues was clearly related to hosting the games. Other projects on the Olympic development agenda, however, were not so obviously relevant to athletic competition. For example, state officials used the certainty of the 2002 deadline to implement an accelerated schedule for reconstructing a section of interstate highway near Salt Lake City. Highway reconstruction had been delayed for years because of concerns over disruptions and funding, but the upcoming games encouraged state officials to propose an ambitious plan for simultaneously designing and building the new highway in order to finish before the Olympics.

Another development project that its advocates successfully linked to the Olympics was light rail. Although an earlier initiative by the Utah Transit Authority (UTA) to build light rail had been halted when voters rejected a proposed tax increase, advocates of light rail were able to use the Olympics to obtain federal money. Federal funds paid for construction of a fifteen-mile line running south from the suburbs into downtown Salt Lake City. UTA officials had greater difficulty, however, obtaining federal funds for an east-west line that would run from the airport through downtown to the east side of the city. An east-west line would have been more relevant to moving Olympic tourists than the commuter-oriented north-south line, but the project ran into trouble first from members of the U.S. House of Representatives, who were skeptical that the project could be built in time for the Olympics, and then from the city council. The city council, UTA, and the Utah Department of Transportation ultimately agreed to a compromise plan for building a scaled-down, east-west rail line that met the federal funding deadline.

Perhaps the most dramatic example of a project that its proponents attempted to justify under the umbrella of the Olympics was the Gateway redevelopment. The Gateway district is a large area, approximately 650 acres located west of Salt Lake's central business district, that was home to light industry, warehouses, and railroad yards. The city's master plan for the Gateway divides this sizable piece of land into five areas, with differing redevelopment goals and timelines (Salt Lake City Planning Division 1998). Mayor Corradini sought to tie redevelopment of the Gateway to the Olympics by proclaiming the need for a large urban space for public Olympic festivities, similar in concept to Atlanta's Centennial Olympic Park (Gorrell 1996). The mayor pushed vigorously for redevelopment and used the pressure of Olympic planning to prompt decisionmaking and attract federal funds. Despite the mayor's efforts to promote the Gateway as part of the city's Olympic needs, the games in fact played only a very small part in the redevelopment plan. For example, in the initial redevelopment, a private developer received approval for more than $18 million in subsidies from the city's redevelopment agency as part of a total $300 million project to build retail space, offices, and housing. In contrast, the only Olympics-related subsidy request was for $750,000 to build housing that might be used by the media during the games (Walsh 1998).

▒ The Bribery Scandal and Its Aftermath

Despite contentiousness over some development projects, early preparations for the games proceeded largely as planned by the SLOC. When difficulties were encountered, such as the cross-country venue or the Snowbasin expansion, the SLOC was able to resolve them to its satisfaction. Even the unforeseen resignation of SLOC President Thomas Welch in August 1997, due to a personal scandal, did not seriously hinder the organizing committee's work. With Welch's departure, Frank Joklik moved from chairman to president, and Robert Garff, a Salt Lake businessman, took over as chairman of the SLOC board of trustees.

Beginning in November 1998, however, the Salt Lake committee and the Olympic movement faced a serious threat. The story began when a television reporter in Salt Lake City obtained a draft letter written to the daughter of an IOC member stating that the SLOC was ending its tuition assistance to her. At first, it appeared that the story might be only a minor embarrassment. Officials of the SLOC simultaneously downplayed the payment as part of a general scholarship program for students from developing nations and blamed any excesses on the defunct bid committee. The stories coming out of Salt Lake City attracted international media attention, however, when IOC member Marc Hodler spoke of the payments as "bribes" and suggested that the Salt Lake City stories were only the tip of the iceberg. In the following months, there were numerous media revelations about college scholarships, expensive gifts, free medical treatment, and even direct cash payments to certain IOC members or their families by the Salt Lake bid committee. The scandal spread to other Olympic cities as stories began to emerge about bid committees in Atlanta, Nagano, and Sydney.

The media stories led to several investigations. In Salt Lake City, the SLOC's ethics panel conducted an internal investigation of bid and organizing committee activities. Both the IOC and the USOC initiated investigations of their own. Committees of the U.S. House and Senate conducted hearings on issues ranging from the tax status of Olympic organizations to the extent of federal aid for American cities hosting the games. The Utah attorney general's office opened an investigation of possible violations of state law. The most serious investigation, however, was by the federal Department of Justice.[8]

At the international level, the bid scandal led to the expulsion of six IOC members, reprimands issued to nine others, and four voluntary resignations. The IOC investigation, headed by Canadian member Richard Pound, presented the view that any fault stemmed from poor judgment by a few IOC members (Report of the IOC 1999). In response to the deluge of negative publicity, the IOC created an ethics commission and filled it with international notables such as Javier Perez de Cuellar, former United Nations secretary-general, and Howard Baker, former U.S. senator. In addition, the IOC 2000 Commission recommended a series of reforms, approved by the full IOC, including a new "bid acceptance" procedure for candidate cities, a ban on visits by IOC members to bid cities, and the disclosure of funding sources for bid cities (Report by the IOC 2000 Commission 1999).

The USOC investigation, headed by former senator George Mitchell, issued a report that blamed the culture of the IOC as well as Salt Lake bid officials. The Mitchell commission recommended that the USOC and IOC create an enforceable set of rules for bid cities and that the USOC prohibit bid cities from offering "assistance programs" (Mitchell et al. 1999, 24–31).

In Salt Lake City, the repercussions of the scandal were surprisingly muted. Before the ethics committee released its report, news of the scandal prompted the resignation of two officials, SLOC President

Frank Joklik and Senior Vice President David Johnson. The SLOC ethics report documented abuses by bid committee officials, including "scholarships" that were merely payments to relatives of IOC members, arranging jobs or lucrative consulting contracts, expensive gifts and travel, free medical care, and direct payments to IOC members and their relatives (Hall et al. 1999).

Written by the ethics committee of a private organization, the purpose of the report was not to identify illegal activity.[9] The committee's report identified the city's two longtime Olympic entrepreneurs, Thomas Welch and David Johnson, as primarily responsible for the inappropriate actions. Members of the board of trustees, who were formally responsible for policy and oversight, stated they were unaware of the scholarship programs and other inappropriate expenditures. As the report noted, "The Board's efforts were focused more on fund raising than on monitoring spending" (Hall et al. 1999, 59).

Several members of the SLOC board of trustees did resign, but not directly because of the scandal. Most of the resignations occurred because a new conflict-of-interest policy was adopted after the scandal. Another casualty of the scandal was Mayor Corradini's desire for reelection. Corradini was closely identified with the Olympic bid, and in the midst of the scandal she suddenly announced she would not seek a third term. Although Corradini stated that the decision was purely personal, questions about the Olympic scandal would have been central to the mayoral campaign had she sought reelection.

The extent of possible damage from the scandal was mitigated by the action of Governor Leavitt and SLOC chairman Robert Garff. Only days before the release of the ethics committee report, Leavitt and Garff publicized a plan to restructure the SLOC. The restructuring plan was one element of a strategic response to the scandal. In essence, the strategy was to acknowledge the seriousness of the inappropriate actions but maintain that these actions were known only to a few bid officials; to shift the discussion from the well-documented actions of Salt Lake bid officials by noting that corruption did not originate with Salt Lake City's bid (without identifying other offending bid cities); and to shift the focus from past misdeeds to the future by asserting that Salt Lake City would be remembered for ending a bad system.

Governor Leavitt's statement, during the press conference announcing the resignation of two SLOC officials, illustrates the elements of this strategy:

It must be made absolutely clear that the actions of a few do not reflect the values, moral expectations, or standards of behavior of this community and state. We deplore it, and revolt at being associated with them. . . . The Olympics have been a shining light, but there is a sinister and dark corner of corruption. This culture of corruption has taken root because of a lack of accountability. . . . This corner of Olympic corruption did not begin in Salt Lake City. But let it end here. (Leavitt 1999)

The SLOC restructuring plan expanded the size of the board of trustees and replaced the executive committee with a twenty-member management committee (SLOC 1999). Governor Leavitt, who had previously expressed the view that board membership should be limited to people with sufficient business experience to manage the games properly, proposed that the size of the board be expanded to allow for greater diversity. Despite the newfound interest in diversity, the selection of members to the management committee ensured that key players in the city's growth elite were still in positions of power. Members of the new management committee included the mayor of Salt Lake City, the governor, one member of the state legislature, the CEOs of a major utility and a major bank, and the president of a large real estate firm. The reorganized committee was still dominated by pro-growth business people, but in response to the scandal, several political leaders were added. In addition, the board of trustees adopted new rules that encouraged board meetings to be held in public, established an attendance policy for board members, and created a new ethics policy for all members of the SLOC.

Reorganization of the SLOC was an important step toward reform. Even more crucial to the strategy for managing the Olympic scandal was a change in personnel. SLOC chairman Robert Garff spoke publicly of the need for a "white knight" to head the scandal-damaged organization. The governor's preferred candidate was W. Mitt Romney. Romney, a successful Boston businessman specializing in corporate turnarounds, had family ties to Utah and was an alumnus of Brigham Young University. Romney's appointment as president of the SLOC drew some criticism both because the governor essentially handpicked Romney and because the selection was seen as yet another example of the white, male, Mormon elite choosing one of their own with little consideration of other candidates. Despite the criticism, Romney's enthusiasm for the job, his engaging and forthright manner, and his attention to the concerns of Olympic supporters and skeptics alike helped him assume the leadership role with minimal difficulty. Romney moved quickly to appoint a former business associate, Fraser Bullock, as vice president and chief financial officer.

One task facing the new management of the SLOC was to adapt the budget to the postscandal realities. Under Frank Joklik's leadership, the arduous task of developing a budget from the ground up, totaling $1.45 billion, had been completed (SLOC 1998). That budget, however, depended on future corporate sponsorship that might not be realized in the postscandal era. Within months of taking their positions, Romney and Bullock announced that the budget had been trimmed $123 million to a total of $1.33 billion. Even with the budget reductions, however, the organizing committee needed to raise more than $100 million only two years before the 2002 games. Despite a vigorous campaign to secure sponsors, the negative connotations of the scandal clearly made the Olympic brand more difficult to sell to image-conscious corporations (e.g., Copetas 1999).

The scandal-induced budget tightening aggravated points of contention between the organizing committee and government entities. A common concern of officials in venue cities was the amount of money the SLOC had budgeted to pay for increased city services, such as garbage collection and fire protection, resulting from Olympic events (Fowler 1999). Although cities and counties anticipate increased tax revenues from the Olympics, these revenues would come in only after local governments had incurred real costs to prepare for the games. According to Salt Lake City's preliminary Olympics master plan, the city might need as much as $23 million in extra Olympic-related services but would receive only about $5.6 million in additional tax revenues from the games (Governor's Office of Planning and Budget 1998b, 3). When officials from venue cities realized the limited prospects of getting help from the organizing committee, they turned to the state legislature. The legislature agreed to divert $13 million from taxes on Olympic ticket sales to defray the costs of Olympic-related services in venue communities (Spangler 2000). Salt Lake City officials subsequently scaled down their proposed Olympic-related expenditures, and a revised master plan put city spending at only about $9 million (Edwards 2000).

For their part, Olympic organizers worried that requests from state and local officials, invoking the Olympics as justification, would threaten federal funding the SLOC considered essential. In the years preceding the games, state and local officials used the Olympics unsparingly to attract more federal funds. For example, Utah officials composed a $300 million "wish list" for transportation projects alone. The state received more than $120 million in discretionary funds from the U.S. Department of Transportation for the 1999 and 2000 fiscal years, in part because of language added to federal law specifying assistance for Olympic cities (*Transportation Equity Act* 1998). Yet the bulk of these discretionary funds went for reconstruction of the interstate highway. Olympic officials worried that funding these big-ticket items would mean insufficient money for more mundane but essential projects such as access roads and park-and-ride lots. As SLOC trustee Spencer Eccles put it: "The bid was never made to expand the airport, the freeways, or to build light rail. What was necessary were roads [at] Snowbasin, the Utah Winter Sports Park, [and] Soldier Hollow" (Gorrell 1999, B-1).

Despite the negative publicity from the scandal and the ensuing concern with cost, public support for holding the games never wavered substantially. Polls conducted in Utah after the scandal showed a slight decrease in the number of people who strongly supported hosting the Olympics, but overall the pattern of support remained similar to the prescandal period (see Table 6.2). The public did regard the actions of the Olympic bid committee as harmful to the city's image; fully 78 percent agreed that the scandal had "tainted" Salt Lake City and Utah, but that did not diminish the desire of most Utahns to host the games.[10]

Nor were people in Utah unique in their response to the scandal. In a nationwide Gallup poll conducted after the scandal, only 8 percent of respondents said their respect for the Olympics had declined a lot, while 42 percent said their respect for the Olympics had not declined at all. A substantial majority did see the need for reform. Fully 77 percent felt that the IOC and local Olympic committees should be required to open their records to public scrutiny.[11] Internationally, the bribery scandal did not appear to dampen interest in viewing the games. According to data from seven nations collected by the IOC, the percentage of people with at least some interest in viewing the games on television did not decline between 1998 and 1999 (L. Roche 1999). Despite media stories on extravagant gifts to IOC members, expulsions from the IOC, and tawdry business dealings in the Olympic family, the Olympic image still holds tremendous appeal for the public generally.

■ Conclusion: Fulfilling the Olympic Dream?

Judgments about the success of Salt Lake City's Olympics hinge on how the goals of hosting the games are defined. From the perspective of the host city, the success of the games should not be judged by whether the organizing committee finishes in the black financially. Even though it may add up to a prodigious amount, the budget kept by the organizing committee does not capture important aspects of the political and economic costs and benefits of the Olympics. Adopting a broader perspective, Olympic proponents in Salt Lake City have articulated two general claims that might serve as criteria for success: that the Olympics would be an engine for local economic development; and that hosting the games would improve the city's image, making it more attractive for business and tourism.

Salt Lake's pursuit of the winter games originated with a desire to promote the local ski industry. When the idea of bidding for the games was revived in the 1980s, proponents spoke both of a desire to establish Salt Lake City as the "winter sports capital" and—at a time when the state's economy was struggling—of the substantial economic benefits that would accrue. As an engine of future economic growth, Olympic-driven development encompassed two distinct goals. One was to create an infrastructure of winter sports facilities that would directly benefit elite athletes and, less clearly, the general public. The referendum campaign, which endorsed spending tax money on a ski jump, bobsled track, and speed-skating oval even before the city won the games, was the centerpiece of this investment strategy. A second goal, less publicly articulated, was to leverage the Olympics as a means to subsidize local development projects. The primary sources of external subsidy were corporations, through their Olympic sponsorships, and the federal government. Federal money has been used to subsidize highway reconstruction, mass transit, and access roads to sporting venues (U.S. General Accounting Office 1999, 2000). Funds from the SLOC have paid modest amounts toward university housing, expansion of a football stadium, and improvements to public sports facilities.

It is too soon to tell whether investments in such development projects will pay future dividends. Clearly, the ability to attract external funds to help pay for activities like rebuilding highways is highly advantageous from the perspective of state and local governments.

The use of federal money for other projects, such as building another road to a private ski resort, appears to provide future benefits to resort owners more than the general public. Similarly, developments with little economic appeal outside of the Olympics, such as a speed-skating oval or bobsled track, are not clearly advantageous. Even with the promised $40 million legacy fund to help maintain such venues, it is not evident that such facilities will ever be economically self-sustaining. Paying tax money to assist the training of elite athletes, though beneficial to the USOC, is an unlikely path to future economic growth.

Of course, there are benefits to government from hosting the Olympics. In Utah, the net tax revenue from the games has been conservatively estimated to be between $80 and $140 million (Governor's Office of Planning and Budget 1998a, 15). The games are not, however, an economic panacea for the host city. Because of the way tax revenues are distributed within the state, Salt Lake City is estimated to get only 6.5 percent of these revenues, even though it is the locus of much Olympic activity and will bear the costs of these activities (Governor's Office of Planning and Budget 1998b, 3). Given the city's investments in Olympic bids and the costs associated with planning and providing services, holding the games appears to be a money-losing proposition for city taxpayers.

What of that other goal of holding the Olympics—improving the city's image? There is little doubt that hosting the Olympics will raise the city's international profile. For a city attempting to make a name for itself as a tourist destination, staging the 2002 winter games is a boon. Yet, as the Olympic bribery story illustrates, image creation is an undertaking fraught with uncertainty. One reason the media found the Olympic scandal to be such an appealing story was that the connotations associated with bribery clashed vividly with the image of the Olympics and of Salt Lake City. Again, it is too early to tell what lasting image will result from the Salt Lake City Olympics internationally or even locally. Although the citizens of Utah continued to support holding the games in Salt Lake City in the aftermath of the scandal, they might not follow the same path again, given the chance. In response to a question asked a year after the scandal, a majority of respondents, 53 percent, said they would not have supported seeking the Olympics if they had known the outcome.[12]

■ Notes

1. Based on survey data from Dan Jones and Associates conducted for KSL Television and the *Deseret News*. In 1999, 34 percent of Salt Lake voters identified themselves as Democrats, 32 percent Republicans, and 32 percent independents. Within Salt Lake City, independent identifiers usually favor Democratic candidates, thus giving Democrats an edge in city elections.

2. Among the twenty-five members of the Utah Winter Games Feasibility Committee in 1985, eleven had ties to major ski resorts or the ski industry association, Ski Utah. Six other members represented various levels of government, including the U.S. Forest Service, the governor's and mayor's offices, and other local government officials. Except for the executive director of the Salt Lake Area Chamber of Commerce, the committee lacked strong representation from downtown businesses. Office space was provided by state government, but most of the financial support appears to have come from the ski industry.

3. This change was adopted by the USOC in June 1989, when Salt Lake City was chosen as the U.S. candidate for the 1998 and 2002 winter games. This new rule, known as the "eighteen-month rule," stipulated that a city chosen by the USOC must begin construction on specific venues within eighteen months of being selected. Since the IOC's decision for the 1998 games would not be made until June 1991, this rule required that Salt Lake City start construction at least six months before knowing the outcome of the IOC process.

4. The arguments for and against public funding were compiled from news reports, editorials, advertisements, and press releases. Jardine (1989) is a good example of the pro-funding argument. Examples of the arguments against public funding include Dick (1989) and Kelner (1989).

5. An interlocal agreement between the State of Utah, Salt Lake City, and the Salt Lake Olympic Bid Committee was signed in May 1991, before the IOC decision on the site for the 1998 winter games. One of the key points of the agreement was that the state would indemnify the city against financial loss or liability (Fowler 1999). It was not certain, however, whether the state's agreement to indemnify the city from loss incurred by a private organizing committee would be binding because the Utah Constitution prohibits the state from lending credit to any "private individual or corporate enterprise or undertaking." When the question of the constitutionality of the agreement reemerged during the bribery scandal, Governor Leavitt publicly stated that the state was "morally" obligated to protect the city from debt. A later deal between the venue cities and the state, however, limited the indemnification. When the venue cities asked the 2000 legislature for financial help with games-related costs, the legislature approved the money under the conditions that venue communities could not impose additional fees for Olympic services and that Salt Lake City waive any claims for reimbursement from the state for the costs of extra city services (Spangler 2000).

6. The Utah Sports Authority and the Utah Sports Advisory Committee originally had fifteen members each. The composition of both groups was amended in 1999 to add positions for active athletes (Utah Code 1999, 63A-7-104 and 111). The amendments also established a legislative oversight board called the Olympic Coordinating Committee (Utah Code 1999, 63A-10-109).

7. The Paralympics are an elite, international sports competition for athletes with disabilities. Since the 1988 summer games and the 1992 winter games, the Paralympics have been staged in the Olympic city, immediately after the Olympic competition. The process of bidding for and staging the Olympic games now includes hosting the Paralympics as well.

8. The Justice Department investigation resulted in federal tax convictions against a local businessman, David Simmons, and a former USOC official, Alfredo LaMont. The investigation also led to federal fraud and conspiracy charges against two former SLOC officials, Thomas Welch and David Johnson (Roche and Camporreales 2000).

9. The SLOC ethics panel had been created in 1997 to revise the SLOC code of ethics and create a policy to avoid conflicts of interest in business dealings. The members of the committee served as volunteers and operated independently of the management or trustees of the SLOC. The five members who reviewed evidence and wrote the report were: Gordon R. Hall, retired chief justice of the Utah Supreme Court; Dean Patricia Hanna, University of Utah; David J. Jordan, partner in a law firm; Professor Barbara Day Lockhart, Brigham Young University; and Merrill R. Norman, a CPA and senior partner in a consulting firm.

10. The wording for this question was: "In your opinion, have the allegations tainted Salt Lake City and Utah in the national and international community?" The 78 percent agreement combines those respondents who said "definitely" (55 percent) and "probably" (23 percent). These data are from a statewide poll of 423 Utahns conducted in January 1999 by Dan Jones and Associates for KSL/*Deseret News*. Data provided courtesy of Dan Jones.

11. The questions were: "As a result of the controversy has your respect for the Olympics—declined a lot, declined a fair amount, declined only a little, or not declined at all?" and "Should the International Olympic Committee and local Olympic organizing and bid committees be required to open their financial records to government and public scrutiny, or not?" These data are from a national telephone sample of 1,013 adult Americans conducted February 26–28, 1999, by the Gallup Organization. Data provided by the Roper Center for Public Opinion Research.

12. From a Dan Jones and Associates poll conducted in December 1999 for KSL/*Deseret News*. The survey was a statewide sample of 405 residents. The question was: "If you knew in 1989 what you know now, would you have favored or opposed seeking the Winter Games?" The 53 percent opposed comes from those respondents who said "probably oppose" (21 percent) and "definitely oppose" (32 percent).

■■ 7 ■■

READING
THE OLYMPIC GAMES

With the worldwide media attention, visiting dignitaries, and the rhetoric of "welcoming the world" and staging the "best games ever," it is easy for city leaders to get caught up in the grand images of an Olympic dream. As the experiences of Los Angeles, Atlanta, and Salt Lake City show, however, the realities of governing urban America make the materialization of Olympic dreams anything but a straightforward proposition. The Olympic games can be an exciting spectacle, but are they good public policy for the cities that host them? That question is at the heart of our concerns, and in this chapter we draw upon the experiences of our three Olympic cities to assess the broader meaning of urban mega-events as public policy.

■ Assessing the Olympics as Urban Mega-event

U.S. cities have come to put greater emphasis on consumption-based development. As public policy, the activities that constitute this form of economic development, such as building convention centers, sports facilities, and entertainment complexes, indicate how globalization and changes in federal policy permeate cities and how cities respond to these changes. Yet the sameness of these urban experiences means that city leaders must rely on place marketing to project a unique image that will bring visitors and investors to their city. As cities seek to differentiate themselves, the Olympic games offer a golden opportunity for city leaders to pursue a growth-oriented policy agenda. Efforts to attract mega-events are thus part of a deliberate strategy to promote local development, and the Olympics have become the preferred mega-event for American cities because of their positive imagery, media attention, and ability to attract corporate sponsorship. As the mega-event strategy unfolds, it generates questions about the future essence of the host city. Although this debate is often couched in terms of economic benefits or city image, a much more important issue must be resolved: Whose city is it?

As we have seen in Los Angeles, Atlanta, Salt Lake City—and indeed would expect to see in any prospective host city—the issue of whose city it is becomes ultimately a struggle over public control and integrity in policymaking. This debate centers on the responsiveness and accountability of local government to a variety of global and local forces. Mega-events, once incorporated into a city's policy agenda, can have a decade-long impact on public policy. In the opening chapter, we identified a series of questions to guide our exploration of the Olympics as an urban mega-event. Having examined the experiences of each of our cities in detail, we return to those questions to summarize our findings and discuss their broader meaning.

▓ How and Why Do Cities Seek to Host Mega-events?

Even though the specifics of launching an Olympic bid differed in each city, the broader pattern that emerged from all three cities was quite clear: Olympic bids are initiated and sustained by elements of the city's growth regime. Indeed, an Olympic bid committee can be seen as a tangible manifestation of a city's growth regime. An Olympic bid does not involve all the individuals who may be part of the informal governing structure of a city, but it does illustrate in a concrete fashion how business resources and governmental authority come together to undertake a policy initiative.

In Los Angeles, the bid for the 1984 games was initiated by a group of downtown business leaders and civic notables. This group, operating through the Southern California Committee for the Olympic Games, raised private funds to finance the bid activities up to selection by the USOC. With these private resources in place, members of SCCOG sought the endorsement of elected officials, including the Los Angeles mayor and city council. Atlanta, unlike LA, did not have an existing organization in place to serve as a vehicle for an Olympic bid. Much of the early work was done by a small group headed by Billy Payne, who became the city's chief Olympic entre-preneur. Payne and his supporters worked to convince key corporate and government leaders to support an Olympic bid. By winning the support of influential corporate executives, lawyers, and elected of-ficials, Atlanta's bid committee was transformed from a fledgling ef-fort into a serious contender. Salt Lake City's bid for the 1998 and 2002 games was formally initiated by the mayor's office and brought together an array of local business leaders and key government offi-cials from Salt Lake City and the surrounding region. In practical terms, however, the bid organization was run by a small group of Olympic entrepreneurs and local business people, with resources supplied by corporate contributions.

Within urban regime theory, there is a well-established expecta-tion that the interests of business will dominate in the policy initia-tives undertaken. Certainly, we found that to be true for the Olympic bids in these cities. In each city, the bid process was funded and con-trolled by representatives of local businesses. According to the pro-cedures outlined by the USOC and the IOC, city governments are formally the entities that bid for the Olympic games. Public officials, however, played only a supporting role in the bid process. The task of elected officials, generally speaking, was to lend an air of govern-mental authority to a process conducted by the city's business inter-ests. Political leaders were involved in varying degrees in each city; yet none of the bid committees or organizing committees could be described as being controlled by public officials. In Los Angeles, for example, the city government's primary concern during negotiations with the IOC was keeping the city financially removed from the games. Despite the presence of former mayor Andrew Young in the Atlanta bid organization, the city played only a minor part in the ac-tivities required to bring the games to Atlanta. In contrast, the mayor of Salt Lake City spoke publicly of the need for city officials to be in control of any bid. As the process unfolded, however, it quickly be-came clear that the presence of local government officials on the bid committee did not mean they were in charge. The case of Salt Lake City illustrates that even if city officials want to, they may not be able to exercise control over an Olympic bid bearing the city's name.

The public reasons given for pursuing the Olympics were strik-ingly similar in each city. In general, Olympic supporters articulated two justifications for going after the games: the city would attract a substantial number of new visitors during the games, which would

generate more revenue for tourism businesses and more tax revenue
for government; and the city would enhance its visibility or prestige
by association with the Olympics. These twin justifications under-
score both the importance of the consumption-oriented development
taking place in U.S. cities and the corresponding need for place marketing. The appeal of tourist dollars is self-evident. Tourist spending
directly benefits businesses providing services, and local governments can capture tax revenues from visitors. Despite their obvious
appeal, mega-events by definition occur for only a short period of
time. As such, the new revenue generated by the event itself would
scarcely warrant the spending required to host the event. Thus the
mega-event is not a viable path to economic growth for cities without the promise of intangible benefits from an enhanced city image.

The prestige of the Olympics has a natural appeal for cities
seeking to craft their image as an exciting, vibrant, and international
place to visit, do business, or live. In Los Angeles, Olympic boosters
spoke of using the games to display the attractions of Los Angeles
on a global stage and of the "intangibles" that would enhance the
city's position in society. Similarly, Atlanta's boosters saw the
Olympics as a vehicle for moving their city from a convention work-
horse to a more exalted "world-class" status. In Salt Lake City, business and political leaders spoke repeatedly of the intangible value of
hosting the games. People in the ski business saw the games as a
way to best their rivals in neighboring Colorado, but political leaders
spoke more broadly of raising city and state visibility both nationally and internationally.

In sum, American cities seek out a mega-event such as the
Olympics when a city has an established growth regime in place and
when members of that business-government coalition endorse the
goal of using the event to embellish the city's image. The symbolic
appeal of the event is critically important because justification for
the event cannot rest solely on its narrow economic benefits. Members of the regime, whether elected officials or business leaders, can
use the positive view that residents and corporate sponsors alike
hold of the Olympics to build widespread support for the premise of
the mega-event strategy. In this sense, city leaders are functioning as
a "symbolic regime" seeking to change the city's image through the
"manipulation of symbols which express the rightness of the cause and
its attractiveness" (Stoker and Mossberger 1994, 209). The Olympics
can be a powerful symbol of international sport, competitiveness, and

world-class standing that helps to unify the various elements of a city behind this particular development endeavor. Once the city has actually won the right to host the games, this symbolic consensus may break down in the scramble to gain the benefits or avoid the costs of Olympic-driven development. By that point, however, the mega-event agenda is already established, and the critical issues of access, representation, responsiveness, and accountability are more difficult to confront.

Largely left out of these strategic calculations, of course, are city residents. Mega-events can serve to orient a host city toward tourism and global business, at least symbolically, but they also establish a pattern of treating the city as a commodity. If cities are to be reimaged into the fantasies of tourists and business executives, what happens to the people who live there?

How Are Policy Decisions Concerning Mega-events Made?

There was no single manner in which policy decisions about each mega-event were made. Yet once again, the broader pattern that emerges from our cities is quite clear. In each case, decisions affecting public policy were made predominantly through the mechanism of a public-private partnership. Although there were examples of conflicting goals and tension within and between the public and private sides, the interests of the private actors within these partnerships tended to prevail overall.

In the United States, the formal responsibilities of preparing for and conducting the Olympic games are in the hands of private, non-profit Olympic organizing committees. Local organizing committees are charged with all aspects of preparation for the conduct of the games themselves, including seeking resources from public and private sources, providing venues for the athletic competition, and catering to the needs of the international media and the extended Olympic family. Although the organizing committee is primarily responsible for the logistics of putting on the games, this is not to say that state and local governments are irrelevant. Only a government entity, a city, can enter into the contractual agreement with the IOC to host the games, and it would be impossible to conduct the games without the cooperation of government officials and the use of public resources. It is true that most of the costs of staging the games in the United States are paid by private businesses, but it is no coincidence that the games are not run by for-profit companies. Without public subsidy, it would not be possible to stage the Olympic games in their present form.

Thus, in the contemporary American context, the task of conducting the Olympic games requires a shared arrangement of responsibilities between public and private actors. Such arrangements have marked advantages for Olympic organizers because they are not subject to the same level of scrutiny that public officials would be. But these arrangements also run the risk of being manipulated—by controlling access, by privileging investors' interests, by separating responsiveness from accountability—for the benefit of Olympic insiders at the expense of the public.

The pattern of the public-private arrangements differed substantially between cities, and the nature of these differences suggest important lessons. The decision-making structure developed in Los Angeles for the 1984 games created a model for other U.S. cities to emulate. This structure, however, was not the product of organizational genius so much as it was of political circumstance. As a result of the legacy of public debt from the Montreal Olympics in 1976 and the uncertainty raised by the Proposition 13 tax limitation movement in California, the overriding concern of public officials in Los Angeles was to limit the city's financial liability for staging the games. In their negotiations with the IOC, the city's representatives forced the IOC to waive its rule requiring the city to be liable for the costs of hosting the games. The games were awarded to LA with the unusual provision that the local organizing committee, the LAOOC, and the USOC would assume financial liability. These circumstances resulted in a set of political arrangements that might best be described as "contractual."

Although formally appointed by the city's mayor, Peter Ueberroth and the members of LAOOC were responsible for conducting what amounted to the first "private" Olympics. Their task was to stage the games in such a way that the costs would be covered by corporate sponsorships. Widespread agreement on this goal among the key players put the LAOOC in a strong position to resist the demands of government officials, neighborhood groups, or local business interests who might have sought to use the games to support an expansive development agenda.

In Los Angeles, government officials endorsed the goal of conducting a "private games" managed by the LAOOC for purposes that pointedly did not include community improvements or support for development initiatives. Public control or oversight of Olympic activities was very limited. But the limited oversight was not problematic since LAOOC's goals were narrowly focused on conducting the games in existing facilities, using corporate resources. The LAOOC pursued these goals while keeping corporate sponsors, local governments, and community groups at "arm's length." In the fragmented local political environment that is Los Angeles, the LAOOC had the advantage of being able to make its own decisions and pursue its own interests without worrying about building political consensus. The LAOOC's chief interest was in promoting the summer games, which became the driving force in the reimaging of Los Angeles as a world-class city.

In Atlanta, however, the organization of the games followed the LA model only in the sense that the Olympic committee was clearly in control. There were potentially three key institutional actors in Atlanta: the private organizing committee (ACOG), the state-created Olympic authority (MAOGA), and the city. Of the three, ACOG was dominant. The political arrangements set out in the Tri-Party agreement meant that neither the city nor the state government had the power to oversee the actions of the organizing committee effectively. Had the goals of ACOG and the city's governing regime been merely to stage the games, the lack of oversight might not have been a problem. Mayor Jackson's vision of scaling the twin peaks of Mount Olympus, by hosting the best games ever and revitalizing downtown Atlanta, linked the summer games to the physical redevelopment of the city. Yet given the political arrangements, ACOG served not only as a vehicle for staging the games, but it also became the most effective organization for pursuing a redevelopment agenda within the city.

Unlike Los Angeles, the goal of using the games to spur both public and private development was widely shared in Atlanta. ACOG's Olympic plans aligned most closely with those of large corporations and important public institutions. Because they fit the desire of both Olympic boosters and regime insiders, projects such as the Olympic Stadium and Centennial Olympic Park were undertaken and completed. ACOG, however, did little to promote the improvement of inner city neighborhoods. The task of trying to leverage the allure of the Olympics to facilitate improvements in neighborhoods was left to the city, which had neither the resources nor the entrepreneurial latitude of ACOG.

In Salt Lake City, the public-private arrangements made more room for public officials than the arrangements in either Los Angeles or Atlanta. The private, nonprofit organizing committee (SLOC) was still chiefly responsible for games preparation, but government officials were more prominent because of the state's commitment of tax dollars during the bid process. When the state legislature agreed to divert sales tax money to be used for the construction of Olympic venues before the city had been awarded the games, it also created a state board to handle the money and a mechanism for legislative oversight and accountability. Although legislative oversight of Olympic activities was never onerous, the public investment did prevent the kind of arm's-length relationship between public and private actors that existed in Los Angeles. An agreement between the bid committee, the mayor of Salt Lake City, and the governor, in which the state indemnified the city from financial loss, meant that the governor played a prominent role in the creation of the Olympic organizing committee once the city was awarded the games. Although there was greater capacity for public oversight in Salt Lake than in either LA or Atlanta, it did not prevent the activities that led to the scandal nor did it mean that public officials controlled the Olympic process. The city's inability to get its preferred location for the medals plaza or to get the SLOC to pay the costs of additional games-related city services illustrates that the private organizing committee could still steer policy outcomes.

Although the nature of the public-private arrangements differed in each city, a common element was that citizens were largely left out of the decision-making process. In general, citizen participation in the process of bidding for or organizing the Olympics is minimal (but for an example of citizen participation in Cape Town's bid for the 2004 games, see Hiller 2000, 449–450). In our cases, the only circumstance that invited citizen participation in Olympic decision-making was the Utah referendum on sales tax money for construction of Olympic venues. The referendum was technically nonbinding, but it did at least encourage citizens to debate the issue and express their preferences on bidding for the Olympics. A 1978 citywide vote in Los Angeles to ensure that no city funding was used for the games paradoxically reduced public accountability during the organizing period. In Atlanta, the issue of public support for the games did not come to the ballot until four years into the Olympic planning process, when voters approved the sale of $150 million in general obligation bonds for improvements in the city's infrastructure.

With the dominance of Olympic proponents over the city's development agenda, the primary forum for citizen participation with respect to the Olympics was piecemeal opposition to specific development projects. The process of bidding for the Olympics may stimulate opposition to the very idea of hosting a mega-event (e.g., Lenskyj 1996), but in none of our cities was there evidence of an organized movement against hosting the games. In part, the lack of opposition speaks to the symbolic power of the Olympics. It is difficult to rally residents against the ideals of international sporting competition. Yet this lack of generalized opposition also reflects the difficulties of taking on an established urban regime (Burbank, Heying, and Andranovich 2000).

What we did find in each city, however, was a pattern of piecemeal resistance against particular Olympic-related developments. In Los Angeles, for example, citizen opposition was generated by an effort to construct athletic venues in the Sepulveda Basin and by developments within Exposition Park. Citizen opposition to the summer games in Los Angeles was not particularly extensive, but it revealed a pattern that would recur in Atlanta and Salt Lake City. When plans for Olympic development encountered opposition from well-organized groups representing economically advantaged residents, such as in Sepulveda Basin, opponents had a good chance of success. On the other hand, when opposition came from residents who were predominately poor, such as in Exposition Park, Olympic developers tended to get their way. A similar pattern was evident in Atlanta, where well-off residents in Blackburn Park got the tennis venue relocated, while opposition to development projects that negatively impacted neighborhoods of poor and minority residents had little success. In Salt Lake City, environmental groups had some success in mitigating the effects of a few proposed Olympic projects, as did middle-class residents who objected to locating a speed-skating oval in their neighborhood. Still, when development plans were of particular importance, Olympic organizers were able to use their superior resources to stymie the actions of opponents.

To conclude, as we have, that Olympic proponents are generally in a stronger position than opponents does not mean that opposition is futile. Opposition can be effective in several ways. First, in all three cities that we observed, there were instances where opponents of various Olympic developments were successful in stopping development or at least mitigating some negative effects. Second, in some cities, well-timed opposition has successfully prevented an Olympic bid from moving forward. One such example occurred in Seattle. In December 1998, a bid committee seeking the 2012 Olympic games for Seattle had to abandon its efforts after it failed to obtain the endorsement of the Seattle City Council (Byrnes 1998a).[1] Finally, in perhaps the most dramatic case, Denver gave up the 1976 winter games after opponents managed to pass statewide and citywide initiatives that effectively prohibited the use of tax money for the games. In sum, though growth regimes can exercise substantial power in pursuit of the mega-event strategy, opponents too can prevail in some circumstances.

▓ What Are the Outcomes of Hosting a Mega-event?

The economic outcomes of the Olympic games tend to be the most highly touted, which is not unexpected given the propensity of civic boosters to equate economic benefits with the public good. Yet the overarching theme we have found is that few of the benefits of being a world-class city—the Olympic dream that helps mobilize public support for hosting the games—directly affect the everyday lives of the host city's residents.

The 1984 games did little to reshape Los Angeles physically, but they had a lasting impact nonetheless. Hosting the Olympics was used to justify a renovation of the airport and a $100 million upgrade in telecommunications infrastructure. But because organizers used existing facilities and venues were spread around southern California, the games did not leave a strong physical legacy. Some new facilities were built, notably a swim stadium, a velodrome, and a new administrative building on the UCLA campus, and some existing facilities were refurbished. But all in all, the spatial impact was minimal. The 1984 games resulted in a banner year for tourism in the city, although the effects across the region were uneven. Perhaps the greatest impact of the games, however, was the image of a successful, "capitalist" Olympics. The tangible evidence of success was a $225 million surplus. This money was shared by the USOC, national sports federations, and the Amateur Athletic Foundation of Los Angeles, but not the City of Los Angeles.

The 1996 Olympic games produced a mixed legacy for Atlanta. Certainly, the preparations for the games by ACOG and local governments boosted spending. Also, to a greater extent than in Los Angeles, the Olympics physically changed parts of the city, most notably with the development of the Olympic Stadium and Centennial Olympic Park. The games also brought the expected influx of tourists, about two million visitors, and the Atlanta region received a substantial economic boost. The games also played a positive role in helping Atlanta land one of six federal empowerment-zone designations. Further, both the state government and the Atlanta Chamber of Commerce have sought to extend the economic legacy of the games by using the Olympics to recruit new businesses and future sporting events.

Still, the Atlanta Olympics also left a legacy of ill will in neighborhoods such as Summerhill that bore the brunt of lost housing and dislocation. The city's efforts to use the Olympics to revitalize urban neighborhoods and create a twenty-four-hour downtown largely fell short. Finally, Atlanta's effort to project the image of a world-class city of the New South met with mixed results. The desire to portray Atlanta as a friendly, progressive city was diluted by negative reports from the international media that focused on transportation problems, the overly commercial look and feel of areas surrounding the venues, and the explosion in Centennial Park. In closing the 1996 Olympics, IOC President Juan Antonio Samaranch did not proclaim the games "the best ever," as is customary, leading to speculation about Atlanta's performance as host and its status as a world-class city.

It is reasonable to expect that the 2002 games will have a positive economic impact because of Olympic-related spending, an influx of tourists, and a net increase in revenues to state and local governments. State and local officials in Utah have already used the games successfully to leverage federal funds for transportation projects that will benefit residents well into the future. Yet given the cost of additional city services and the distribution of state tax revenues, the games may not be an economic panacea for Salt Lake or the other venue cities. Furthermore, the bribery scandal has tarnished the luster of hosting the Olympics, and conflict over Olympic-related projects has aggravated disputes over growth and maintaining the quality of the environment. With questions about the future economic viability of athletic facilities for elite athletes and the lingering effects of the Olympic scandal, the 2002 games are likely to leave a mixed legacy at best for Salt Lake City.

The Olympic dreams of the growth regimes in LA, Atlanta, and Salt Lake City were only partially realized. Certainly, playing host to the Olympic games does bring the spotlight of global media coverage to the host city. But while the decade-long period from bid initiation to the closing ceremonies led to increased infrastructure development and enhanced sports and entertainment facilities in all three cities, the Olympic spectacle has not led to urban regeneration or revitalization.

▨ What Can the Conduct of Mega-events Tell Us About Urban Politics Generally?

We have argued that the process of undertaking the Olympics as an urban mega-event can best be described as a product of an active growth regime. A city's Olympic committees are a tangible manifestation of the concept of a growth coalition. In all three cities, the Olympic committees were composed mostly of local business people and public officials dedicated to seeking economic development. Once the bidding moved from the national to the international level, the composition of the bid team took on a more corporate look in all three cities. Business people dominated the Olympic organizations because they were the most active members, and they provided the resources to sustain the effort, which became more important at the international level.

As Clarence Stone has noted, regimes exist because they provide a way to overcome the weaknesses of city governments; that is, a regime provides "the capacity to assemble and use needed resources for a policy initiative" (1989b, 227). From the evidence in our cases, the existence of a growth regime is vital to an Olympic bid. Without an established business-government network in place to provide a substantial level of resources over an extended period of time, an Olympic bid would simply not occur.

Thus the initiation of the mega-event strategy should be seen as a by-product of regime politics. A mega-event is sought not because it is appealing in a narrow cost-benefit sense, but because the event fits into the larger purpose of an urban regime's desire to promote growth. The existence of a growth regime by itself, however, is not sufficient to start a city down the mega-event path. Another necessary ingredient is a desire among growth elites to establish or modify the city's image. In each city, business leaders and politicians alike referred to the intangible benefits associated with being an "Olympic city" as one of the main reasons for initiating the bid.

Although the roots of the mega-event strategy are firmly planted in regime politics, the evidence from our cases suggests that the nature of mega-event development is not fully captured by the view of urban politics given by regime theory. In response to criticism of the regime concept, Stone (1998) has argued that regimes are important in theoretical terms because they act as an intervening variable between external forces, such as economic trends or federal policy, and local policy outcomes. In Stone's view, the best way to understand the observable variation in local development policy is to incorporate the effect of local political arrangements. While we agree with Stone's assessment of the theoretical utility of the regime concept and have acknowledged the importance of regimes for understanding the mega-event strategy, the view that development policy outcomes are largely determined by actors within the local growth regime does not adequately explain development driven by mega-events. More specifically, in examining how an event influences the local development agenda, it is evident that once the mega-event has been secured, many key decisions are outside of local control.

Once the mega-event has been obtained and the planning process is under way, its success depends less on players in the regime and more on external actors. In all three cities, the success of the Olympic mega-event as a mechanism for local development was heavily dependent on nonlocal actors, ranging from multinational corporate sponsors to nonprofit organizations such as the USOC and the IOC. And the magnitude of the Olympic event required substantial coordination between the host city and other governments in the region that served as hosts for particular venues. Each city was also highly dependent on the state and federal governments either for resources or authority. Thus the appeal of an event such as the Olympic games is that it can attract nonlocal resources, such as corporate sponsorship or federal money, to subsidize local development projects. But this approach means that the goals of local development are subject to the decisions and conditions of external actors. One of the outcomes of the Olympics as a vehicle for economic development is that the ability of local leaders to deliver tangible benefits becomes highly dependent on the actions of regime outsiders.

In theoretical terms, the evidence from these cities suggests the need to broaden the spatial scale as well as deepen the understanding of linkages between political actors, in order to provide a more complete explanation of urban politics as cities increasingly compete for consumption-oriented business in the global economy. The variety of intergovernmental and intersectoral relations that are built into the structure of the mega-event strategy highlights the need for regime theory to integrate the complexity of interdependence into analyses of the political arrangements of cities. The capabilities of city leaders to negotiate satisfactory terms for the host city, to maintain alliances over an extended time period, to engage in boundary-spanning activities to influence private and third-sector decisions, and to obtain resources from state or federal officials must play a more prominent role in explaining urban outcomes. Questions of access, representation, responsiveness, and accountability must be addressed as well, to better understand under whose rules the game is being played. Furthermore, if the competition for hosting mega-events becomes riskier or more costly or both, then we would expect to see multicity bids in order to spread the risk or cost more widely. Developing a better understanding of how regimes operate and how mega-event policy can be used to achieve certain political, economic, and social ends may also permit the public or community-based organizations to exert some control over the local economic development process.

■ Conclusion

In this postfederal era, U.S. cities will undoubtedly continue to be concerned with place marketing, city image, and long-term strategies for subsidizing their development as consumption locations. As such, the allure of hosting a mega-event will remain.[2] The symbolic value of the Olympics will continue to allow the advocates of growth to set the terms of the policy debate in cities. These terms have been narrowly defined around the goals of consumption-oriented economic development—the Olympic dream of a growth regime. As a public policy instrument that has a decade-long planning horizon and no broad public-participation requirement, the Olympic mega-event provides an opportunity for development interests to make their vision the local policy agenda. The experiences of Los Angeles, Atlanta, and Salt Lake City indicate that, despite the rhetoric, the materialization of Olympic dreams serves only narrow purposes. Without change, the long time frame needed for planning, the use of public-private partnerships to design and implement Olympic development, and the absence of meaningful citizen participation add up to an extended business-as-usual theme under the rhetoric and symbolism of Olympic dreams.

■ Notes

1. Olympic bid proponents did not give up without a fight. After the Seattle City Council first refused to vote on a resolution of support for the bid in October, bid proponents used their political connections to try to circumvent the city council by seeking a governmental endorsement of the bid from the Puget Sound Regional Council, a voluntary planning organization composed of various governmental bodies (Byrnes 1998b). This end run was stopped when the regional council agreed to consider the matter only under the conditions that the Seattle City Council endorse the idea and that the USOC approve. When neither condition could be met, the regional council declined to proceed, and the Seattle bid committee voted to disband.

2. Nine cities are competing to be America's choice to host the 2012 summer games: Cincinnati, Dallas, Houston, Los Angeles, New York City, San Francisco, Tampa, and a combined bid from the cities of Baltimore and Washington, D.C. (Wanninger 1998).

■■ ACRONYMS ■■

ACOG	Atlanta Committee for the Olympic Games
AEDC	Atlanta Economic Development Commission
AHA	Atlanta Housing Authority
ANUFF	Atlanta Neighborhoods United for Fairness
AOC	Atlanta Organizing Committee
ARCO	Atlantic Richfield Company
CDA	Community Development Association (LA)
CDBG	Community Development Block Grant
CODA	Corporation for Olympic Development in Atlanta
GAAF	Georgia Amateur Athletic Foundation
GWCC	Georgia World Congress Center
IOC	International Olympic Committee
LAOOC	Los Angeles Olympic Organizing Committee
LDS	Church of Jesus Christ of Latter-Day Saints
MAOGA	Metropolitan Atlanta Olympic Games Authority
OUI	Olympics for Utah, Incorporated
SCCOG	Southern California Committee for the Olympic Games
SLOC	Salt Lake Olympic Organizing Committee
SNI	Summerhill Neighborhood Inc.
UAF	Utah Athletic Foundation
URPS	Utahns for Responsible Public Spending
USA	Utah Sports Authority
USAC	Utah Sports Advisory Committee
USOC	United States Olympic Committee
UTA	Utah Transit Authority

■■ REFERENCES ■■

Abrahamson, Alan, and David Wharton. 2000. Inside IOC's books: A tangled web of wealth, mystery. *Los Angeles Times,* July 23, I-1.

Allen, Frederick. 1996. *Atlanta rising: The invention of an international city, 1946–1996.* Marietta, GA: Longstreet Press.

Anderson, Martin. 1964. *The federal bulldozer: A critical analysis of urban renewal.* Cambridge: MIT Press.

Andranovich, Greg, and Gerry Riposa. 1993. *Doing urban research.* Newbury Park, CA: Sage.

———. 1998. Is governance the lost hard "g" in Los Angeles? *Cities* 15 (3): 185–192.

ANUF is too much. 1990. *Atlanta Journal Constitution,* November 30, A-18.

Appadurai, Arjun. 1990. Disjuncture and difference in the global cultural economy. *Theory, Culture, and Society* 7 (2): 295–310.

Argue, John. 1985. Interview by Kenneth Reich, March 19. Transcript available at the Amateur Athletic Foundation of Los Angeles, Paul Ziffren Sports Resource Center.

Atlanta Committee for the Olympic Games (ACOG). 1997. *Official report of the Centennial Olympic games.* Vol. 1, *Planning and organizing.* Atlanta, GA: Peachtree Publishers.

Atlanta neighborhoods need CODA successor. 1996. *Atlanta Journal Constitution,* December 23, A-10.

Atlanta Organizing Committee (AOC). 1990. *Atlanta: A city of dreams.* Vol. 2, *Atlanta's official bid for the 1996 Olympic games.* Atlanta: AOC.

Autman, Samuel A. 1994. Debate on Olympic bid denied kids. *Salt Lake Tribune,* October 14, B-1.

Baade, Robert A. 1996. Professional sports as catalysts for metropolitan economic development. *Journal of Urban Affairs* 18 (1): 1–17.

Baade, Robert A., and Allen R. Sanderson. 1997. The employment effect of teams and sports facilities. In *Sports, jobs and taxes,* ed. Roger G. Noll and Andrew Zimbalist, 92–118. Washington, D.C.: Brookings Institution.

Baim, Dean V. 1994. *The sports stadium as a municipal investment.* Westport, CT: Greenwood Press.

Baker, Erwin. 1977. City council votes to bid for 1984 Olympics. *Los Angeles Times,* May 13, III-10.

Barker, Norman. 1984. Whole community will reap lasting benefits. *Los Angeles Times,* July 22, V-3.

Barnekov, Timothy K., Daniel Rich, and Robert Warren. 1981. The new privatism, federalism, and the future of urban governance: National urban policy in the 1980s. *Journal of Urban Affairs* 3 (4): 1–14.

Barnes, William R., and Larry C. Ledebur. 1998. *The new regional economies: The U.S. common market and the global economy.* Thousand Oaks, CA: Sage.

Beattie, Lane. 2000. *Annual report of the state Olympic officer relating to the state budget impacts of the 2002 Olympic winter games.* Salt Lake City: State of Utah.

Belcher, Jerry. 1978. LA's '32 Olympics—bright days amid dark times. *Los Angeles Times,* May 21, II-1.

Berman, Marshall. 1982. *All that is solid melts into air: The experience of modernity.* New York: Simon and Schuster.

Blackmon, Douglas A. 1994. Mayor mounts big push before vote. *Atlanta Journal Constitution,* July 17, B-7.

Blackmon, Douglas A., and David Pendered. 1994. Mayor vows new push for bond vote. *Atlanta Journal Constitution,* March 9, A-1.

Booker, Lorri Denise, and Cynthia Durcanin. 1990. Leery advocates worry city's poor neighborhoods will be 1996's big losers. *Atlanta Journal Constitution,* September 23, R-22.

Boorstin, Daniel J. 1965. *The Americans: The national experience.* New York: Vintage.

———. 1971. *The image: A guide to pseudo-events in America.* New York: Atheneum.

Boyarsky, Bill. 1983. Raiders add new element to coliseum neighborhood. *Los Angeles Times,* January 24, I-1.

———. 1984. Arcadia expects to take Olympic events in stride. *Los Angeles Times,* March 12, II-1.

Boyer, M. Christine. 1992. Cities for sale: Merchandising history at South Street Seaport. In *Variations on a theme park: The new American city and the end of public space,* ed. Michael Sorkin. New York: Noonday Press.

Bradley, Thomas. 1985. Interview by Kenneth Reich, May 9. Transcript available at the Amateur Athletic Foundation of Los Angeles, Paul Ziffren Sports Resource Center.

Burbank, Matthew J., Charles H. Heying, and Greg Andranovich. 2000. Antigrowth politics or piecemeal resistance? Citizen opposition to Olympic-related economic growth. *Urban Affairs Review* 35 (3): 334–357.

Byrnes, Susan. 1998a. Defeat accepted on Olympics bid. *Seattle Times,* December 17, B-2.

———. 1998b. Resolution could kill Olympic bid—city may not back regional council. *Seattle Times,* December 3, B-3.

Calleia, Anton. 1985. Interview by Kenneth Reich, April 23. Transcript available at the Amateur Athletic Foundation of Los Angeles, Paul Ziffren Sports Resource Center.

Campbell, Colin. 1999a. He's affable, but he's still wrong. *Atlanta Journal Constitution,* February 25, A-8.

———. 1999b. King and Spalding finally reveals its Olympic earnings. *Atlanta Journal Constitution,* August 26, F-1.

Caraley, Demetrios. 1992. Washington abandons the cities. *Political Science Quarterly* 107 (1): 1–30.

Char, Sudhanva, and Bob Holmes. 1995. The 1996 Atlanta summer Olympics and their impact on African-Americans. In *The Status of Black Atlanta 1995,* ed. Bob Holmes, 39–66. Atlanta, GA: Southern Center for Studies in Public Policy, Clark Atlanta University.

Clark, Terry N., and Edward G. Goetz. 1994. The antigrowth machine: Can city governments control, limit, or manage growth? In *Urban innovation,* ed. Terry N. Clark, 105–145. Thousand Oaks, CA: Sage.

Clarke, Susan E., and Gary L. Gaile. 1992. The next wave: Postfederal local economic development strategies. *Economic Development Quarterly* 6 (2): 187–198.

———. 1998. *The work of cities.* Minneapolis: University of Minnesota Press.

Clayton, Janet. 1981. Olympics stirring fear in south central. *Los Angeles Times,* September 13, II-1.

Cochrane, Allan, Jamie Peck, and Adam Tickell. 1996. Manchester plays games: Exploring the local politics of globalization. *Urban Studies* 33 (8): 1319–1336.

Copetas, A. Craig. 1999. IOC pays high price to look good—way too high, critics say. *Salt Lake Tribune,* December 10, A-1.

Danielson, Michael N. 1997. *Home team: Professional sports and the American metropolis.* Princeton: Princeton University Press.

Davis, Mike. 1987. *Chinatown,* part two? The "internationalization" of downtown Los Angeles. *New Left Review* 164 (July-August): 65–86.

———. 1990. *City of quartz.* New York: Verso.

DeFrantz, Anita. 1988. The long term impact of the LA Olympics. In *Hosting the Olympics: The long term impact,* Report of the 1988 Seoul International Conference, 55–62. Cambridge: MIT Press.

DeLeon, Richard E. 1992. *Left coast city: Progressive politics in San Francisco, 1975–1991.* Lawrence: University Press of Kansas.

Dick, Gale. 1989. Some things voters should know. *Utah Holiday,* October 19, 8.

Dickerson, Jeff. 1991. If Techwood's a cesspool, why haven't we helped? *Atlanta Journal Constitution,* March 22, A-14.

Dolan, Maura. 1984a. A wrinkle in the Olympic welcome mat. *Los Angeles Times,* February 12, I-3.

———. 1984b. Being hosts pleases some, appalls others. *Los Angeles Times,* February 12, I-3.

Dommel, Paul R. 1979. Block grants for community development: Decentralized decisionmaking. In *Fiscal crisis in American cities: The federal response,* ed. L. Kenneth Hubbell, 229–255. Cambridge, MA: Ballinger.

Doyle, Don H. 1990. *New men, new cities, new South: Atlanta, Nashville, Charleston, Mobile, 1860–1910.* Chapel Hill: University of North Carolina Press.

Dunning, Eric. 1999. *Sport matters: Sociological studies of sport, violence, and civilization.* New York: Routledge.

Dyreson, Mark. 1998. *Making the American team: Sport, culture, and the Olympic experience.* Urbana: University of Illinois Press.

Economic Research Associates. 1984. *Community economic impact of the 1984 Olympic games in Los Angeles and southern California.* Los Angeles: ERA.

———. 1986. *Executive summary: Community economic impact of the 1984 Olympic games in Los Angeles and southern California.* Updated June 1986. Los Angeles: ERA.

Edwards, Alan. 2000. S.L. to reap some gold? *Deseret News,* September 9, B-1.

Eisinger, Peter K. 1988. *The rise of the entrepreneurial state: State and local economic development policy in the United States.* Madison: University of Wisconsin Press.

———. 2000. The politics of bread and circuses: Building the city for the visitor class. *Urban Affairs Review* 35 (3): 316–333.

Elkin, Stephen L. 1987. *City and regime in the American republic.* Chicago: University of Chicago Press.

Erie, Steven P. 1992. How the urban West was won: The local state and economic growth in Los Angeles, 1880–1932. *Urban Affairs Quarterly* 27 (4): 519–554.

Erikson, Robert S., Gerald C. Wright, and John P. McIver. 1993. *Statehouse democracy: Public opinion and policy in the American states.* New York: Cambridge University Press.

Espy, Richard. 1979. *The politics of the Olympic games.* Berkeley: University of California Press.

Essex, Stephen, and Brian Chalkley. 1998. Olympic games: Catalyst of urban change. *Leisure Studies* 17 (3): 17–206.

Euchner, Charles C. 1993. *Playing the field: Why sports teams move and cities fight to keep them.* Baltimore: Johns Hopkins University Press.

———. 1999. Tourism and sports: The serious competition for play. In *The tourist city,* ed. Dennis R. Judd and Susan S. Fainstein, 215–232. New Haven: Yale University Press.

Evensen, Jay. 1989. Olympic boosters at odds over public money. *Deseret News,* January 11, B-3.

———. 1998. Samaranch deserves blame in bid scandal, too. *Deseret News,* December 13, AA-1.

Fainstein, Susan S. 1990. The changing world economy and urban restructuring. In *Leadership and urban regeneration: Cities in North America and Europe,* ed. Dennis R. Judd and Michael Parkinson, 31–47. Newbury Park, CA: Sage.

Fainstein, Susan S., and Dennis R. Judd. 1999a. Cities as places to play. In *The tourist city,* ed. Dennis R. Judd and Susan S. Fainstein, 261–272. New Haven: Yale University Press.

————. 1999b. Global forces, local strategies, and urban tourism. In *The tourist city,* ed. Dennis R. Judd and Susan S. Fainstein, 1–17. New Haven: Yale University Press.

Fainstein, Susan S., and Robert James Stokes. 1998. Spaces for play: The impacts of entertainment development on New York City. *Economic Development Quarterly* 12 (2): 150–165.

Fairbank, Canapary, and Maullin. 1983. Survey research: Coliseum/Exposition Park venue, Westwood/UCLA venue. Memo. Don Matso, VP Public Relations Office files, UCLA University Research Library Special Collection 1403, box 119, folder 13.

Feagin, Joe R., Anthony M. Orum, and Gideon Sjoberg, eds. 1991. *A case for the case study.* Chapel Hill: University of North Carolina Press.

Fidel, Steve. 1994. S.L. Olympic bid promoters urged to outline the risks, too. *Deseret News,* September 7, A-1.

Fish, Mike. 1992. Atlanta Olympic watch identity crisis: MAOGA questions own authority. *Atlanta Journal Constitution,* February 8, A-10.

Fitzpatrick, Tim. 1988. Financing may be crucial for 1998 Olympic bid. *Salt Lake Tribune*, November 14, B-1.

Fogelson, Robert M. 1967. *The fragmented metropolis: Los Angeles, 1850–1930.* Cambridge: Harvard University Press.

Foglesong, Richard. 1999. Walt Disney World and Orlando: Deregulation as a strategy for tourism. In *The tourist city,* ed. Dennis R. Judd and Susan S. Fainstein, 89–106. New Haven: Yale University Press.

Foskett, Ken. 1993a. Olympic stadium reaps suspicion planted 30 years ago. *Atlanta Journal Constitution,* March 7, A-14.

————. 1993b. Protesters rally against Olympic stadium site. *Atlanta Journal Constitution,* July 9, G-3.

————. 1993c. Stadium deal gains swing vote. *Atlanta Journal Constitution,* March 10, A-1.

Foskett, Ken, and Bert Roughton, Jr. 1993. Olympic stadium gets Fulton OK. *Atlanta Journal Constitution,* March 10, A-1.

Foster, Mark S. 1976. Denver 1976. *Colorado Magazine* 53 (2): 163–186.

Fowler, John E. 1999. *Annual report of the state Olympic officer relating to the 2002 Olympic winter games.* Salt Lake City: State of Utah.

Fox, Catherine. 1994. Turning asphalt avenues into people places. *Atlanta Journal Constitution,* June 12, N-6.

French, Steven P., and Mike E. Disher. 1997. Atlanta and the Olympics: A one-year retrospective. *Journal of the American Planning Association* 63 (3): 379–392.

Friedmann, John. 1995. Where we stand: A decade of world city research. In *World cities in a world-system,* ed. Paul L. Knox and Peter J. Taylor, 21–47. New York: Cambridge University Press.

Fry, Earl H. 1995. North American municipalities and their involvement in the global economy. In *North American cities and the global economy,* ed. Peter Karl Kresl and Gary Gappert, 21–44. Thousand Oaks, CA: Sage.

Fulton, William. 1997. *The reluctant metropolis: The politics of urban growth in Los Angeles.* Point Arena, CA: Solano Press.

Fun and games—and money. 1977. *Los Angeles Times,* July 17, VIII-4.

George, Alexander L., and Timothy J. McKeown. 1985. Case studies and theories of organizational decision making. *Advances in Information Processing in Organizations* 2: 21–58.

Gittell, Marilyn, Kathe Newman, Janice Bockmeyer, and Robert Lindsay. 1998. Expanding civic opportunity: Urban empowerment zones. *Urban Affairs Review* 33 (4): 530–588.

Gladstone, David L. 1998. Tourism urbanization in the United States. *Urban Affairs Review* 34 (1): 3–27.

Gordon, Margaret T., Hubert G. Locke, Laurie McCutcheon, and William B. Stafford. 1991. Seattle: Grassroots politics shaping the environment. In *Big city politics in transition,* ed. H. V. Savitch and John Clayton Thomas, 216–234. Newbury Park, CA: Sage.

Gorrell, Mike. 1995. Foundation to ensure "games" don't end with Olympics. *Salt Lake Tribune,* August 4, E-1.

———. 1996. Gateway project to figure in S. L. games? S. L. mayor seeks Olympic green space. *Salt Lake Tribune,* July 18, D-1.

———. 1999. Trustees urge SLOC to make sure Olympic projects are first to get federal funding. *Salt Lake Tribune,* November 12, B-1.

Gottdiener, Mark. 1997. *The theming of America: Dreams, visions, and commercial spaces.* Boulder, CO: Westview.

Gottdiener, Mark, Claudia C. Collins, and David R. Dickens. 1999. *Las Vegas: The social production of an all-American city.* New York: Blackwell.

Governor's Office of Planning and Budget. 1998a. *2002 Olympic winter games: Economic, demographic, and fiscal impacts.* Salt Lake City: State of Utah.

———. 1998b. *2002 Olympic winter games: Estimated local government Olympic revenues.* Salt Lake City: State of Utah.

———. 1999. Estimated resident and destination skier visits in Utah (1960–1997). Internet document accessed at: www.governor.state.ut.us.

Gratton, Reg. 1999. The media. In *Staging the Olympics: The event and its impact,* ed. Richard Cashman and Anthony Hughes. Sydney, Australia: University of New South Wales Press.

Grosfoguel, Ramón. 1995. Global logics in the Caribbean city system: The case of Miami. In *World cities in a world-system,* ed. Paul L. Knox and Peter J. Taylor, 156–170. New York: Cambridge University Press.

Gust-Jenson, Cindy. 1994. Letter from the executive director, Office of the Salt Lake City Council, December 28. Utahns for Responsible Public Spending Papers, University of Utah Marriott Library Special Collection 1548, box 1, folder 4.

Hall, C. Michael. 1992. *Hallmark tourist events: Impacts, management and planning.* London: Bellhaven Press.

———. 1996. Hallmark events and urban reimaging strategies: Coercion, community, and the Sydney 2000 Olympics. In *Practicing responsible tourism: International case studies in tourism planning, policy, and development,* ed. Lynn C. Harrison and Winston Husbands, 366–379. New York: John Wiley.

Hall, Gordon R., Barbara Day Lockhart, Merrill R. Norman, Patricia Hanna, and David J. Jordan. 1999. Report to the Board of Trustees. February 8. Salt Lake Olympic Organizing Committee.

Hannigan, John. 1998. *Fantasy city: Pleasure and profit in the postmodern metropolis.* New York: Routledge.

Hansen, Jeffrey. 1980. Council to get valley citizens' reports on Olympics facilities in Sepulveda Basin. *Los Angeles Times Valley Edition,* March 20, F-6.

Harding, Alan. 1995. Elite theory and the growth machine. In *Theories of urban politics,* ed. David Judge, Gerry Stoker, and Harold Wolman, 35–53. Thousand Oaks, CA: Sage.

Harris, Lyle V. 1993. Techwood dorm deal "in the bag" AHA says. *Atlanta Journal Constitution,* February 20, B-7.

———. 1994. Water woes. *Atlanta Journal Constitution,* February 7, C-1.

———. 1996a. More than 40 companies interested in street sales of food and souvenirs. *Atlanta Journal Constitution,* March 1, D-3.

———. 1996b. Signs of displeasure. *Atlanta Journal Constitution,* July 17, S-1.

Henry, Bill, and Patricia Henry Yeomans. 1984. *An approved history of the Olympic games.* Los Angeles: Southern California Committee for the Olympic Games.

Herson, Lawrence J. R., and John M. Bolland. 1990. *The urban web: Politics, policy, and theory.* Chicago: Nelson-Hall.

Heying, Charles H. 1995. Civic elites, civic institutions, and the urban growth dynamic. Ph.D. diss., University of North Carolina at Chapel Hill.

Hill, Alma E. 1993a. Atlanta 1996 communities raise a ruckus over CODA. *Atlanta Journal Constitution,* November 11, G-1.

———. 1993b. Neighborhood leaders' first reaction: Wrong priority. *Atlanta Journal Constitution,* November 19, A-7.

———. 1993c. Neighborhood plan unveiled CODA action will cost $220 million. *Atlanta Journal Constitution,* October 20, C-4.

———. 1993d. Olympic panel appoints redevelopment official. *Atlanta Journal Constitution,* June 18, D-3.

———. 1995. A blueprint for the homes of the Olympics: Summerhill banking on townhouse development to revive neighborhood. *Atlanta Journal Constitution,* March 16, E-8.

Hill, Alma E., and Bert Roughton, Jr. 1992. New city board will plan, guide '96 renovations. *Atlanta Journal Constitution,* October 10, A-1.

Hill, Christopher R. 1994. The politics of Manchester's Olympic bid. *Parliamentary Affairs* 47 (3): 338–354.

———. 1996. *Olympic politics.* 2nd ed. Manchester: Manchester University Press.

Hiller, Harry H. 2000. Mega-events, urban boosterism and growth strategies: An analysis of the objectives and legitimations of the Cape Town 2004 Olympic bid. *International Journal of Urban and Regional Research* 24 (2): 439–458.

Hiskey, Michelle. 1993. Residents reject plan. *Atlanta Journal Constitution,* February 9, C-1.

————. 1994. Protesters descend on Olympic groundbreaking. *Atlanta Journal Constitution,* October 18, B-1.

————. 1997. The ballpark. *Atlanta Journal Constitution,* March 23, G-5.

Holcomb, Briavel. 1999. Marketing cities for tourism. In *The tourist city,* ed. Dennis R. Judd and Susan S. Fainstein, 54–70. New Haven: Yale University Press.

Horan, Cynthia. 1991. Beyond governing coalitions: Analyzing urban regimes in the 1990s. *Journal of Urban Affairs* 13 (2): 119–135.

Hoxworth, Dan H., and John Clayton Thomas. 1993. Economic development decisionmaking in a fragmented polity: Convention center expansion in Kansas City. *Journal of Urban Affairs* 15 (3): 275–292.

Hrebenar, Ronald J., Melanee Cherry, and Kathanne Greene. 1987. Utah: Church and corporate power in the nation's most conservative state. In *Interest group politics in the American West,* ed. Ronald J. Hrebenar and Clive Thomas, 113–122. Salt Lake City: University of Utah Press.

Hula, Richard C. 1990. The two Baltimores. In *Leadership and urban regeneration: Cities in North America and Europe,* ed. Dennis R. Judd and Michael Parkinson, 191–215. Newbury Park, CA: Sage.

Hume, Ellen. 1979. Olympic bid hits snag in capital. *Los Angeles Times,* May 23, I-1.

Hunter, Floyd. 1953. *Community power structures: A study of decision makers.* Chapel Hill: University of North Carolina Press.

Jardine, James. 1989. We can't have it both ways. *Utah Holiday,* October 19, 8–9.

Jarvis urges delay in Olympic action. 1977. *Los Angeles Times,* December 23, II-2.

Johnson, William Oscar. 1990. The push is on. *Sports Illustrated.* August 27, 36–51.

Jones, Grahame L. 1999. World Cup 2002 is all set to draw FIFA's attention. *Los Angeles Times,* December 5, D-13.

Jorgenson, Chris. 1992. Clergy join fight against ice oval. *Salt Lake Tribune,* June 30, B-3.

Judd, Dennis R. 1983. From cowtown to sunbelt city: Boosterism and economic growth in Denver. In *Restructuring the city: The political economy of urban redevelopment,* ed. Susan S. Fainstein, Norman I. Fainstein, Richard Child Hill, Dennis R. Judd, and Michael Peter Smith, 167–201. New York: Longman.

————. 1999. Constructing the tourist bubble. In *The tourist city,* ed. Dennis R. Judd and Susan S. Fainstein, 35–53. New Haven: Yale University Press.

Judd, Dennis R., and Susan S. Fainstein, eds. 1999. *The tourist city.* New Haven: Yale University Press.

Judd, Dennis R., and Michael Parkinson. 1990. Urban leadership and regeneration. In *Leadership and urban regeneration: Cities in North America and Europe,* ed. Dennis R. Judd and Michael Parkinson, 13–30. Newbury Park, CA: Sage.

Judd, Dennis R., and Todd Swanstrom. 1998. *City politics: Private power and public policy.* 2nd ed. New York: Longman.

Kalich, Veronica Z. 1998. A public choice perspective on the subsidization of private industry: A case study of three cities and three stadiums. *Journal of Urban Affairs* 20 (2): 199–219.

Keahey, John. 1995. Some Olympic donors going for the gold. *Salt Lake Tribune,* February 19, C-1.

Keating, Larry, and Carol A. Flores. 2000. Sixty and out: Techwood Homes transformed by enemies and friends. *Journal of Urban History* 26 (3): 275–311.

Kelner, Alexis. 1989. Utahns should reject proposal to use sales tax for Olympics. *Salt Lake Tribune,* October 8, A-28.

Kilgore, Margaret. 1977. Two tourism units merge to attract more visitors to LA. *Los Angeles Times,* August 25, II-8.

Killanin, Lord. 1983. *My Olympic years.* New York: William Morrow.

Knight, Richard V. 1989. The emergent global society. In *Cities in a global society,* ed. Richard V. Knight and Gary Gappert, 24–43. Newbury Park, CA: Sage.

Knox, Paul L. 1995. World cities in a world-system. In *World cities in a world-system,* ed. Paul L. Knox and Peter J. Taylor, 3–20. New York: Cambridge University Press.

Kruger, Arnd. 1999. The unfinished symphony: A history of the Olympic games from Coubertin to Samaranch. In *The international politics of sport in the 20th century,* ed. Jim Riordan and Arnd Kruger, 3–27. New York: Routledge.

Laccetti, Susan. 1991. Opponents of stadium site hold vigil at Payne's Dunwoody home. *Atlanta Journal Constitution,* February 4, A-4.

Ladd, Helen F., and John Yinger. 1989. *America's ailing cities: Fiscal health and the design of urban policy.* Baltimore: Johns Hopkins University Press.

Larson, James F., and Heung-soo Park. 1993. *Global television and the politics of the Seoul Olympics.* Boulder, CO: Westview.

Lauria, Mickey. 1997. Introduction. In *Reconstructing urban regime theory: Regulating urban politics in a global economy,* ed. Mickey Lauria, 1–9. Thousand Oaks, CA: Sage.

Law, Christopher M. 1993. *Urban tourism: Attracting visitors to large cities.* New York: Mansell Publishing.

Lawson, Craig. 1985. Intergovernmental challenges of the 1984 Olympic games. *Publius* 15 (3): 127–141.

Leavitt, Michael O. 1999. Press release: Governor's public statement regarding the Olympics. Salt Lake City, January 8.

Lenskyj, Helen Jefferson. 1996. When winners are losers: Toronto and Sydney bids for the summer Olympics. *Journal of Sport and Social Issues* 20 (4): 392–410.

Leonard, Stephen J., and Thomas J. Noel. 1990. *Denver: Mining camp to metropolis.* Denver: University Press of Colorado.

Levitt, Susanna H. 1990. The 1984 Olympic arts festival: Theatre. Ph.D. diss., University of California, Davis.

Lindblom, Charles E. 1977. *Politics and markets: The world's political economic systems.* New York: Basic Books.

Logan, John R., and Harvey L. Molotch. 1987. *Urban fortunes: The political economy of place.* Berkeley: University of California Press.

Logan, John R., and Todd Swanstrom. 1990. Urban restructuring: A critical view. In *Beyond the city limits: Urban policy and economic restructuring in comparative perspective,* ed. John R. Logan and Todd Swanstrom, 3–24. Philadelphia: Temple University Press.

Logan, John R., Rachel Bridges Whaley, and Kyle Crowder. 1997. The character and consequences of growth regimes: An assessment of 20 years of research. *Urban Affairs Review* 32 (5): 603–630.

Los Angeles Chamber of Commerce. N.d. *Answers to most often asked questions about the 1984 Summer Games.* Los Angeles: Chamber of Commerce.

Los Angeles Olympic Organizing Committee (LAOOC). 1980. *First official report of the organizing committee of the games for the XXIII Olympiad.* Los Angeles: LAOOC.

———. 1983. Public relations plan. Don Matso, VP Public Relations Office files, UCLA University Research Library Special Collection 1403, box 123, folders 3, 5, 6, 17.

———. 1984a. Exposition Park area impact study. Don Matso, VP Public Relations Office files, UCLA University Research Library Special Collection 1403, box 119, folder 5.

———. 1984b. Exposition Park community relations plan. Don Matso, VP Public Relations Office files, UCLA University Research Library Special Collection 1403, box 119, folder 6.

———. 1985. *Official report of the games of the XXIIIrd Olympiad, Los Angeles, 1984.* Vol. 1, *Organization and planning.* Los Angeles: LAOOC.

MacCargar, Victoria. 1985. Tourism set record in 1984, thanks to Olympics. *Los Angeles Times,* May 26, V-4.

Maloney, Larry. 1996. Atlanta 1996. In *Historical dictionary of the modern Olympic movement,* ed. John E. Findling and Kimberly D. Pelle, 194–200. Westport, CT: Greenwood Press.

Mannheim, Jarol B. 1990. Rites of passage: The 1988 Seoul Olympics as public diplomacy. *Western Political Quarterly* 43 (2): 279–295.

Meagher, Ed. 1977. Stick to a tight Olympic budget, LA warned. *Los Angeles Times,* December 22, II-1.

Mitchell, George J., Kenneth Duberstein, Donald Fehr, Roberta Cooper Ramo, Jeffrey G. Benz. 1999. Report of the Special Oversight Commission. March 1. Colorado Springs, CO: United States Olympic Committee.

Mohl, Raymond A. 1985. *The new American city: Urban America in the industrial age, 1860–1920.* Arlington Heights, IL: Harlan Davidson.

Mollenkopf, John H. 1983. *The contested city.* Princeton: Princeton University Press.

———. 1998. Urban policy at the crossroads. In *The social divide: Political parties and the future of activist government,* ed. Margaret Weir, 464–505. Washington, D.C.: Brookings Institution Press.

Molotch, Harvey L. 1976. The city as growth machine: Toward a political economy of place. *American Journal of Sociology* 82 (2): 309–332.

Monkkonen, Eric H. 1988. *America becomes urban: The development of U.S. cities and towns, 1780–1980.* Berkeley: University of California Press.

Moran, Michael. 1991. *The politics of the financial services revolution: The USA, UK and Japan.* New York: St. Martin's.

Mullins, Patrick, Kristin Natalier, Philip Smith, and Belinda Smeaton. 1999. Cities and consumption spaces. *Urban Affairs Review* 35 (1): 44–71.

Newman, Harvey K. 1995. Atlanta welcomes the world: Preparations for the 1996 Olympic games by the city's hospitality business. Paper presented at the Urban Affairs Association Annual Meeting, Portland, OR.

———. 1999. *Southern hospitality: Tourism and the growth of Atlanta.* Tuscaloosa: University of Alabama Press.

Nixon, Howard L. 1988. The background, nature, and implications of the organization of the "capitalist Olympics." In *The Olympic games in transition,* ed. Jeffrey O. Seagrave and Donald Chu, 237–251. Champaign, IL: Human Kinetics.

Noll, Roger G., and Andrew Zimbalist. 1997. The economic impact of sports teams and facilities. In *Sports, jobs and taxes,* ed. Roger G. Noll and Andrew Zimbalist, 55–91. Washington, D.C.: Brookings Institution.

Nurse, Doug. 1999. Conyers horse park a potential cash cow. *Atlanta Journal Constitution,* November 18, JR-1.

Olympic torch continues to be passed in Utah. 1995. *Salt Lake Tribune,* June 17, H-8.

Olympics paranoia. 1994. *Salt Lake Tribune,* October 17, A-6.

Orlov, Rick. 1979. LA panel backs Olympics study. *Valley News,* September 5, I-1.

———. 1980. Merchants tell of traffic jam fear if Olympic games held in LA. *Valley News,* February 6, I-5.

Pace, Steven, spokesperson for Utahns for Responsible Public Spending. 1995. Interview by Douglas McGee, May 25. Unpublished transcript. Salt Lake City, UT.

Paddison, Ronan. 1993. City marketing, image reconstruction and urban regeneration. *Urban Studies* 30(2): 339–350.

Pagano, Michael, and Ann O. Bowman. 1995. *Cityscapes and capital: The politics of urban development.* Baltimore: Johns Hopkins University Press.

Page, Stephen. 1995. *Urban tourism.* New York: Routledge.

Palmer, Kenneth T. 1984. The evolution of grant policies. In *The changing politics of federal grants,* Lawrence D. Brown, James W. Fossett, and Kenneth T. Palmer, 5–53. Washington, D.C.: Brookings Institution.

Parker, Robert E. 1999. Las Vegas: Casino gambling and local culture. In *The tourist city,* ed. Dennis R. Judd and Susan S. Fainstein, 107–123. New Haven: Yale University Press.

Pearce, Philip L. 1988. *The Ulysses factor: Evaluating visitors in tourist settings.* New York: Springer-Verlag.

Pendered, David. 1994. Chamber, banks, waste firm top contributions to bond campaign. *Atlanta Journal Constitution,* July 13, D-5.

Perelman, Richard B. 1985. *Olympic retrospective: The games of Los Angeles.* Los Angeles: Los Angeles Olympic Organizing Committee.

Perry, David C. 1990. Recasting urban leadership in Buffalo. In *Leadership and urban regeneration: Cities in North America and Europe,* ed. Dennis R. Judd and Michael Parkinson, 258–276. Newbury Park, CA: Sage.

Peterson, Paul E. 1981. *City limits.* Chicago: University of Chicago Press.

———. 1993. The changing fiscal place of big cities in the federal system. In *Interwoven destinies: Cities and the nation,* ed. Henry G. Cisneros, 187–210. New York: Norton.

Picking up the check. 1993. *Atlanta Journal Constitution,* March 24, A-12.

Pierre, Jon. 1999. Models of urban governance: The institutional dimensions of urban politics. *Urban Affairs Review* 34 (3): 372–396.

Pope, S. W. 1997. *Patriotic games: Sporting traditions in the American imagination, 1876–1926.* New York: Oxford University Press.

Private dollars, public dream: Here's who bankrolled the bid. 1995. *Salt Lake Tribune,* June 18, B-1.

Purcell, Mark. 2000. The decline of the political consensus for urban growth: Evidence from Los Angeles. *Journal of Urban Affairs* 22 (1): 85–100.

Quesenberry, P. 1996. The disposable Olympics meets the city of hype. *Southern Changes* 18: 3–14.

Ray, Barbara J. 1995. Leveraging the mega-event: Atlanta's efforts to boost its infrastructure and host the 1996 Olympics. Paper presented at the Urban Affairs Association Annual Meeting, Portland, OR.

Regalado, Jaime. 1992. Political representation, economic development policy making, and social crisis in Los Angeles, 1973–1992. In *City of angels,* ed. Gerry Riposa and Carolyn Dersch, 159–180. Dubuque, IA: Kendall-Hunt.

Reich, Kenneth. 1977a. Bernardi seeks June vote on Olympic aid. *Los Angeles Times,* November 9, I-3.

———. 1977b. LA picked for Olympic bid. *Los Angeles Times,* September 26, II-1.

———. 1978a. Bradley entrusts Olympic hopes to private panel. *Los Angeles Times,* June 4, I-1.

———. 1978b. Council cautious on Olympic stand. *Los Angeles Times,* January 17, I-1.

———. 1978c. IOC accepts LA terms reported. *Los Angeles Times,* August 16, II-1.

———. 1978d. IOC, not LA, will control '84 Olympics, Killanin says. *Los Angeles Times,* March 23, II-1.

———. 1978e. LA delegation awaits IOC reply to Olympic bid. *Los Angeles Times,* May 14, I-3.

———. 1978f. Lake Placid's tip for LA Olympics panel: Be wary. *Los Angeles Times,* February 10, II-1.

———. 1978g. Mayor to form Olympic panel. *Los Angeles Times,* April 18, II-1.

———. 1978h. Olympics cost measure due for ballot. *Los Angeles Times,* February 22, II-1.

———. 1978i. Only pessimism emerges from long Olympic talks. *Los Angeles Times,* June 20, II-1.

———. 1979a. Bradley shakes up Olympics liaison post. *Los Angeles Times,* May 2, II-1.

———. 1979b. 59 named to Olympic games panel. *Los Angeles Times,* January 27, II-1

———. 1979c. Rep. Wilson, after polling district, says he'll oppose any federal Olympics aid. *Los Angeles Times,* July 11, II-4.

———. 1981a. Bradley drops plan for Olympic rowing site in valley. *Los Angeles Times,* April 9, II-1.

———. 1981b. Rowing course skirmish reviewed. *Los Angeles Times,* March 25, II-5.

———. 1981c. Special taxes may pay part of bill for Olympics security. *Los Angeles Times,* December 20, II-1.

———. 1981d. Use of basin for 84 Olympics opposed. *Los Angeles Times,* January 12, II-1.

———. 1984. UCLA and Westwood will have the welcome mat out for the Olympics. *Los Angeles Times,* April 22, B-1.

———. 1986. *Making it happen.* Santa Barbara, CA: Capra Press.

Reid, S. A. 1996. Remodeling public housing. *Atlanta Journal Constitution,* July 21, C-2.

Report by the IOC 2000 commission to the 110th IOC session. 1999. Lausanne, Switzerland: International Olympic Committee.

Report of the IOC *ad hoc* commission to investigate the conduct of certain IOC members and to consider possible changes in the procedures for the allocation of the games of the Olympiad and the Olympic winter games. 1999. Lausanne, Switzerland: International Olympic Committee.

Rice, Robert. 1988. Mayor refuses to lead cheers for games. *Deseret News,* December 3, B-1.

———. 1989. Swaying USOC included massages. *Deseret News,* June 8, B-1.

Riess, Steven A. 1981. Power without authority: Los Angeles' elites and the construction of the coliseum. *Journal of Sport History* 8 (1): 50–65.

Ritchie, J. R. Brent. 1984. Assessing the impact of hallmark events: Conceptual and research issues. *Journal of Travel Research* 23 (1): 2–11.

Rivera, Nancy. 1984. LA visitors bureau hopes games' image will pay off. *Los Angeles Times,* October 31, IV-2.

Robertson, Martin, and Yvonne Guerrier. 1998. Events as entrepreneurial displays: Seville, Barcelona and Madrid. In *Managing tourism in cities: Policy, process, and practice,* ed. Duncan Tyler, Yvonne Guerrier, and Martin Robertson, 215–228. New York: John Wiley.

Robinson, Jonathan. 2000. Turner plans $1.2 billion expansion and more CNN online. *New York Times,* July 3, C-7.

Roche, Lisa Riley. 1994a. Bid backers to do battle at home. *Deseret News,* November 20, A-1.

———. 1994b. Huntsman still opposes bid for games. *Deseret News,* December 2, B-1.

———. 1999. World still holds games in high regard, IOC says. *Deseret News,* November 10, B-1.

Roche, Lisa Riley, and Hans Camporreales. 2000. Welch, Johnson are indicted. *Deseret News,* July 20, A-1.

Roche, Maurice. 1992. Mega-events and micro-modernization: On the sociology of the new urban tourism. *British Journal of Sociology* 43 (4): 563–600.

———. 1994. Mega-events and urban policy. *Annals of Tourism Research* 21 (1): 1–19.

Rood, Rodney. 1977. Consider, for a moment, the benefits of hosting the Olympics. *Los Angeles Times,* December 6, IV-6.

Rosentraub, Mark S. 1996. Does the emperor have new clothes? A reply to Robert A. Baade. *Journal of Urban Affairs* 18 (1): 23–31.

———. 1997. *Major league losers: The real cost of sports and who's paying for it.* New York: Basic Books.

Rosentraub, Mark S., David Swindell, Michael Przybyiski, and Daniel R. Mullins. 1994. Sport and downtown development strategy: If you build it, will jobs come? *Journal of Urban Affairs* 16 (3): 221–240.

Rothman, Hal K. 1998. *Devil's bargains: Tourism in the twentieth-century American West.* Lawrence: University Press of Kansas.

Roughton, Bert, Jr. 1990a. Fight vowed over '96 stadium site. *Atlanta Journal Constitution,* November 29, A-1.

———. 1990b. Groups say no to new stadium. *Atlanta Journal Constitution,* December 15, C-4.

———. 1991a. Atlanta Olympics update '91. *Atlanta Journal Constitution,* July 21, F-3.

———. 1991b. Summerhill plan would create new town. *Atlanta Journal Constitution,* March 10, B-1.

———. 1992a. Atlanta Olympic watch: Watchdog asks ACOG who will be the master. *Atlanta Journal Constitution,* February 1, A-10.

———. 1992b. Atlanta Olympics update '92 the challenge. *Atlanta Journal Constitution,* September 20, H-6.

———. 1993a. ACOG still stings after King calls it elitist club for whites. *Atlanta Journal Constitution,* March 6, B-6.

———. 1993b. Jackson makes plea on behalf of CODA. *Atlanta Journal Constitution,* December 22, C-4.

Rutheiser, Charles. 1996. *Imagineering Atlanta: The politics of place in the city of dreams.* London: Verso.

———. 1997. Making place in the nonplace urban realm: Notes on the revitalization of downtown Atlanta. *Urban Anthropology and Studies of Cultural Systems and World Economic Development* 26 (1): 9–42.

Rybczynski, Witold. 1996. Little-town blues: It takes more than an Olympics to make a city world class. *Saturday Night,* November, 146.

Salt Lake City Bid Committee. 1994. *Salt Lake City candidate to host the XIX Olympic winter games, 2002.* Vol. 1. Salt Lake City: SLC Bid Committee.

Salt Lake City Planning Division. 1998. The Gateway specific plan. July. Salt Lake City, UT: SLC Planning Division.

Salt Lake Olympic Organizing Committee (SLOC). 1998. Budget. Internet document accessed at: www.slc2002.org/info/budget/plan/part6.

———. 1999. Organization. Internet document accessed at: www.slc2002.org/info/organization.

Salter, Sallye. 1994. Some owners rolling up sleeves to fight Olympic park. *Atlanta Journal Constitution,* January 10, C-1.

———. 1999. Today's topic: Commercial real estate: Centennial Park redevelopment. *Atlanta Journal Constitution,* June 16, D-2.

Sanders, Heywood T. 1992. Building the convention city: Politics, finance, and public investment in urban America. *Journal of Urban Affairs* 14 (2): 135–160.

Saporta, Maria. 1994. Olympic development co-chair named. *Atlanta Journal Constitution,* August 9, F-1.

Sassen, Saskia. 1988. *The mobility of labor and capital: A study in international investment and labor flows.* Cambridge: Cambridge University Press.

———. 1991. *The global city: New York, London, Tokyo.* Princeton: Princeton University Press.

———. 1996a. Cities and communities in the global economy: Rethinking our concepts. *American Behavioral Scientist* 39 (4): 629–639.

———. 1996b. *Losing control? Sovereignty in an age of globalization.* New York: Columbia University Press.

Sbragia, Alberta M. 1990. Pittsburgh's "third way": The nonprofit sector as the key to urban regeneration. In *Leadership and urban regeneration: Cities in North America and Europe,* ed. Dennis R. Judd and Michael Parkinson, 51–68. Newbury Park, CA: Sage.

Schneider, Mark, and Paul Teske. 1993. The antigrowth entrepreneur: Challenging the "equilibrium" of the growth machine. *Journal of Politics* 55 (3): 720–736.

Schockman, H. Eric. 1996. Is Los Angeles governable? Revisiting the city charter. In *Rethinking Los Angeles,* ed. Michael J. Dear, H. Eric Schockman, and Greg Hise, 57–75. Newbury Park, CA: Sage.

Shachar, Arie. 1995. World cities in the making: The European context. In *North American cities and the global economy,* ed. Peter Karl Kresl and Gary Gappert, 150–170. Thousand Oaks, CA: Sage.

Shaiken, Bill. 1988. *Sport and politics: The Olympics and the Los Angeles games.* New York: Praeger.

Shlay, Anne B., and Robert P. Giloth. 1987. The social organization of land-based elite: The case of the failed Chicago 1992 World's Fair. *Journal of Urban Affairs* 9 (4): 305–324.

Short, J. R., L. M. Benton, W. B. Luce, and J. Walton. 1993. Reconstructing the image of an industrial city. *Annals of the Association of American Geographers* 83 (2): 207–224.

Simson, Vyv, and Andrew Jennings. 1992. *The lords of the rings: Power, money, and drugs in the modern Olympics.* New York: Simon and Schuster.

Singleton, Gregory H. 1979. *Religion in the city of angels: American Protestant culture and urbanization, Los Angeles, 1850–1930.* Ann Arbor: UMI Research Press.

Soble, Ronald. 1977. Olympics still have Canada seeing red. *Los Angeles Times,* July 1, I-1.

Sonenshein, Raphael J. 1993. *Politics in black and white: Race and power in Los Angeles.* Princeton: Princeton University Press.

Sorkin, Michael, ed. 1992. *Variations on a theme park: The new American city and the end of public space.* New York: Noonday Press.

Soto, Lucy. 1996. We will not be defeated. *Atlanta Journal Constitution,* July 31, S-34.

Spangler, Jerry. 2000. Legislation pleases Romney. *Deseret News,* March 2, A-14.

Standeven, Joy, and Paul De Knop. 1999. *Sport tourism.* Champaign, IL: Human Kinetics.

Starr, Kevin. 1990. *Material dreams: Southern California through the 1920s.* New York: Oxford University Press.

Stewart, Robert W. 1984. Green missing in Westwood display of colors. *Los Angeles Times,* July 26, I-3.

Stoker, Gerry. 1995. Regime theory and urban politics. In *Theories of urban politics,* ed. David Judge, Gerry Stoker, and Harold Wolman, 54–71. Thousand Oaks, CA: Sage.

Stoker, Gerry, and Karen Mossberger. 1994. Urban regime theory in comparative perspective. *Environment and Planning C: Government and Policy* 12 (2): 195–212.

Stone, Clarence N. 1980. Systemic power in community decision making: A restatement of stratification theory. *American Political Science Review* 74 (4): 978–990.

———. 1987. The study of the politics of urban development. In *The politics of urban development,* ed. Clarence N. Stone and Heywood T. Sanders, 3–22. Lawrence: University Press of Kansas.

———. 1989a. Paradigms, power, and urban leadership. In *Leadership and politics,* ed. Bryan D. Jones, 135–159. Lawrence: University Press of Kansas.

———. 1989b. *Regime politics: Governing Atlanta, 1946–1988.* Lawrence: University Press of Kansas.

———. 1993. Urban regimes and the capacity to govern: A political economy approach. *Journal of Urban Affairs* 15 (1): 1–28.

———. 1998. Regime analysis and the study of urban politics, a rejoinder. *Journal of Urban Affairs* 20 (3): 249–260.

The fight over sites. 1979. *Los Angeles Times,* August 30, II-10.

The southland. 1978. *Los Angeles Times,* May 3, I-2.

Tomlinson, Alan. 1996. Olympic spectacle: Opening ceremonies and some paradoxes of globalization. *Media, Culture and Society* 18 (4): 583–602.

Towns, Hollis R. 1998. Housing: Drawing the line at the poorest of the poor. *Atlanta Journal Constitution,* February 15, G-5.

Transportation Equity Act for the 21st Century. 1998. U.S. Public Law 105–178. 105 Cong., 2nd sess., June 9, 1998.

Turner, Melissa. 1992a. All Payne had to say to get first sponsorship was "yes." *Atlanta Journal Constitution,* March 5, A-14.

———. 1992b. Circle the rings, "ambush" ads hit. *Atlanta Journal Constitution,* March 3, A-6.

———. 1993. Sponsorship drive walks fine line. *Atlanta Journal Constitution,* September 19, H-3.

———. 1994. Coke chief challenges peers to do more for city. *Atlanta Journal Constitution,* March 18, C-1.

———. 1996a. After the games: Polling America. *Atlanta Journal Constitution,* August 11, C-5.

———. 1996b. Forming an Olympic legacy. *Atlanta Journal Constitution,* December 22, G-8.

———. 1997. Remains of the games. *Atlanta Journal Constitution,* July 13, H-6.

———. 1999a. ACOG account: Millions left to spend. *Atlanta Journal Constitution,* April 1, A-1.

———. 1999b. Memo: Bidders alert to IOC "sleaze bags." *Atlanta Journal Constitution,* September 18, F-1.

———. 1999c. Olympic bid defense: System corrupt. *Atlanta Journal Constitution,* September 17, A-1.

———. 1999d. Payne profited from land deals near horse park. *Atlanta Journal Constitution,* May 30, A-1.

———. 1999e. Philips Arena: A new downtown: "Defining moment." *Atlanta Journal Constitution,* September 12, P-15.

———. 1999f. Stakes raised in games bid probe. *Atlanta Journal Constitution,* August 8, E-1.

———. 1999g. "We did not bribe anyone," Billy Payne says of the city's bid for games. *Atlanta Journal Constitution,* February 20, A-1.

UCLA chancellor's memorandum. 1984. Regents of the University of California committee on finance memorandum, Activities of the 1984 Summer Olympics, February 13. Don Matso, VP Public Relations Office files, UCLA University Research Library Special Collection 1403, box 349, folder 8.

Ueberroth, Peter, with Richard Levin and Amy Quinn. 1985. *Made in America: His own story.* New York: William Morrow.

Unger, Henry. 1996. Braves' new stadium swells franchise value. *Atlanta Journal Constitution,* February 22, C-2.

U.S. General Accounting Office. 1999. *Olympic games: Preliminary information on federal funding and support.* Washington, D.C.: GAO.

———. 2000. *Olympic games: Federal government provides significant funding and support.* Washington, D.C.: GAO.

U.S. Olympic Committee (USOC). 1997. To bid or not to bid? Yes for the 2007 Pan Am; no for the 2008 Olympics. *Olympic Beat* 12 (July): 1.

U.S. Travel Data Center. 1998. *The economic review of travel in America.* Washington, D.C.: Travel Industry Association of America.

———. 1999a. *Profile of travelers who attend sports events.* Washington, D.C.: Travel Industry Association of America.

———. 1999b. *Survey of state tourism offices, 1998–99.* Washington, D.C.: Travel Industry Association of America.

Urry, John. 1990. *The tourist gaze: Leisure and travel in contemporary societies.* Newbury Park, CA: Sage.

Usher, Harry. 1985. Interview by Kenneth Reich, April 14. Transcript available at the Amateur Athletic Foundation of Los Angeles, Paul Ziffren Sports Resource Center.

Vending tarnished Atlanta. 1997. *Atlanta Journal Constitution,* July 26, A-10.

Venturi, Robert, Denise Scott Brown, and Steven Izenour. 1977. *Learning from Las Vegas.* Rev. ed. Cambridge: MIT Press.

Waitt, Gordon. 1999. Playing games with Sydney: Marketing Sydney for the 2000 Olympics. *Urban Studies* 36 (7): 1055–1077.

Walsh, Rebecca. 1998. Gateway developers ask for tax money. *Salt Lake Tribune,* September 18, B-1.

———. 2000. Choosing Olympic icons may turn thorny. *Salt Lake Tribune,* November 17, A-1.

Wanninger, Richard. 1998. Olympic, Pan Am U.S. bid cities gather in Colorado Springs. *Olympic Beat* 13 (June) 1: 8.

Watson, Robert P. 1996. Appendix B: The U.S. Olympic Committee. In *Historical dictionary of the modern Olympic movement,* ed. John E. Findling and Kimberly D. Pelle, 395–404. Westport, CT: Greenwood Press.

Weatherby, James B., and Stephanie L. Witt. 1994. *The urban West: Managing growth and decline.* Westport, CT: Praeger.

Weeks, Russell. 1988a. Utah '98 Olympic bid? Mayor's chief of staff visits Minnesota. *Salt Lake Tribune,* November 12, E-1.

———. 1988b. We must move fast, DePaulis says of Olympic bid. *Salt Lake Tribune,* November 15, B-1.

Weinstein, Henry. 1980. Details of financing for Raiders revealed. *Los Angeles Times*, February 25, I-3.

Whitt, Richard. 1996a. Marketer sues over ill-fated Olympic deal. *Atlanta Journal Constitution,* September 27, B-7.

———. 1996b. The city's Olympic plan: Olympic money lost. *Atlanta Journal Constitution,* January 13, C-8.

Whitt, Richard, and Melissa Turner. 1996. False profits: Dreams of Olympic gold turn into nightmare. *Atlanta Journal Constitution,* September 22, D-6.

Wilcox, David. 1994. Lessons for tourism industries from the 1984 Olympics at Los Angeles. Speech in Sydney, Australia, March 2. Available at the Amateur Athletic Foundation of Los Angeles, Paul Ziffren Sports Resource Center.

Wilkinson, Brian. 1989. Key players: Who's who in Utah's Olympic organizations. *Utah Business,* October, 40–59.

Williams, J. D. 1960. *The defeat of home rule in Salt Lake City.* Eagleton Institute Case Studies in Practical Politics. New York: Holt, Rinehart and Winston.

Wilson, Wayne. 1996. Los Angeles 1984. In *Historical dictionary of the modern Olympic movement,* ed. John E. Findling and Kimberly D. Pelle, 169–177. Westport, CT: Greenwood Press.

Wolfe, Mark R. 1999. The wired loft: Life-style innovation diffusion and industrial networking in the rise of San Francisco's multimedia gulch. *Urban Affairs Review* 34 (5): 707–728.

Wolman, Harold. 1986. The Reagan urban policy and its impacts. *Urban Affairs Quarterly* 21 (3): 311–335.

Wong, Kenneth K., and Paul E. Peterson. 1986. Urban response to federal program flexibility: Politics of community development block grants. *Urban Affairs Quarterly* 21 (3): 293–309.

World Tourism Organization. 1992. *Recommendations on tourism statistics.* Madrid, Spain: WTO.

———. 2000. *Tourism highlights 2000.* Madrid, Spain: WTO.

Wright, Gerald C., John P. McIver, Robert S. Erikson, and David P. Holian. 2000. Stability and change in state electorates, Carter through Clinton. Paper presented at the Midwestern Political Science Association Annual Meeting, Chicago.

Zukin, Sharon. 1982. *Loft living: Culture and capital in urban change.* Baltimore: Johns Hopkins University Press.

———. 1991. *Landscapes of power: From Detroit to Disney World.* Berkeley: University of California Press.

Zukin, Sharon, et al. 1998. From Coney Island to Las Vegas in the urban imaginary: Discursive practices of growth and decline. *Urban Affairs Review* 33 (5): 627–654.

■■ INDEX ■■

195

■■ ABOUT THE BOOK ■■

What drives cities to pursue large-scale, high-profile events like the Olympic games? What are the consequences for citizens and local governments? Investigating local politics in three U.S. cities—Los Angeles, Atlanta, and Salt Lake City—as they vied for the role of Olympic host, this book provides a compelling narrative of the evolving political economy of modern mega-events.

The authors reveal how the mega-event strategy typically is initiated by a coalition of public and private elites; how citizen involvement is managed and often curtailed; and how latent development agendas are revived and refocused to leverage Olympic opportunities. In assessing the impact of mega-event-driven growth, they look beyond the tax revenues and stadium costs to offer a nuanced examination of the ways Olympic dreams affect local governance and social conditions in urban economies.

Matthew J. Burbank is assistant professor of political science at University of Utah. **Gregory D. Andranovich** is associate professor of political science at California State University, Los Angeles. **Charles H. Heying** is assistant professor of urban studies and planning at Portland State University.